"Bartlett understands the power of stories to c
produce a future that is more violent. Other
peace. At a time when so many are weaponizi
harm, Anthony invites us to rediscover the Bi
and into deep conviviality."

—BRIAN D. MCLAREN, author of *Faith after Doubt*

"A rigorous expositor, Bartlett profoundly re-dimensions our historic as-
sumptions about divinely sanctioned violence. . . . In an age that often looks
outside of the Bible for wisdom, Bartlett draws attention back to sacred
Scripture as a culturally pivotal source of revelation—about God and
ourselves."

—GENA ST. DAVID, author of *The Brain and the Spirit*

"Say goodbye to biblical delusions and a religion of self-justifying purity
with its necessarily violent God. Instead, discover faith—a new self and a
new God in a new world, beyond a poisoned religious imagination. Tony
Bartlett . . . takes us on a new, consistent, and compelling interpretative
journey through Hebrew Scripture, Jesus, and Paul. A master class in reading and teaching the Bible."

—SCOTT COWDELL, author of *René Girard and the Nonviolent God*

"Humanity needs the hope this book represents! Bartlett teaches us to understand the Bible as the story of new creation, showing us how to read
Revelation's transformative signs and so engage in the work of bringing
harmony to creation. We look around at the current 'apocalyptic' violence
which threatens our survival, and the good news of this book becomes urgent: God in Jesus Christ has launched a project of human transformation
from violence to nonviolence!"

—PAUL NUECHTERLEIN, Curator, Girardian Reflections on the Lectionary

"A biblical theology of nonviolence: this book, both seasoned and entirely
fresh in its rigorous 'biblicality,' persuasively reads the Christian canon as
a cohesive story of re-signification and transformation towards non-retaliation. Exciting in the bold sweep of its storytelling yet firmly grounded in
the generative matrix of the text, it opens up striking re-encounters with
Exodus, Job, the Suffering Servant, Jonah, Jesus, Paul, and the Slaughtered
Lamb."

—BRIGITTE KAHL, Union Theological Seminary

Signs of Change

Signs of Change

The Bible's Evolution of Divine Nonviolence

ANTHONY BARTLETT

CASCADE *Books* · Eugene, Oregon

SIGNS OF CHANGE
The Bible's Evolution of Divine Nonviolence

Cascade Books
An Imprint of Wipf and Stock Publishers
199 W. 8th Ave., Suite 3
Eugene, OR 97401

www.wipfandstock.com

PAPERBACK ISBN: 978-1-6667-0372-6
HARDCOVER ISBN: 978-1-6667-0373-3
EBOOK ISBN: 978-1-6667-0374-0

Cataloguing-in-Publication data:

Names: Bartlett, Anthony, author.
Title: Signs of change : the bible's evolution of divine nonviolence / Anthony Bartlett.
Description: Eugene, OR : Cascade Books, 2022 | Includes bibliographical references and index.
Identifiers: ISBN 978-1-6667-0372-6 (paperback) | ISBN 978-1-6667-0373-3 (hardcover) | ISBN 978-1-6667-0374-0 (ebook)
Subjects: LCSH: Girard, René, 1923–2015. | Violence—Religious aspects—Christianity. | Semiotics.
Classification: BS680.V55 B38 2022 (print) | BS680.V55 B38 (ebook)

Cover art, *Morning Aspen*, by Vahe Yeremyan, 2021, used with permission.
Epigraph quotation from Cixin Liu, *The Three-Body Problem*.

To all the *maskilim*, men and women, who helped find and reveal the path, and to all the seekers and pilgrims who now are traveling upon it

God is the newness of everything that is and is coming to be.
God is ever newness in love.

— Ilia Delio

It was impossible to expect a moral awakening from humankind itself, just like it was impossible to expect humans to lift off the earth by pulling up on their own hair. To achieve moral awakening required a force outside the human race.

— Cixin Liu

The authentic knowledge about violence and all its works to be found in the Gospels cannot be the result of human action alone . . . A nonviolent deity can only signal his existence to mankind by having himself driven out by violence—by demonstrating that he is not able to establish himself in the Kingdom of Violence.

— René Girard

CONTENTS

Preface

READ THIS BOOK IF you're picking up the Bible for the very first time. But especially read it, and take it to embrace, if you've read the Bible many times before.

Just like the weight of the sun continues to determine the orbit of wandering earth, the Old Testament, aka the Hebrew Bible, shapes the reading of the New Testament which, nevertheless, claims to give it its final meaning. Thus, any reading of the New Testament carries inside it a guiding concept from the Old. It is vital then to make plain and conscious that reflexive significance. The present book sets out to show a theological nonviolence emerging consistently in the Old Testament, and thus help the determination of the New as fully the revelation of a nonviolent God.

I always loved the storytelling and language of the New Testament. There's an irreplaceable drama there. A man dies, and somehow everyone is involved in his death. A spiritual and human movement is born in its aftermath, and ultimately, after some centuries, a triumphant church is built on its memory. But what is that death, and how does its story somehow fulfill everything that went before?

In the Middle Ages, they said the answer was easy. The death paid everyone's debt to a God of righteous anger, beginning with the church which, as it were, holds a title to the payment made. But as time went on, it becomes more and more repugnant to think of Jesus this way. His death is a revelation, not a compensation; a luminous crack in a false narrative, not a feudal honor payment.

In the Department of Religion where I did my PhD, the thought of René Girard was not popular. It had something to do with the Frenchman's realist approach to the universe, as opposed to any systematic uncertainty of everything. I was not there to study Girard, but he formed a background to my research, and I had to be circumspect in bringing him up. On one occasion when I did, as part of a formal examination project, one particular professor gave voice to a profound sense of scandal. He quoted Girard's keystone book, *Things Hidden*. "God is not violent," he huffed incredulously, as if he were being required to accept a proposition like the ultimate nature of reality is blue spaghetti.

On the surface, his reaction was about Girard's audacity in making a *decision* about such a big metaphysical term as "God," but more and more I came to see that what was really offensive was making a decision about violence. Afterwards, I was always grateful to that professor, because he alerted me to how that statement was so important. To say God is non-violent says something truly profound about "God," in contrast to the way of being of the world. That is why that truly smart professor zeroed on it. It was and is a scandal.

A few years later, I was at a conference in San Francisco where Girard himself gave a paper, and it seemed that he had repented his scandal. Someone on the panel asked him what seemed a straightforward enough question, "Is God nonviolent?" To my surprise, he replied directly, if enigmatically, "I don't know." I was floored. Had he forgotten what he wrote in *Things Hidden*, the thing that so rattled the esteemed professor?

But whatever the enigma of his answer (later career ambivalence, a bad day, or did I even mishear?), I am prepared to overlook it. Really. As the Italians say, *i libri hanno il loro destino* (books have their own destiny), and my personal love affair with the biblical text had been given its full freedom and self-awareness by the thought of the nonviolent God in *Things Hidden*. This present book is its coming to expression. It arrives some years after those other occasions, but it was always there seeking its pages.

In order to write it, I had first to deal with the technical question of how it is possible to emerge from a previous language and concept of violent divinity. *Theology Beyond Metaphysics* gave the theoretical explanation with its argument of semiotic openness: the possibility of progressive change in human meaning through the use of signs and the relations they mediate. In particular, the intervention of the gospel narrative in the primary scene of human meaning was shown to provide a generative new beginning of nonviolence, rather than age-old generative violence. This necessarily applies to theology, hand in hand with anthropology.

It amounts to a radical conversion of original meaning, from violent difference to the indifference of nonviolent love. This is the real story going on in the New Testament, far removed from the payoffs of the

Middle Ages. And as *Theology Beyond Metaphysics* showed, the thought of semiotics was also evolving in that biblically enchanted period, moving toward its modern and postmodern breakthrough.

Signs of Change both depends on this previous argument and demonstrates and illustrates it, showing in historical and literary detail the morphing of signs within the fabric of biblical writing. Everything moves towards the revelation of divine nonviolence in Jesus and the new creation that results. The book is an adventure story within an adventure story, and thus a comprehensive retelling of the whole story. Read it for fun, and possibly finish it for faith. It is my love letter to the text, and to the nonviolent God who stands behind it, the fountainhead of biblical signs and their one-day transforming destiny.

Acknowledgments

THE ROAD THAT LEADS to this book has several richly storied waystations. Apart from standard academic teaching, I credit Liberation Theology, and some of its practitioners whom I personally encountered, with setting me on the way. They alerted me to reading the Scripture neither in a purely dogmatic nor scientific-critical sense, but as a mirror and echo of human life as undergone by any of the oppressed and violated of the earth. Among the practitioners, Eloy Sanchez from Ecuador, currently living in Rome, stands at the head. It was Eloy who first helped me see and understand that human beings are authentic protagonists of the Bible, as much (by God's design) as Godself. On a different track are the Little Brothers of Jesus, and, among them, Carlo Carretto who welcomed me for a year as part of his community in Spello, Italy, some decades back. Although not a biblical scholar, Carretto communicated an emphatic sense of the dynamism of the Gospels. He encouraged my own fledgling reading of the texts; but the Spirit-filled urgency of his communication left the most enduring mark. Among the members of the fellowship around him was Franco Pignotti. Franco also first introduced me to the work of René Girard, and in that first encounter I caught some of Franco's own sensibility to the historical nerve of Girard's exegesis. It is but one of the reasons Franco remains a friend to this day. Finally, and again, I continue to thank the members of the Wood Hath Hope and Bethany Center community here in Syracuse, New York. Without the constant practice of reading and interpretation done with and by this community, none of these pages would be possible.

Abbreviations

ASV	American Standard Version (Bible)
BCE	Before Common Era
CE	Common Era
JB	Jerusalem Bible
KJV	King James Version (Bible)
LXX	Septuagint
NASB	New American Standard Bible
NISB	New Interpreter's Study Bible
NIV	New International Version (Bible)
NRSV	New Revised Standard Version (Bible)
TBM	*Theology Beyond Metaphysics*

INTRODUCTION

FOR MOST PEOPLE WHO grew up as Christians, there was never any problem in the various stories of God decreeing the extermination of peoples, or moving directly to wipe them out by flood, fire, or otherwise unprovided death. God is God, and God can do whatever God wants. As Noam Chomsky has remarked, "The bible is probably the most genocidal book in the literary canon."[1] It is only perhaps in the last decades of the twentieth century that this kind of free pass for divine violence began to be questioned. Looking back on a century of horror, beginning in the meat-grinder of the First World War, marching onward through the lethal weaponry of the Second, linked also to the mechanized genocide of the Shoah, and ending with the continuous slaughter of various colonial and post-colonial wars, how could humanity not question any kind of theological sanction for this wrenching history of violence?[2]

Yet we also recall that the great conflagrations of the twentieth century had little to do with religion. God seemed largely absent. Perhaps that was part of it. Where, before, the presence of God on the scene of violence made it somehow righteous and inevitable, now the naked face of violence itself stood forth, and suddenly we could see it had a life of its own, not tied to any metaphysical "God." Humanity saw itself and it became disgusted, and the disgust filters back through the revered texts of religion, especially the Bible—suggesting that who or whatever "God" is, divinity has been perversely implicated in an all-too-human violence. The question then becomes one of transcendence.

1. Chomsky, *Final Edition*, 14.

2. Phyllis Trible's *Texts of Terror* (1984) can stand as a landmark, underscoring the violence in biblical stories. According to Walter Brueggemann's foreword, her writing "lets us notice in the text the terror, violence, and pathos that more conventional methods have missed" (x).

Transcendence is a term for ultimate power and meaning, a final source of truth. In the past, the undisputed use of violence went along with supreme authority, and supreme authority automatically meant disposing of untrammeled violence. It was a closed circle: one thing implied the other. Now, however, the transcendence of violence is seriously questioned. Human beings continue to use violence, but we make less and less pretense about its honorable status. There have been enough accounts of abused victims to induce a healthy cynicism about the unblemished virtue of victors.

The Bible has always had a struggle of transcendence. The founding event of the chosen people—liberation from Egypt—involved the slaying of the firstborn. This included the firstborn of Pharaoh, himself an incarnation of the god, Horus. As James G. Williams put it, the Exodus struggle with Pharaoh was actually "God versus the Egyptian gods."[3] If the Lord brought his children out of Egypt, it was at the cost of the children of the Egyptians and those of their state-sanctioned god and ruler. But hidden in the clash-of-Titans rivalry between the Lord and the Pharaoh is a very different struggle. The Lord had made a choice for the suffering Hebrews, the worthless migrants of the second millennium BCE, while the Pharaoh represented a millennial Egyptian civilization, one of the greatest the earth has known. What does it mean to institute a new transcendence on behalf of the powerless? Is it simply a battle to the death against the powerful—a vengeful revolution from below? Or does it perhaps involve the slow and painful communication of an entirely different way of knowing, of understanding ultimate value and truth? Is not the Bible, by definition, a slow-burning question mark about transcendence itself? The question is inevitably posed at first in terms of which "god" has the greatest firepower at his disposal, the greatest ability to inflict misery. But little by little, the hollowness of that formula is exposed, and something very different emerges. "Not by might, nor by power, but by my Spirit, says the LORD of hosts" (Zech 4:6).

It's unthinkable to establish a truly new source of meaning by simply imposing a fresh dynasty or empire on people. That will become simply a matter of "Meet the new boss, same as the old boss." In modern terms, a revolutionary state ideology will claim to represent a true break in history,

---

3. Williams, *Bible, Violence and the Sacred*, 76. At Exodus 4:22–23, the Lord commands Moses to say to Pharaoh, "Thus says the Lord, Israel is my firstborn son, and I say to you, 'Let my son go that he may serve me'; if you refuse to let him go, behold, I will slay your firstborn son."

only to prove itself finally just another form of the status quo. In contrast, biblical Scripture has always struggled with the unfathomable identity (the unseeable face) of Israel's God, and, hand in hand, it has engaged in a struggle with the root conditions by which we establish human meaning itself. It has taken millennia for us to get round to understanding and seeing this double movement for what it truly intends.

In *Theology Beyond Metaphysics*, I showed how our signs and the relations they communicate inherently shift and change, transforming the way we see the world and how we live in it. Signs are not metaphysics, fixed in an eternal order. They are an open-ended, pliant, an ever-transforming system of communication and meaning. I traced the beginning of the question to the moment in which language was first "invented" by a group of neurally sophisticated hominids. Here the thought of René Girard provided a momentous breakthrough, identifying the violent origins and conditions of the first signified thought and meaning—what he broadly calls "the sacred." Girard's discoveries have a marked biblical connection, providing an essential starting point for understanding the Bible as the injection of a radical new meaning source in the subsoil of human existence. However, not only does the Bible "reveal the victim" (Girard's pivotal claim), by the same token and more primordially, it brings with it the possibility of a transformative humanity—one of compassion, nonviolence, and peace. This is indeed a new transcendence, and it has been working in and through the Bible's diffusion through Western culture since the first centuries of the Common Era.

The very prevalence of violence in the Bible, alongside a progressive theme of nonviolence, suggests that this is the true problem that the text has been struggling with all along. It is out of the biblical reaction against oppression that a deeper, more truly radical revolution of compassion and forgiveness is born. What is really striking is to see an emergent questioning of the default of violence and an alternative possibility of genuinely nonviolent humanity. Afterward, among Christians and Christendom, it is once again because of our ingrained actual humanity that this more radical revelation has only slowly been recognized, and more often than not honored in the breach rather than the observance.

Our latter-day response, therefore—of disgust at violence in the Bible—has to acknowledge a parallel and actually more powerful principle: one of positive nonviolence, one which we have gleaned not in reaction against but actually *from* the Bible. The present book sets out to present a coherent narrative of this biblical principle, tracing it from the Old

Testament to the New, and showing both its struggle against the "natural" transcendence of violence and, at the same time, its essence as the most profound and creative content of revelation. The journey maps its way along a ribbon of key "code creations," borrowing an idea from Umberto Eco.[4] Eco refers to the ability of an artist to produce new meanings in a given medium, to the extent even of making something available that had never been seen or understood before. He applied the thought primarily to instances of fine art, but there is obviously no reason to refuse its use with respect to writing. Thus, the biblical journey demonstrates a sequence of genetic shifts up to and including the figure of Jesus. These biblical shifts run largely counter to their surrounding ecosystems; they are what might perhaps be named a genome of redemption, running painfully contrary to their environment, but slowly, irreversibly, changing the actual ecology around them.

I owe an incalculable debt to the work of Girard. But, ultimately, I march to a different drum. Both *Theology Beyond Metaphysics* and this present book press the transformative message of the gospel and depend for their method on a thought of semiotics. Although Girard derived a great deal from semiotics in both the material and structure of his arguments, his claimed method was rational and scientific. My approach is both semiotic and evangelical, looking to actual religious effects and outcomes, and above all the concrete word of the gospel producing them.

Girard's later work evinced a terminal mood, emphasizing the destabilizing effect of the gospel in society, claiming that "Violence can no longer be checked . . . the apocalypse has begun," and any "optimism" should be abandoned.[5] Short of real and genuine conversion, the apocalyptic breakdown of culture is what the gospel provokes, and we are manifestly in that moment, subject only to an "implacable law of the escalation to extremes."[6]

What Girard's thought was processing was not so much the gospel (he always protested he was not a theologian), but what we might call anthropo-mimetics, a rational analysis of the human world as such. In contrast, the gospel is eruptive and self-validating. It comes with a verbal announcement, carrying the germ of a radical change in human constitution, one carried out in the depths of the artificial cultural-evolutionary

4. Eco's actual term is "code invention." See Bartlett, *TBM*, 128–30.
5. Girard, *Battling to the End*, 210, 132.
6. Girard, *Battling to the End*, xiv.

construct that is the human. Once this change is effected (conversion), the individual concerned really is in a totally new human situation—what the gospels call "the kingdom of God" or "Holy Spirit." This clearly impacts the individual, but it cannot help also impact the world in which the individual exists, as a communicative, organic whole. In analytic evolutionary terms, human beings cannot produce this transformation themselves—how can lions evolve the imagination of lambs? What we might call "the gospel nerve," allowing human beings to see their own constitutive violence must come necessarily from outside, beyond the human organism. Nevertheless, once the possibility is set in motion, it then must belong to the repertoire of the human, since it must set itself up semiotically, in shared signs and possibilities of meaning. Once introduced as an evolutionary possibility, this alternative transcendence must begin to offer an inherent possibility of the human construct. What begins as alien is quickly endemic.

What I am claiming, therefore, is that at that heart of the Girardian project lies an effect he did not clearly take account of, but which is crucial for the results he intuits. *Theology Beyond Metaphysics* showed that the very revelation of original violence depends essentially not on a rational synthesis but a mutation of signs which is the heart of the gospel. Girard's own argument depends intimately on the autonomous revelation of transformative meaning found in biblical signs and language, one that inescapably intends forgiveness and nonviolence.

Attempting here to describe the actual biblical pathway by which this revelation came about is very likely a new thing. But claiming a privileged pathway in and through the texts is not new. Luther's often mentioned "canon within the canon" is among the most famous.[7] And the overall Christian Bible almost demands a highway, given its structure of a story over time with a host of bewildering items between. The question has always been, "What are God's intentions? What is God's plan?" Augustine encouraged what he called a *plena narratio* (the full story) of God's work. This included, not just the teaching of Scripture, but the recent successes of the church, its irresistible spread, and the support of

---

7. "Those apostles who treat oftenest and highest of how faith in Christ alone justifies, are the best evangelists. Therefore are St. Paul's epistles more a gospel than Matthew, Mark and Luke. For these do not set down much more than the story of the works and miracles of Christ; but the grace which we receive through Christ, no one so boldly extols as St. Paul, especially in his letter to the Romans" (Luther, *Preface to the Exposition of 1 Peter* (1523), quoted in Kidd, *Documents Illustrative of the Continental Reformation*, 55).

the emperors.[8] Later, in the aftermath of the barbarian invasion of Rome in 410 CE, he would take a more nuanced view, but in every case it was a matter of some consistent account of the Bible story and its impact in the world. I am offering here a *plena narratio* in terms of a vital selection: a thread of evolutionary mutations which eventually produced the new *anthropos* proclaimed by Paul. The difference is that, whereas Augustine saw a steady progression from the sovereign narrative of salvation to the contemporary "heavenly" victory of the church, I am digging behind a rational anthropology of original violence, dependent on the Bible, to its transformative preconditions in the same Bible. It is an archaeological narration, one that reveals the conditions not of a triumph, but the essential transformation of the meaning of triumph itself.

It is worth making a strategic, scene-setting pause here on this monumental figure, Augustine of Hippo. There is surely no other Western thinker who has produced so much writing forming a narrative of God's work, and whose compositions have had such resounding effect. Augustine did not so much expound theology as practice it and create it by writing, more or less continually, on the multiple situations that presented themselves throughout his life. He had something to say on almost every topic, with the confidence to insist dogmatically, and yet also sometimes to change his mind. Nevertheless, there is no doubt his final legacy has a characteristic signature, including the soul's destined enjoyment of the eternal vision of God, God's predestined gift of grace by which this is carried through for individuals, and the role of the church in effecting the unique community in which these goals are represented. I am certain that almost anyone reading that sentence will have a deep sense of recognition. Traces of what is called Neoplatonism are not hard to identify even in this description. But the point is not just to recognize the elements of an influence, but to acknowledge its world-historical effect. As Jerome, translator of the Bible into Latin, said in a letter to Augustine in 418 CE: "You are known throughout the world; Catholics honor and esteem you as the one who has established anew the ancient Faith." The Latin is *conditor antiquae rursum fidei*, which could be translated as "founder all over again of the ancient faith," putting Augustine somewhere up there with Jesus or the Spirit.[9] Rounding out the parallels with New Testament source personalities, Diarmaid MacCulloch writes: "Augustine's impact

---

8. Markus, *Saeculum*, 32

9. Jerome, *Letter 195*, quoted in TeSelle, *Augustine the Theologian*, 341.

on Western Christian thought can hardly be overstated; only his beloved example, Paul of Tarsus, has been more influential, and Westerners have generally seen Paul through Augustine's eyes."[10] With these comments, we get a sense of the formidable cultural gravity exercised by Augustine and the inescapable fact flowing from it that a constructed account of the Bible's meaning has been created for us by him and his worldview.

As already suggested, Augustine's is a story of the soul, and at once, with that very expression, we are deep within a heavy texture of meaning. While Augustine was in Milan before his conversion, "some books of the Platonists" were given to him.[11] It is widely agreed that these were accounts of the Neoplatonist philosophy of Plotinus.[12] Plotinus taught a heady but deeply consoling vision of an original fall of the soul away from ontological unity with the divine One, a fall which was itself the source of material reality, and, at the same time, the soul's fraught but exhilarating spiritual journey back to the One.[13] There is a specialized academic discussion about how much and how essentially Augustine brought this doctrine into his emerging Christian theology.[14] It seems clear that in his earliest works, post-conversion, the future doctor of the church understood the soul as created separate from the body and, in that state, sinning somehow and so becoming part of the earth.[15] As he began to read and grasp the Bible more thoroughly, he understood the soul and

10. MacCulloch, *Christianity*, 301.

11. Augustine, *Confessions*, VII:9.

12. Rombs, *Augustine and the Fall*, 26.

13. Plotinus, *Enneads*.

14. Robert O'Connell is the primary name associated with belief in Plotinus' core influence on Augustine; see *St. Augustine's Early Theory of Man, A.D. 386–391*, and *The Origin of the Soul in St. Augustine's Later Works*. Other scholars responded, claiming Augustine's biblical orthodoxy, but no one argues there was no influence. See Rombs, *Augustine and the Fall*, 5, 3-15. See O'Connell: "(T)he view of us humans as fallen souls is either the root, or so very close to the root of Augustine's entire intellectual synthesis, that virtually all the significant particularities of that synthesis slide into sharper focus, become more naturally intelligible, once we envisage them as emerging from that root vision" (O'Connell, *Augustinism*, 211).

15. See Augustine, *Refutation of the Manichees*, II:3-4. Augustine interprets Genesis 2:5 allegorically: "*before it was on the earth* is to be understood as meaning before the soul sinned. When it has befouled itself with earthly lusts, after all, it is rightly said to have been born upon the earth, or to be upon the earth" (Augustine, *Refutation of the Manichees*, II:4). In other words, the soul sinned and by reason of its sin came to earth. Thus, "It seems almost certain that the young Augustine thought of the soul as having fallen into bodily life" (Rombs, *Augustine and the Fall*, 163).

body as a composite creature, with both parts made simultaneously by God. However, the root difference between the two parts, one spiritual and one material, remained an unshakeable feature in his thinking. In true Platonic fashion, the soul is the center of rational thought,[16] but because of original sin it was now vulnerable to being overwhelmed by the passions of the flesh. So, the body—although originally good—becomes the locus of a fearful moral and legal struggle for the destiny of the soul. In the Plotinian scheme, the issue is not so much the body as matter as such, with a desire by the immortal soul for its own realm of property and authority—as opposed to simple devoted contemplation of the One. This is what actually produces the lower material universe.[17] In some of Augustine's descriptions we can clearly sense the drama of this scheme:

> So [the soul] turns away . . . from [God] and slithers and slides down [*moveturque et labitur*] [literally: "falls"] into less and less which is imagined to be more; it can find satisfaction neither in itself nor in anything else as it gets further away from him alone who can satisfy it.[18]

And the sense of dirt and contamination is not far away. In the same writing Augustine exhorts the soul:

> Come, see if you can [contemplate God], O soul weighed down with the body that decays (Wis 9:15) and burdened with many and variable earthly thoughts, come see if you can—God is truth. Come, hold it in that first moment in which so to speak you caught a flash from the corner of your eye when the word "truth" was spoken, stay there if you can. But you cannot: you slide back into these familiar and earthly things. And what weight is it, I ask, that drags you back but the birdlime of greed for the filth you have picked up in your wayward wanderings.[19]

Augustine references here the Wisdom of Solomon, a late biblical work, influenced by the Greek thought world. But when Augustine deals with Genesis, specifically chapters two and three, he is facing a much more

---

16. For example, Augustine, *De Immortalite Animae*, 2.2, 6, 10; *De ordine*, 2.43, in Rombs, *Augustine and the Fall*, 52.

17. Plotinus, *Enneads*, 4, 8, 6.

18. Augustine, *De Trinitate*, 10.7, quoted in Rombs, *Augustine and the Fall*, 87, brackets original. *De Trinitate* is a work which was revised over years and published toward the end of Augustine's career.

19. Augustine, *De Trinitate*, 8.3, quoted in Rombs, *Augustine and the Fall*, 87. Rombs remarks that "birdlime" is a "favorite circumlocution for the body" (88).

material and existentialist account. To specify what is "fallen," he must equate the fall of the soul with the episode of the first parents' disobedience, beginning with Eve. There was in her "that love of her own independent authority and a certain proud over-confidence in herself," as a result of which she took the fruit at the instigation of the serpent.[20]

But then, at that moment, the eyes of both first parents are opened and they saw that they were naked (Gen 3:7). Augustine follows through with the most audacious, head-spinning interpretation. What are their eyes opened for, "if not for lusting after each other, as a punishment for the sin, a punishment conceived by the death of the flesh itself?" He continues:

> No sooner then they had transgressed the commandment than they were inwardly stripped stark naked, bereft of the grace which they had offended against by a kind of feverish delusion, and by the proud love of their own independent authority; then they turned their eyes on their own genitals and lusted after them with that stirring movement they had not previously known . . . When they forfeited this condition [of immortality through the tree of life], then their bodies contracted that liability to disease and death which is present in the flesh of animals—and thus also that motion of the genitals which stirs in animals the desire to mate, and so ensures the birth of the young to take the place of those which die.[21]

And that is how it happens, how the circle is closed—between the Plotinian fall of soul, the biblical transgression of the first parents, the act of sex, and the inevitability of death. All that needs to be added is the (apparent) Pauline doctrine of the inherited sin of Adam. Augustine, along with his Latin contemporaries, read Romans 5:12 as "in whom all have sinned," where modern translations have "in as much as all have sinned."[22] For Augustine, there is a necessary arc of connection between Adam's sin and the punishment of death exacted of every human.[23] And Augustine's vivid account of the drama of Eden nails involuntary sexual arousal as the indisputable evidence of this punishment of death entering into human history. After Adam, all humanity comes by way of mortal

---

20. Augustine, *Literal Meaning of Genesis*, XI:30.

21. Augustine, *Literal Meaning of Genesis*, XI:31.

22. For example, Augustine, *Literal Meaning of Genesis*, VI:9, X:11.

23. For Augustine, this life is a penal condition, and thus, in justice, it must be the result of voluntary sin (Rombs, *Augustine and the Fall*, 67, 93).

generation, *mortali generatione*, and the soul must shamefully recognize its responsibility for this condition.[24]

Augustine has married Plotinus and Genesis in a triumphant synthesis, mashing the elevated Plotinian odyssey of the soul with Genesis' second creation account and its earthy picture-book story. But there is a proverbial fly in the ointment. In order for us truly to sin in Adam, we must have been present in the titular first parent in a *real* way, not simply allegorically. We had to be *really and substantially* there if we are legally to have committed the sin at the source of all our penal suffering. But how is this to be the case? It cannot be because we inherit Adam's flesh; because the flesh does not contain the true self, the willing, responsible self; only the soul does. Augustine tends to speak in forceful but general terms. "God created man aright . . . but man was willingly perverted and justly condemned and so begot perverted and condemned offspring. For we were all in that one man, seeing that we all *were* that one man who fell into sin . . ."[25] But, again, how does this work?

There were two major theories for the origin of the soul at his time. One was "creationism," meaning God creates each soul for each separate embryo. This has the advantage of suggesting the entirely spiritual nature of the soul, derived directly from God's hand. The other theory is known as "traducianism," which means an actual portion of Adam's soul was passed down to all subsequent humans. The difficulty here is the obvious (Stoic) materialism of the concept, militating against a purely spiritual soul not existing within space. Such a view of things was obviously not congenial to Augustine's wider thought, but when the greatest doctrinal struggle of his later career erupted, the battle with Pelagius and his followers, he was forced to entertain its possibility. Pelagians did not believe in the morally crippling effect of original sin—they held that the human will was capable of responding adequately to the strict demands of the gospel and was not in need of an exceptional work of grace to do so. So, when it came to the origin of the individual spiritual soul in humans, it was natural for them to accept that God created each soul individually, without responsibility for or contaminated by the sin of Adam.

Augustine was more concerned to defend his teaching of "original sin" than he was to maintain a consistent metaphysical order. He was, in

24. "(F)or all that, in this very punishment the rational soul gave an indication of its natural nobility by feeling embarrassment at this animal motion in these organs of its flesh, and covering it with shame" (Augustine, *Literal Meaning of Genesis*, XI:32).

25. Augustine, *City of God*, XIII:14, emphasis original.

the end, more a lawyer and religious legislator than a pure philosopher. An argument he makes in his final extended treatment of Genesis (finished around 415 CE) is noteworthy both for its flexibility on the issue of traducianism and its finding a final court of appeal in the popular practices of North African Christians upheld by the Catholic Church:

> We must be on our guard, indeed, against errors that may be implied in holding that the soul does not descend from Adam's soul. For instance, we must not make God seem to be the author of sin if he gives the soul to a body in which it must necessarily sin . . . But since the universal Church holds to the custom of rushing to the sacrament with living infants to provide for them, there is only one explanation, namely each child is Adam in body and soul, and therefore the grace of Christ is necessary for him. At that age the infant in his own person has done no good or evil, and thus his soul is perfectly innocent *if it has not descended from Adam.*[26]

Augustine has come around in his own circle of argument, but finally he is unable to tie the two ends together. There is a fundamental disconnect between a spiritual soul and a physical inheritance from Adam, but Augustine did not care. So long as he had the authority of the church and popular piety embracing both things, the show could go on. This is what points us most clearly to the Augustinian construct as construct. The fact that at a key point the theoretical foundations are absent or contradictory would seem to disqualify the whole edifice. But it does not happen: the consistent, splendid "supplementarity" of Augustine's writing makes it work. This was the North African's genius, to grasp and effect a synthesis that combined both metaphysical essences, spiritual experience, popular institutional practice, and written mastery second to none.

I have given space to these details because, unarguably, Augustine's is the paradigm for a constructed theological narrative in Western Christianity. His effect continued through the Medieval world and into the Reformation, and out the other side. The work in the present book obviously gives a very different *plena narratio*, shifting the biblical travail in a distinctly new direction. The Bible does not pivot around the fall of the soul, and sex as the proof, but around a holistic account of the human organism and its motifs of mimetic desire and violence—signaled clearly and emphatically throughout Genesis. We have inherited a broad

---

26. Augustine, *Literal Meaning of Genesis*, X:11, quoted in Rombs, *Augustine and the Fall*, 179–80. My italics.

semiotic Augustinianism, but with Girard's irruptive reading of the Bible, alongside the materialism of neurological mimesis, we are in a decisively new situation. It is important, I think, to flag the dramatic difference with Augustine in order to plead a decisively new dynamic of evangelism. The biblical journey to divine nonviolence is something emerging today in ever greater relief; all that remains is for Christianity to embrace it with the same imaginative and spiritual fervor with which it once embraced the Augustinian *narratio* of the soul.

All language reaches out through relation, and this relation can change. Within the ocean of human words and sign-making the biblical writing is born and progressively swims upstream to reveal the victim at its source. To produce a relation to the victim goes against the grain of culture—it is the one thing that should *not* have a relation, if the myth of sacred meaning is to be preserved. But via a progressive story of non-violence, forgiveness, and love, it has become possible to bring that relation to the surface. Once again, this revelation of nonviolence is more fundamental than that of the victim, for the latter is dependent on it. This revelation of forgiveness and nonretaliation is in fact the core biblical revelation, its true apocalypse, because it shows the true and definitive character of Godself.

The present book offers a coherent story of that deeper revelation. In many ways, its evidence is simple and straightforward. It does not offer treatises on the character of covenants and their relationships. It does not give complex schemes of different divine dispensations. It simply claims that at the level of human signs something new is progressively revealed and it seeks to show that. To some degree, therefore, it skirts what has been a classic landscape of Old Testament study, that of the covenants, kings, and the political function of prophets. It claims another, deeper story is growing in the margins of the national narrative and offers a series of seminal essays establishing this story. But a lot of that older, familiar story is filled in as it progresses. Exodus is a liberation of an actual oppressed class in relation to a thousand-year empire; Genesis as a preface to the Torah, and especially Exodus, foregrounds everything with the question of violence and its resolution through forgiveness; Job is an earthquake at the very core of the Scripture, upending the Deuteronomic ethic of the guilty party; the figure of the servant from the Isaiah prophetic tradition following the exile is the first vital sketch of divine nonviolence, arising in circumstances of military loss, weakness, and the emergence of an alternative theology of compassion;[27] Ruth is the story of an outsider woman who in her unarmed womanhood makes the whole story turn toward redemption; Daniel is the inbreaking of a new sense of God's action and identity precisely out of a crisis of violence; and Jonah is sheer fable which in its exuberant invention is the canon's purest semiotic artifact. Then at length to Jesus and Paul. Putting Jesus in the progression increases the energy of the sequence enormously, like a tidal current sweeping up against a gulf of water, creating a vortex where they meet. I attempt to show how Jesus' intervention produced a definitively new semiotic space, one in continuity with what goes before but gathering it all to a genuine quantum leap. Paul is the supreme interpreter of this event, so close to the sources and giving extraordinary expression to the transformed *anthropos* resulting from faith in Christ. To understand Paul as an intrinsic part of this sequence is to recruit the apostle of "justification" to an evangelism of divine nonviolence, which in the end become one and the same thing. Finally, there is a very brief appendix on the Lamb of Revelation. It is necessary to attach short remarks on this topic since Revelation seems so easily to relapse into violence at the end of the New Testament. It does anything but. The Lamb "standing as having been slain" (Rev 5:6) registers as the final unconquerable sign of the entire sequence—the worthy emblem of the whole biblical journey to nonviolence.

Signs give birth to relations. As we shall have cause to see, the relation to the sign of Christ is named faith, or faithfulness. To make everything hinge on salvation/loss of the immortal soul is to promote a mimetic economy grounded in external objects and original violence. To nurture the nonviolent relation of faith, derived from the whole biblical journey, is to enter a door into a new creation, something beginning now and promising ultimate fulfilment. We cannot foresee the end state, but biblical semiotics surely point the way.

---

27. The author of the post-exilic material in Isaiah 40–55 is commonly named Second Isaiah

1

Exodus

Cry of the Oppressed

WE BEGIN WITH EXODUS. And necessarily so.

The wretched of the earth groan beneath the lash of the oppressor. Intolerable economic conditions and brutal treatment are the norm. A slave class has no future, other than toil without end until they die. But even to talk like this is too much a language of the modern world.

The Romans said *servus non habet personam* ("A slave has no identity"). In the same vein, they cried *vae victis*: "Woe to the defeated!" When it came to war against a major rival city, their Senator Cato ended his speeches declaring, *Carthago delenda est*: "Carthage must be wiped out!" The very word "subjugation" comes from the Roman practice of *passum sub iugum,* meaning "to pass under a yoke," signifying that those who previously resisted Roman might are now no more than expendable beasts of burden. Why and how could this way of the world be changed?

Ancient Wisdom got as far as recognizing the unfairness of the poor man's lot, but its conclusion was not resistance, rather a final acquiescence. Why? Because the gods create the situation and endorse it.

The gods "gave perverse speech to the human race. With lies and not truth, they endowed them forever. Solemnly they speak in favor of a rich man. 'He is king,' they say, 'riches go to his side.' But they harm a poor man like a thief, they lavish slander upon him and plot his murder."[1]

---

1. Lambert, *Babylonian Wisdom Literature*, 87.

Without a different semiotics, the "other" is not even an underclass. She is historically invisible, or at least totally insignificant, and will be kept so. Unless there arrives a completely different "transcendental signifier," a "god-of-the-Hebrews," the demand for deep social justice has no status. It cannot give rise to authentic, self-standing speech.

Unless the underclass find a voice, and a transformed status, there is no hope.

What then is this strange fire in the desert? Who is this God who stirs himself on their behalf? The God of the Hebrews who must reveal his name and interpret its meaning, so little known is he?

It has to start with a name, a name that *will be what it will be.* That will bring about what it will bring about. A new name means changed everything. It means changed meaning.

Pharaoh will laugh, and rightly so. His way of things is already a millennium old. He knows the future—according to Pharaoh. An underclass will always result from established social and military might. But such people count for nothing, and less than nothing, next to his sovereign power.

In the Ancient Near East, we know of an identified underclass. They are called *Hapiru*—"a loosely defined, inferior social class composed of shifting and shifty population elements without secure ties to settled communities."[2] Constant warfare, displaced peasantry, disinherited clans, refugees, scattered warriors: this creates the perfect conditions for outlaws, mercenaries, indentured labor, slaves. I am not setting out a sociological thesis as such, but it is certainly plausible to argue along these lines. And, once we do, the historical scene-setting swiftly provides the necessary background for a semiotic revolution like the Bible. Just on the face of it, the ancient syllables represented by *'apiru* are phonetically close to *ibri* (Hebrew). Thus, the appellation "Hebrew" presents as a cognate or dialect form of *Hapiru/Habiru.*

If we dig into the folk memories preserved in Genesis, we have instant confirmation of this connection. The very first time the term "Hebrew" is introduced in the Bible, it comes abruptly—without explanation—in relation to Abram. It comes after his story has explicitly begun as the account of a refugee from the cities of Ur and Haran. Abram's nephew, Lot, has been taken captive in an attack on the city of Sodom. We hear that the patriarch has at his command an armed force of three

2. Redmount, "Bitter Lives," 98.

hundred and eighteen men, and he goes directly to attack and rout the "kings" who had captured his relative (Gen 14:13–16). There is no doubt that in this instance, Abram/Abraham is a marauding warlord without settled abode, exactly fitting the category of *Hapiru*. So, when the text says, "Abram the Hebrew," it pretty naturally means "Abram the *Hapiru*." (The rather desperate expedient of deriving the term from the ancestor Eber, in the lists given in Genesis 10 and 11, fails because it is arbitrary, and because *Eber* could well be itself a variant form of *Hapiru/Habiru*.)[3]

Other examples come to mind. The scandalous way Abraham disposes of his wife in situations of social and material insecurity strongly suggests the *Hapiru* world (Gen 12:10–20, 20:1–18). Abraham effectively offers his wife as a concubine/prostitute, because that is what objectively desperate men do (see Gen 20:11–13). If your only saleable asset is women, then these will be offered in a deal with those who have both wealth and power. It is not a matter of morality, but survival.[4]

Against a backdrop like this, we begin to accept that the people who will become Israel are drawn sociologically from the disenfranchised underclass of the ancient near-eastern world known as *Hapiru*. A few of them are perhaps indeed the bearers of folkloric traditions of God-led ancestors. But most simply we can understand them as a highly disparate group gathered together under the leadership and ideals of a spiritual visionary, someone named "Moses." This happened directly in Egypt, and afterward in a transformative revolt of "tribes" in Canaan.[5]

3. Mendenhall, *Ancient Israel's Faith and History*, 31. Mendenhall in fact translates *Eber* as "transgressor," which is the same basic meaning as *Hapiru*, "transgressor," "outlaw."

4. The story is repeated yet again in respect of Isaac and his wife (Gen 26:1–11). It is impossible this could be anything but embedded memory of profound insecurity and lack of status.

5. Two main scholarly names associated with this thesis are Georg Mendenhall (*The Tenth Generation* and *Ancient Israel's Faith and History*) and Norman Gottwald. The latter's *Tribes of Yahweh* is a landmark contribution to Old Testament research clarifying the role of oppressed and marginalized Canaanite peoples, including 'apiru (his rendering of the name, closest to the Egyptian writing), in the formation of Israel. Gottwald argues that proto-Israelites should be understood to include 'apiru as a key socio-historical component, involving an overlap between militarized outlaws and disaffected villagers, within a general revolt model of the settlement of Canaan (Gottwald, *Tribes of Yahweh*, 202–3, 407–8). In this situation, a radical cadre of outsiders constituted the necessary trigger to the wider uprising. "[T]he catalyst to the rise of Israel is seen as deriving from a group of outsiders who entered Canaan with enthusiastic adherence to the deliverer God Yahweh and who supplied a militant stimulant to revolution among the native Canaanite underclasses" (Gottwald, *Tribes of Yahweh*,

This understanding of the origins of the biblical people seems the most persuasive reconstruction out of the literary and archeological evidence, but it is not precisely the character of the argument here.

No, really the argument is because the situation fits the story, and the story changes the world. The semiotics of liberation from Egypt has to come from a powerless, dispossessed people whose name is held by others as a token of contempt. "[T]he Egyptians could not eat with the Hebrews, for that is an abomination to the Egyptians" (Gen 43:32). From where else and for whom else could such a story arise? An imaginative novel might construct a story of an oppressed people who are set free under the leadership of a charismatic individual. But that is modern fiction. The telling of stories like this depends on a primary semiotic breakthrough that established the very possibility of such meaning. In a world where meaning is construed on the side of the powerful and is practiced by a scribal class hired by the powerful, how can a revolutionary meaning break in unless there is some singular event setting it in motion? Because we are today heirs of the biblical narrative, it is difficult, if not impossible, to project ourselves back three-and-a-half-thousand years and conceive a world without that narrative. But that condition must necessarily have been the case at some point: there had to be a world without the Exodus.

And, so, insistently, we have to answer the question of how the Exodus narrative arises.[6] The Bible is self-evidently diffuse and syncretic enough to exclude a single "genius writer" (if indeed such an ahistorical author is conceivable at all), so we are again left with the need for some distinctive generative event, or series of events. It does not have

---

210). See also Frank Moore Cross, *From Epic to Canon*, 69: "The *'apiru*, the client class, despised or feared by Canaanite nobility before Israel's appearance in Canaan, in Israel become the *'ibrîm*, a class or group—only later carrying ethnic overtones—with whom Israel identified and who had special status in early Israelite legal lore." Also, specifically in relation to the Israelites in Egypt, see Fohrer, *History of Israelite Religion*, 71: "[T]he Moses host was sent to live in the land of Goshen (Wadi et-Tumelat) and . . . were forced to provide compulsory labor for the building projects of the Pharaoh, the more since Ramses II (1301–1234) built the store cities Pithom and Raamses (Tanis) mentioned in Exod.1:11, and used *'apiru* for the work." And, "According to Egyptian evidence, such groups of Asiatic nomads frequently sought refuge in Egypt in the period between 1500 and 1200 B.C., and the Egyptians brought *'apiru* back with them as prisoners and slaves" (Fohrer, *History of Israelite Religion*, 71).

6. I capitalize Exodus throughout as I am referring to a major semiotic theme. The word also refers to a book and to an event, an actual escape. In the latter instance, I could use lower case. But for the sake of simplicity, and because the theme is always implied, I stick with the capitalized word.

to be much—it does not have to be the cinematic Red Sea crossing with walls of water on either side. Indeed, such a dramatic show could easily overwhelm an inner content of liberation and simply establish a violent transcendence. No, what is required is the germ of new meaning via an experiential transcendence breaking into the world. Or, more simply put, there has to be something like the burning bush, a voice, a name, and an intention to set free, all received by an individual and a group around him willing to spend their lives for its sake.

Story of Liberation

So it is, the God of Exodus erupts on the scene, an irresistible force of new semiosis. The first chapters of the book are an explosion of new meaning on a plane of brute and hopeless fate. The God who introduces himself to Moses in the burning bush is a God of relationship, not empire, and "he" (for that is how the text styles him) introduces himself as such: "The God of Abraham, the God of Isaac, the God of Jacob." Three names to establish a community between God and his people. From there on, this God continues to speak and act with unquenchable energy, driving forward to the full liberation of his people from the power of Pharaoh. The effect also comes in the course of a dramatic struggle, together with pleas and threats, and the hardening of Pharaoh's heart, a phenomenon which is both the action of Pharaoh and of God. The story recognizes the resistance to liberation offered by the agents of oppression, and the relentlessly mimetic character of such a confrontation. Because God offends the Pharaoh, the Pharaoh offends back, and because it is a struggle of rivals in which God must triumph, the Bible understands God as the agent of Pharaoh's own obduracy. This is the character of mimetic, violent struggle—the reading of which in the chapters of Exodus engages us intimately and compellingly.

After introducing himself, God says:

> I have observed the misery of my people who are in Egypt. I have heard their cry on account of their taskmasters. Indeed, I know their sufferings, and I have come down to deliver them from the Egyptians, and to bring them up out of that land to a good and broad land, a land flowing with milk and honey . . . (Gen 3:7–8a)

The assumption at one level is that "my people" are the physical descendants of Abraham, Isaac, and Jacob, and that God is upset by the harms his unique people are suffering. But the multiplication of notes of oppression tells us something quite different. It says that equally valid is the experience of a marginalized, enslaved class as such: misery, cry, taskmasters, sufferings, deliverance, Egyptians. This is what alerts and engages the reader and creates the sign-value of the story, its irruptive power in human culture as a narrative of oppression and its overturning by God. The same insistent notes are repeated at 3:9: "The cry of the Israelites has now come to me; I have also seen how the Egyptians oppress them." And earlier at 2:23: "The Israelites groaned under their slavery, and cried out. Out of the slavery their cry for help rose up to God. God heard their groaning, and God remembered his covenant with Abraham, Isaac and Jacob. God looked upon the Israelites, and God took notice of them." It's almost impossible not to hear the groaning.

It is this audible cry that made Exodus the critical source of Liberation Theology. I was in Latin America in 1978, the tenth anniversary of the watershed Medellín Conference of Latin American Bishops that gave the go-ahead to understanding and preaching the gospel as liberation of the oppressed. The theme of Exodus was everywhere, catching priests, nuns, teachers up by the hairs of their heads. It was a semiotic shift for me personally, enabling me to understand the reading of the Scripture with a new and vital dynamic, different from the stale dilemmas of archeological digs and doctrinal disputes. The Medellín Conference declared,

> [T]he God whom we know in the Bible is a liberating God, a God who destroys myths and alienations, a God who intervenes in history in order to break down the structures of injustice and who raises up prophets in order to point out the way of justice and mercy. He is the God who liberates slaves (Exodus), who causes empires to fall, who raises up the oppressed.

Gustavo Gutiérrez quotes this in his seminal *A Theology of Liberation*, reading the Exodus as an integral salvation—spiritual, revelatory, political.[7]

The same energy went on to inform many other fronts of human inequity, giving rise to a theological language of liberation for multiple historical scenes of oppression. James H. Cone's *God of the Oppressed* is thick with reference to Exodus. "The Exodus was the decisive event in

---

7. Gutiérrez, *Theology of Liberation*, 69.

Israel's history, because through it Yahweh was revealed as the Savior of an oppressed people. The Israelites were slaves in Egypt; thus, their future was closed. But Yahweh 'heard their groaning . . . he took heed of it.'"[8] Cone underlines how and why the Exodus story was taken up by black churches; the central image and dynamic of the biblical story "met their historical need."[9] Phyllis Trible refers to the Exodus as a "compelling . . . theme of freedom from oppression" which "speaks forcefully to Women's Liberation."[10] Rosemary Radford Ruether in a theological critique of sexism tells us that the God of the Bible is "One who does not take the side of the powerful but who comes to vindicate the oppressed . . . the prophetic God who takes the side of the poor, drowns the horsemen of Pharaoh and leads the slaves out of Egypt."[11]

But this is only the beginning. What we have to grasp is that this vital energetic step in new semiosis is only the first step on a journey of transformation that has a thousand trails yet to travel. As Liberation Theology beat a path into the many ramified channels of human oppression, it came to understand that one person's liberation may yet involve another's oppression. Especially feminist and womanist theology recognized that what counted as liberation for some people might still imply forms of hierarchy and oppression for others.[12] Oppression is complex and multiple and not easy to overcome in one splendid orgy of revolution. A journey of transformation is not the same as one of liberation, although it embraces the same ultimate end. This is why the biblical pathway will have several further passes to travel in order to reach its final account of trans-semiosis. It is also the reason for the present book, laying out a wider and deeper concept of human change than the first exuberant but simplistic expectations of liberation. To overcome the devious, twisting paths of dehumanization, a more concealed root has to be reached, beyond the massive and obvious unfairness of the Pharaoh.

The complexity is reinforced by a parallel observation, looking at what emerges in the Bible after Exodus. Liberation from Egypt is necessarily embedded in a wider narrative of the nation and identity of Israel, with all that implies. When "Israelite" is read in the text, we may very

8. Cone, *God of the Oppressed*, 58.

9. Cone, *God of the Oppressed*, 55.

10. Trible, "Depatriarchalising in Biblical Interpretation," 34.

11. Ruether, "Religion for Women," 309.

12. See, for example, Ruether, *Sexism and God-Talk*, and Douglas, *What's Faith Got to Do with It?*

easily hear "the nation of Israel," and this note is certainly anachronistic as the nation does not yet exist. But the very possibility of that connotation being heard—within the overall sweep of the first six books of the Bible—demonstrates it was very likely part of the intent of the compilers: they were creating the founding epic of the nation Israel. It is established opinion among scholars that a great deal of the biblical material was written down, or achieved its received form, during the period of the monarchies, or even later.[13] So, the question then becomes urgent: if this material is written retrospectively, and from the perspective of established societies with centralized identities, how do we critically distinguish and evaluate these different layers and continue to assert the foundational quality of the Exodus story?

Unpicking the Story

From one perspective, the very maintenance of the Exodus traditions within a national narrative testifies to their internal power and status. After all, which nation wants to celebrate its origin as miserable slaves: as prisoners and pawns of a genocidal imperial power? Yes, there are the plagues and the drowning of Pharaoh's chariots, asserting ultimate victory over Egypt. But this is victory by the hand of God, not by force of national arms, and the brute fact of slavery remains. To preserve a record of total helplessness, even via an experience of a redemptive God, is not what you would expect for the heart of a successful national epic. Again, yes, the Book of Joshua goes on to record military triumph in what becomes a fairly standard feat of arms, but that only makes the escape from Egypt stand out by contrast. In addition, serious questions can be raised against the historical accuracy of Joshua's account. The perspective that sees it simply as national propaganda serves to underline the utterly different semiotics of Exodus.[14] The theophoric name *Isra-el*

13. See Cohen, *From the Maccabees to the Mishnah*, 182.

14. "Careful examination of the archeological evidence has almost thoroughly destroyed the Conquest Model" (Calloway and Shanks, "Settlement in Canaan," 62). The overall biblical text backs up this archaeological conclusion at multiple points. One of the most notable is the instance of the central highland city of Shechem: there is no mention of conquest of this city in Joshua, and yet it is the strategic site of a covenant ritual among the tribes at the end of the book (Josh 24:1–28). The choice of the city strongly suggests the inhabitants were at least partly committed to the ideology of the Exodus group, and then are invited into full participation. "The assembly at Shechem (Joshua 24) makes sense as a ritual incorporation of part of the Canaanite populace,

also hints at the possibility of a Canaanite group identified around the divine name *El* prior to the arrival and impact of the Yahweh outsiders. The "conquest" of Canaan may then look more like a revisionist reading of progressive religio-political developments, and nothing like an actual historical blitzkrieg led by Joshua. At some point, however, the two cultural strands—the Canaanite peasantry and the Exodus group—and their respective "gods," were fused together, leading step-by-step to the weaving of a national story.[15]

It is never, therefore, simply the historical nature of the "conquest" that is the question; it is very much a matter of what core values the Yahweh group brings with them. Richard Elliott Friedman has argued strongly that the original group out of Egypt was solely the Levites, the biblical "tribe" which had no territory of its own and who subsequently came to act as priests for the rest of the twelve.[16] There is much about the Levites that is pretty striking, including their ferocious violence (for example, Exodus 32:25–29, where Levites kill three thousand of their own people). They come across as the shock-troops of Mosaic and Yahwist faith, a militant party driving forward the radical novelty of a religious code for liberated slaves. Friedman's thesis fits that of Gottwald's ("a

purged of their oppressive kings, newly tribalized, who throw off the Baal religion and accept Yahweh of the Israelites, who has helped them in their victories" (Gottwald, *Hebrew Bible*, 156).

15. Smith, *Early History of God*: "Yahweh, originally a warrior-god from Sinai/Paran/Edom/Taiman, was known separately from El at an early point in early Israel . . . In time El and Yahweh were identified . . ." (32–33). Smith sees the path of identification as an organic process in overall Israelite religion in the period of Judges and early monarchy. "The convergence of titles and imagery of deities to the personage of Yahweh appears to have been part of a wider religious development of conflation of religious motifs in Israelite tradition" (58). This is opposite to the position of Margaret Barker. Barker sees El and Yahweh as essentially different divine entities, embedded in early Israelite religion. The editors of the Exodus narratives are seventh and sixth-century "Deuteronomists" responsible for imposing their Yahwistic singularity on the tradition. "If the keynote of the Deuteronomists was an emphasis on the sacred history, the Exodus and the saving acts of Yahweh to the exclusion of all other gods, then it is easy to see that any traces of earlier religious practices in Jerusalem, had they been concerned with things other than the sacred history, the Exodus and the cult of Yahweh alone, would have had little chance of surviving" (Barker, *Great Angel*, 13). It goes without saying that Barker's perspective is not founded in the liberative historical narrative of Exodus. The thesis of two cultural deities progressively merged into one is well explained by an in-breaking group of refugees from Egypt carrying their memory of liberation with them, and through the vigor of the memory asserting a single and singular semiotics.

16. Friedman, *Exodus*.

group of outsiders . . . with enthusiastic adherence to the deliverer God Yahweh"[17]), but for Friedman less from the socio-historical aspect than from their crucial role in the formation of the biblical literary traditions. He points to a consistent body of laws and texts coming from the Levites, and within these the distinctive redemptive effect of Yahweh. It seems perhaps that there is certain circularity in Friedman's approach—the Levites are known from their considerable profile in the biblical stories, and therefore we know who "they" were right at the beginning of the story of Exodus. They become the clear-cut religious protagonists of Exodus, the group that brought their dramatic religion with them to Israel. However, I don't think anything human is that plain. We have to remember the big hint about diffuse origins of the Moses group given us by the text itself. At Exodus 12:38, we are told of a "mixed multitude" which came out of Egypt "with the Israelites" (*rab ereb*—also translated as "foreign mob"). We can be sure of the phenomenon of any motivated group moving in a common direction inevitably attracting a larger mass of people. A strong ideological core to the Exodus experience makes a lot of sense, but that doesn't mean there weren't hangers-on, fellow travelers and johnny-come-latelys deeply embedded in the mix and all along the way.[18]

Friedman does, however, give major substance to the impact of the Exodus experience on the content and meaning of what came to constitute the Bible and, with that, wider culture. He calls it a "necessary part—a *foundational* part—of religion, literature and history ever after."[19] One of the many compelling features he points to is that there are fifty-two instances of the rule "do not mistreat aliens (strangers)" in the three biblical writings he attributes to the Levites (what are known as the E, P, and D sources[20]). He quotes the Canadian scholar Glen A. Taylor. "In

17. Gottwald, *Tribes of Yahweh*, 210; see n. 5 above.

18. The genetic diversity of the present-day Jewish Levite line as described by Friedman suggests indeed it was ideology, not tribal bloodline, that counted. At that early stage, presumably anyone could have joined the ranks of the deeply persuaded (Friedman, *Exodus*, 109–12).

19. Friedman, *Exodus*, 83.

20. From "Elohist," "Priestly" and "Deuteronomist" (Friedman, *Exodus*, 62). Adding the Yahwist source (known as "J," from the German spelling), we complete the four sources of what is known as the Documentary Hypothesis. The argument of four separate written sources behind the first five books of the bible (the Torah) emerged in the nineteenth century and has been hugely influential ever since. Friedman's *Who Wrote the Bible?* is a ringing endorsement of the hypothesis, going so far as to speculate on the character and identity of some of the authors, as well as specifying the historical

ancient Near Eastern laws, while there is usually protection and provision given to the marginalized (i.e., widows and orphans), there is typically no mention of provision for the sojourner, or foreigner, as Deuteronomy provides. This is an emphasis unique to the Hebrew law codes."[21] What is the reason for this exceptional emphasis? Friedman responds according to the text. "All three Levite sources answer word-for-word the same: 'Because you were aliens in Egypt.'"[22] Behind major literary sources in the composition of the Bible lies an indelible experience of alienation, state-lessness, human insecurity—and rescue from it. It is this bedrock which makes up the core of the biblical narrative, and nothing else can account for the vitality and urgency of what comes after. It is because the biblical text remembers the *human transformation* of the Exodus that everything after nourishes the vibrant possibility of ever more of the same.

And so, we return to the drama of a God who hears the groaning of the Israelites. God remembers his covenant with Abraham, Isaac, and Jacob. The mention of covenant ties the story to a formal legal commitment by God to the Patriarchs and their descendants. It is this formal commitment which provides, on one level at least, the main architecture of the story, moving the whole thing forward through history, reaching through into the period of the monarchy. God commits Godself to this group, and has done so pre-emptively from an earlier time, while moving

---

stresses behind their work. According to Friedman, the E and J documents come from the Northern and Southern Kingdoms (Israel and Judah), respectively. They were written somewhere between ninth and eight centuries BCE, in the golden age of Israelite monarchies, before the rise of new imperial powers in Mesopotamia. They seem to have been combined after the fall of the Northern Kingdom to the Assyrians (722 BCE), probably when northern refugees brought their manuscripts to Jerusalem. The merging with the southern account was pressed by the need to reconcile sibling rivals now living side-by-side. Friedman's conclusions are necessarily part of ongoing academic debate and shifts of opinion, but they supply a vital opportunity for popular critical appropriation of the Bible. The Documentary Hypothesis is currently challenged by what is called the Supplementary Hypothesis, which believes there is essentially one original source (D, seventh century) and later supplements or additions. In particular, J, composed in the later period of exile, provided a benign corrective to the D viewpoint, underlining God's unilateral commitment to Israel, rather than a bilateral, breakable covenant. See Van Seters, *Pentateuch*, and Kugler and Hartin, *Introduction to the Bible*, 49–50. The idea of a corrective fits well with the approach here, understanding the first book of the Bible as a profound, proleptic critique of the logic of violence and punishment itself. We will return to the great concluding novella of forgiveness in Genesis in the next chapter.

21. Friedman, *Exodus*, 63; see Taylor, "Review of Lundbom 'Deuteronomy.'"

22. Friedman, *Exodus*, 63; from Exod 22:21; Lev 19:33–34; Deut 10:19.

progressively into the future. In the immediate circumstances, God will make a collective covenant with the people of Israel at Sinai, related in both the Book of Exodus and the Book of Deuteronomy (where the mountain is called Horeb). It is often noted that the covenant genre in the Pentateuch reflects ancient vassal treaties, especially Hittite and Assyrian.[23] But in the place of the political overlord—a figure who is usually not obliged to more than vague formulae of goodwill toward the inferior party—the God of the Israelites enters into profound undertakings on behalf of his chosen. In the Exodus narrative, this covenant God turns up to pay his dues in full in concrete and dramatic form. From the other side, the newly minted people of Yahweh are now expected to keep their own detailed obligations and practices. What we see, then, in the covenant formulation is a radical and transformative use of contemporary political semiotics. The sign system of treaty relationship becomes a vehicle of religious relationship, one of enormous vitality and centered always in the Exodus. God fulfills his commitments by setting slaves free and leading them to a promised land. In return, the people are brought into a living relationship demanding transformative behaviors.

By means of covenant semiotics, the Exodus thus becomes an operative theme for all subsequent history. The writers of the Old Testament are able to express relationship with God in a dynamic, historical, detailed, and deeply personal fashion. Commenting particularly on the Book of Deuteronomy, Walter Brueggemann says, "This hugely creative interpretive act that pushed Israel's theological horizon in a covenantal direction was accomplished by a small interpretive cadre working with great intentionality."[24] By definition, almost, it is a crucial interpretive minority which creates the semiotic codes which go on massively to impact subsequent generations. The production of transformative patterns of meaning in a written text does not need a "biblical number" of writers/editors. On the contrary, a half-dozen scribes working consistently could do it. But what *is* needed is a genuinely transformative momentum for them to be working within, an event or set events which permanently changed core human relationships. That is what we call Exodus.

23. Boadt, *Reading the Old Testament*, 176–81.

24. Brueggemann, *Old Testament Canon and Christian Imagination*, 90. Friedman says the cadre was Jeremiah and his scribe, Baruch! (*Who Wrote the Bible?*, 147).

Exodus of Prophets and Kings

Another instance of "crucial minority" is of course the company of Israel's prophets, and to understand the impact of Exodus, we need to see the way prophets inhabit the theme and make it operative. Friedman tells us that seven of the prophets refer to the Exodus in thirty-three verses.[25] One of the striking things about the list is the way the eighth-century prophets figure so emphatically (Hos 2:15, 11:1, 12, 9, 13, 13:4; Amos 2:10, 3:1, 9:7; Mic 6:4, 7:15; Isa 11:16, 19:20–22). The eighth century BCE is the dawn of the great written prophecies of Israel, and their use of the theme tells us the meaning of Yahweh for these crucial minorities belonged intimately to the Exodus experience. It also tells us that the intentional semiotics of Exodus emerged at least a century before the formulations of Deuteronomy and quite likely helped prompt them into being.

> "When Israel was a child I loved him, and out of Egypt I called my son." (Hos 11:1)

> "I have been the Lord your God ever since the land of Egypt; you know no God but me, and besides me there is no savior." (Hos 13:4)

> "[T]here shall be a highway from Assyria for the remnant that is left of his people, as there was for Israel when they came up from the land of Egypt." (Isa 11:16)

The prophet Amos makes most drastic use of the theme. From a critical perspective, Amos' prophecy comes to an end at chapter 9, verse 8a: "The eyes of the Lord God are upon the sinful kingdom, and I will destroy it from the face of the earth."[26] The voice of doom falls like a hammer on an anvil. It follows a verse which deliberately undoes the semiotics of Exodus, telling us that bringing Israel "up from the land of Egypt" is no different from similar interventions God made for the Philistines and Arameans. So, all the wonder of Exodus is reduced to just another instance of God's sovereign management of the nations. But an earlier passage uses the semiotics in another way—as precisely the reason why

---

25. Friedman, *Exodus*, 78.

26. The final line at 8b has obviously been added by a revisionist hand, along with the much more upbeat oracles from 9 through 15. See *New Interpreter's Study Bible*, 1290.

God will now *punish* his people. The unique work of salvation morphs seamlessly into a project of retributive violence.

> Hear this word that the Lord has spoken against you, O people of Israel, against the whole family that I brought up out of the land of Egypt: You only have I known of all the families of the earth; therefore I will punish you for all your iniquities. (Amos 3:1–2)

We can recognize here an inversion of Exodus semiotics, one paradoxically confirming their continuing power for the writer and his audience. Amos brings a harsh twist in those semiotics, setting underway a path of "covenant punishment" that will culminate in the dire list of threatened disasters in Deuteronomy 28. Amos says *because* God has chosen the Israelites, he will punish them; Deuteronomy says *if* the Israelites do not keep the covenant, unparalleled disaster (which very likely has already happened) will be unleashed by God against them. What we learn here is that biblical semiotics are *unfolding* semiotics. They are a set of signs that, like all human signs, have numerous possible subordinate, parallel, or developing pathways. We will have cause to return below to Deuteronomy's strict invocation of covenant punishment and what this might mean for Jewish and Christian theology. The thing to bear in mind is that the Deuteronomic pathway is one among others, and, as we have just suggested, an inversion of meaning can also have the effect of continuing to strengthen core meaning upon which the inversion depends! Exodus as meaning does not reach a dead-end because of Amos-style judgments (the editorial history of Amos itself demonstrates this). It is capable of springing fresh beginnings, as we shall also continue to see, and precisely because its inversion does not exhaust it.

The rise of the monarchy offers a powerful parallel structure of meaning, one that stands in counterpoint if not contrast to Exodus. Monarchy is the normal development of an emerging state apparatus organizing for purposes of identity and security, as the Bible itself recounts. The people said to the priest and judge, Samuel, "[W]e are determined to have a king over us, so that we also may be like other nations, and that our king may govern us and go out before us and fight our battles" (1 Sam 8:19–20). The fact of the monarchy's existence provided the centralization of resources and stability that doubtless enabled the production and publication of manuscripts such as, perhaps, the E and J documents, and almost certainly D, under Josiah.[27] Someone has to pay for the education, work, and materials of scribes, and it is very much in the interests of the king to have a school of such people in his employ, committed to his overall policy and, in many cases, dynasty. So it is that we meet one of the primary paradoxes of the Bible story: a people and a meaning based in escape from an oppressive king and his state apparatus turn to exactly those political features in order to maintain themselves. Just before the words of the people to Samuel, the prophet said this to them:

> These will be the ways of the king who will reign over you: he will take away your sons and appoint them to his chariots and to be his horsemen, and to run before his chariots . . . and some to plow his ground and to reap his harvest, and to make his implements of war and the equipment of his chariots . . . He will take the best of your fields and vineyards and olive orchards and give them to his courtiers . . . He will take one-tenth of your grain and of your vineyards and give it to his officers and his courtiers . . . He will take one-tenth of your flocks, and you shall be his slaves. (1 Sam 8:11–17)

Et cetera. A people founded in escape from state slavery will institute one of their own; and yet, it will also be the very institutions of centralized power that provide the tools for institutional memory of that escape! The monarchy becomes a very non-transformative pivot around which a transformative set of texts survive and continue to exert their influence.

The figure of King Solomon emerges as the very greatest in terms of fame and wealth, standing at the apex of what is effectively an Israelite Empire. He is also an icon of Wisdom, a theme and connection memorably referenced by Jesus in the New Testament (e.g., Luke 7:35, 11:31). He seems to play, therefore, this paradoxical role to the full: that of political and imperial regression, while also offering an arc of positive semiosis through the ages. Walter Brueggemann in his fiery treatment, *The Prophetic Imagination*, tells us,

> Solomon managed what one would think is not possible, for he had taken the Mosaic innovation and rendered it null and void. In tenth-century Jerusalem it is as though the whole revolution

---

27. See the narrative at 2 Kgs 22:3—23:3, where it is the combination of the king, the high priest, and a key group of scribes and courtiers who "find" and promulgate "the scroll of the Torah." See Friedman, *Who Wrote the Bible?*, 101–02, for the generally accepted thesis that this scroll was the Book of Deuteronomy, or at least a first draft and basis.

Israel and Judea, there was still a powerful truth left, and what that was had to be related ultimately to the Exodus experience. Exodus provided the primary impetus and held the deep code for still further biblical mutation as we go forward.

What Is His Name?

Without the regenerative semiosis of Exodus, none of the future would be possible. We need, therefore, to dwell again and further in the actual drama of the writing, in the change of meaning that is being rehearsed there. An unknown God—unknown, as regards his proper name and nature, either to Moses or the Hebrews—reveals Godself. Doing so sets in motion a sense of absolute divine relation to and on behalf of the oppressed. This is the writing of the E source, which, according to Friedman, comes from a community of Moses-loyal priests located at the ancient Israelite shrine of Shiloh.[31] The reflection they share understands the revelation of the name of God not in an abstract philosophical sense, but in a sense of unquenchable life in relationship with those to whom he is speaking. Thus the "being" of this God is not pure metaphysical existence, but pure immediate relation. God's name is given in three variants. First "I am who I am" which also can mean "I will be what/who I will be" (Exod 3:14a). Then he tells Moses to say, "I AM has sent me" (Exod 3:14b). Finally, he adds that Moses is to say, "Yahweh has sent me" (Exod 3:15). The third iteration is presented as "Lord" in many translations, following the Jewish practice of replacing this divine name, too holy to speak, with a superscript, *Adonai*, meaning "Lord." Commentators tell us this name, Yahweh, is yet another form of the verb "to be" which can be translated as "He is" or "He will be."[32]

The triple declaration to Moses of a name derived from the verb "to be" provides an intense set of signs of a God-in-relation. His insistent being is for the sake of relation with the Israelites. Moses needs to have this name given to him by God, because it is God's identity, containing its own warrant, a pledge of the Godself-in-relation. This is very different from Aquinas' remote *ipsum esse*, although that Latin thought had to be at some level influenced by it.[33] *Yah* (a short or primitive form, e.g., Exod

31. Friedman, *Who Wrote the Bible?*, 72
32. Stalker, "Exodus," 179c.
33. Bartlett, *TBM*, 83–5.

15:2)[34] is absolute life related to those who don't have life—life in the midst of death, creative life in relation As such, the name forms a prodigious breakthrough of meaning, a semiotic supernova. Reading that text today still communicates a sense of awe and primary revelation.

Thus, the urgency of the condition of the oppressed is matched by an equivalent urgency of divine relationship. The two codes interpret each other, inasmuch as the condition of the oppressed victim would not reach a distinct historical value without the absolute relation of the divine. Nor would the relation with Yahweh, the God who revealed himself to Moses, achieve the clarity of its truth without it erupting on the scene of human desolation. This God, this *Yah*, cannot be known unless he comes entirely stripped of the trappings of worldly structure. The meeting of God in the desert is a core feature of the Abrahamic religions, an indispensable mark of their authentic realization. In terms of a scene of emptiness as the only place where the otherness of God can truly be apprehended, it is also the classic contemplative setting. But Exodus is not the simplicity of a mystic's solitary meeting with God, in isolation from the world. It is the arrival of the biblical God on the scene of human meaning in order to challenge and transform it.

This God necessarily touches the world where the world is least integrated with itself, where the world frays away into the spaces hidden to and by the world's triumphant self-identity. God arrives in the unrecorded space, the desert, the place which is not the metropolis, the wasteland which no one wants and hardly anyone lives in. From there, he addresses those without identity living within the metropolis. Moses had to leave Egypt to find God in the land of Midian, in order then to return with this God *to* Egypt. God then arrives among the victims of human violence, the offcasts of a sacred system already in place, the detritus of sacred order who should not be seen or recognized in the company of imperial power. Now, arriving from the desert, God starts with them, raising them to historical view and agency, giving them a story, a writing, a book. But at least at the beginning, and in the concrete circumstances, it seems such an intervention cannot happen without an accompanying, reciprocating violence on the part of the violated.

We are told that the liberation of the Hebrews will come at the cost of the dispossession of others. After God promises to bring them to a land flowing with milk and honey, God directly adds, "to the country

34. Stalker, "Exodus," 179c.

of the Canaanites, the Hittites, the Amorites, the Perizzites, the Hivites, and the Jebusites" (Exod 3:8). As already discussed, it is highly unlikely a straightforward dispossession of other peoples actually happened. But what the text provides is a sense of sovereign decision and power and, ultimately, an ideology of separation from non-Exodus cultures.[35]

At the actual point in the story, the signaled intention massively emphasizes the sense of the God of Exodus' determination and decision. The God who will set these people free will carry them through to a land where they can dwell permanently, and for the sake of which others must take second place and, if necessary, be deprived. The contradiction is immediately apparent to contemporary eyes, but at the primary level of the Exodus picture it should not scandalize. We already see God as a rival of Pharaoh and the whole project of Exodus is nothing short of a personal duel with this semi-divine king—a military struggle carried through by a God who is committed against the Egyptians for the sake of his own (un)people. In the historical conditions of historical oppression and homelessness, there can hardly be another possibility—both real and conceptual—than some form of revolution and overthrow of established control. It is, as we have seen, what *Hapiru* do! What is essential is the powerful dynamic of the narrative from start to finish, its assured sense that the God of the Hebrews will bring this about and nothing can stop his will.

We have not yet arrived at the fuller revelation of a God whose ways are not those of *homo violentus*. We will have to wait for the political collapse of Israel, much later, for that. At the same time, this should not blinker us to the semiotic vigor and value of the Exodus account. We are dealing with a breakthrough within the field of generative violence, one that goes to the roots of the human structure and raises them to view, thus shaking that actual structure to the foundations. The victim is now visible and to be counted as part of history. It is this that provides the true raw energy of Exodus, not in any supposed revenge of the conquered. The promise of the land is a way of affirming the historical endurance of the revelation, not the establishment of another state controlling its borders with force of arms.

35. Cf. Deut 7:1–2: "When the Lord your God brings you into the land that you are about to enter and occupy, and he clears away many nations before you . . . and when the Lord your God gives them over to you and you defeat them, then you must utterly destroy them." According to Friedman, this is likely written in the midst of the Josaianic reform at the end of the seventh century BCE (*Who Wrote the Bible?*, 117–35).

In this perspective it becomes doubly necessary to view the text also within the broader sweep of the whole Bible. It's only when the deeper implications of liberation are plumbed in the semiotic continuum of the Scripture that it is possible to think of the "other," of the non-Israelite, of "the Samaritan," as also a subject of God's mercy. Indeed, precisely because of the perceived contradiction in Exodus, it is critical that further books are written over the course of time, exactly as happened. The Bible is always an ongoing semiosis, rather than an everlasting single point, both departure and arrival together, always the same. It is a journey toward the improbable, and the initially inconceivable, meaning of divine nonviolence. But our next sketch of biblical semiotics already confirms the direction. In Genesis, we will see directly how the functional xenophobia of Exodus is already canceled out in that pre-emptive text.

Meanwhile, the signs of the Exodus story march forward. The ten plagues can be seen as ten direct acts of aggression by God against Pharaoh and Egypt. They are ordered according to a pattern of escalating divine power and terror. They first originate in water (snakes/sea monsters, blood, frogs), then on land (gnats, flies, cattle), then in the air (boils from thrown ash, hail, locusts). Finally, darkness and death of the firstborn strike from the heavens. Their purpose is both to set the Israelites free and to show them that the Lord is indeed their God, the divine "I AM" (Exod 10:2). Again, there is no escaping the generative violence in bringing about these goals. But at the same time, the choreographed progression suggests a theatre of action, one designed to bring about a formative change both in Pharaoh and in those who read or listen to this account. The plagues can all be given naturalistic explanations, including the last—i.e., some sort of pathogen in foods contaminated by prior plagues, then given to the privileged firstborn. But the semiotic drama is always what counts, the breaking in of Yahweh into a human history dominated by Pharaoh, overturning it and in the process creating a people.

The plagues should, therefore, be read as continued interpretants, or really re-interpretants, of the status quo. And the final liberation of the people—the Passover—is the definitive change of human meaning and the paradigm case of such. The interweaving of the death of the firstborn with the account of the first Passover heightens the distinction between the freedom of the Israelites and the doom of the Egyptians. In contrast with the Egyptians, the firstborn of the Israelites (including animals) belong to the Lord (Exod 13:11–13). They were redeemed at the price of life itself (that of the Egyptians), and afterward in Canaan the Israelites are to acknowledge this with an animal sacrifice. Even so, the authority of Pharaoh is now surrendered to the Lord for the sake of a totally different way of life. The fact that Jesus can be seen as himself interpreting Passover, by offering himself as the Lamb of self-giving, reinforces the whole sequence as a chain of new meaning, one reaching its final term in nonviolence.

There is in fact another way of historically interpreting Exodus which seems to set the whole thing on its head—the Egyptian way. In James Williams' book, *The Bible, Violence and the Sacred,* he gives the viewpoint of Hellenistic-era Egyptian writers, like Manetho, a priest (third century BCE), and Apion, a scholar (first century CE).[36] These Egyptians were familiar with the biblical story, probably through Jews living in Alexandria, and they countered the Exodus narrative by claiming that the Israelites did not escape—they were in fact expelled! Because the Hebrews were infected with various diseases and could have brought harm on the Egyptians, they were thrown out. This is a plausible account—from the Egyptian viewpoint. Many centuries separated these Egyptians from the Pharaoh of the Exodus, but the mindset of blaming victims is perennial. It could easily have been the case that what was understood as liberation by the Hebrews was seen in fact by the Egyptians as a necessary casting-out. The fact that in the Bible account the Egyptians are described as giving the Hebrews trinkets of gold and silver as they go (Exod 3:22, 11.2) reinforces the possibility of their seeing them as possessing a power of curse needing to be mollified. The text even says that the Pharaoh "will drive you away" (Exod 11:1). The parallel *Hapiru* story of Abram and his wife, Sarai, in Egypt (Gen 12:10–20) is clearer still. It tells us explicitly that Pharaoh releases Sarai from his harem, and sends her and her husband on their way, because he discovers, via an *affliction of plagues,* that he has broken a powerful taboo. "Why," he says, "did you not tell me that she was your wife?" (Gen 12:18).

The existence of two very different interpretations related to the Exodus underscores a semiotic analysis. What on the one side is expulsion, on the other is liberation. In the one case (the Egyptian), you are dealing with the sacred victim, alternately hated and placated. In the other (the Israelite), the God of liberation intervenes to set in motion a totally different way of understanding and appropriating human existence. Yahweh—he who is and causes to be—first appears on the side of the rejects of history. His action thus begins to dismantle the semiotic apparatus

36. Williams, *Bible, Violence, and the Sacred,* 89, 270, n. 35.

of scapegoating and othering, leading step by step and inevitably to an alternative semiotics of compassion and love. Reading the Bible this way obviously discounts a literalist approach. Instead, it accepts the historical critical method as clearing the ground of "mythologized" accounts. But when we then understand that a deeper process of semiotic change is underway in the whole complex—of both history and writing—we suddenly achieve a very different sense of revelation. What is much more important than either elusive brute fact or inerrantist authority is the progression of interpretation and meaning. The true miracle of revelation is the connection with a God-in-relation who has begun a journey of human change, starting with the dispossessed. Only those dispossessed of this world's apparatus of assured meaning are able to embark on this journey. For sure they will seek, very quickly, to re-appropriate that assured meaning for themselves (hence kings, battles, and temples). But that is not what's important. What is irreducible is the labor of semiotic change engaged so brilliantly in Exodus. Once that journey is begun and the clock is started on its inevitable years of wandering, we are in the presence of transformative process that is and will be its own vindication.

Tell them that I AM has sent you!

2

Genesis

A Biography of God and Humans

IN THE THIRTY SECOND chapter of the first book of the Bible, Jacob, the father of the Twelve Tribes of Israel, has a personal wrestling match with a mysterious figure simply called a "man" (Gen 32:24–31). He subsequently recognizes this man to be nothing less than the person of God.

The episode is shrouded in a dreamy darkness and fear. It is similar in tone to Abraham's experience in Gen 15:7–18, where God appears and makes a covenant via a ritual of dismembered animals, fire, and smoke. In the Jacob wrestling-passage, the name used for God is Elohim, unlike the earlier, chapter fifteen story where it is Yahweh. As already highlighted, since the nineteenth century, commentators have seen these differing divine names in Genesis as signals of different literary sources employed in the compilation of the final book.

Interestingly, the name Elohim is used for God in the first part of one of the most clamorous Genesis texts, the one relating to Abraham and the sacrifice of Isaac in Gen 22:1–14. This would make these two memorable stories—the sacrifice of Isaac and Jacob wrestling with God—stand-out episodes from what is called the "Elohist" literary source.

But if this is the case—that they come from the same literary tradition—then it would seem that Jacob has brought Elohim down a notch or two. The God who asked to have Jacob's father, Isaac, sacrificed to him on top of a mountain is now the loser in a wrestling match down by the ford of a river.

We might naturally begin to ask whether there is anything intentional in the transitions, either in the sources, between individual sources, or the final editorial compilation. Critically speaking, beyond broad outlines, this would be difficult to establish, but it might also be that a semiotic shift is evidence itself of theological movement. The shift could potentially be "in the mind of the writer," or it could be something that works unconsciously, spontaneously in the flow of the text. For the study of biblical semiotics, therefore, a strict historical hypothesis is not necessary. All that is needed is to see the operative changes in the signs. Indeed, to talk of different sources, Genesis through Kings, is already a semiotic analysis in its own right on the plain surface of the book itself. There are different authors and voices collected together in a single work: so, there must be some code or codes that bring the differences into unity, and yet still preserve their particularity at least to some degree. What is important is both to discover a sense of what the unifying code is and, alongside, to understand what the different shifts may imply. There is a sort of alternating current running through the Bible text, shifting back and forth between the various sources, flashing up various differential themes and concerns. As suggested, a sensitivity to these sources already represents a built-in semiotic reading, a perceived play of meanings, one that necessarily includes possibilities of transformation.

So, in this instance, we can see that where Elohim first appears remote, unquestionable, absolute, at a certain point there is a relinquishing of power; and it all comes in relation to sacrifice and violence. We will see this play out in quite an extraordinary way as this particular episode continues, but first we need to lay out in more detail the overall structure and content of the traditional first book of the Bible. This will help us begin to grasp the revolutionary dynamic the text creates.

Genesis consists in basically two parts: the first eleven chapters, which comprise the creation accounts and prehistories of the human race; then, from twelve on, there are thirty-nine chapters of patriarchal sagas telling of Abraham, Isaac, Jacob, and Joseph.[1] The creation stories present God's deeds in setting up the world; the prehistories demonstrate human behavior in conflict with God's goals, followed by God's actions in response. God's responses often seem little better than the same reactive strategies typical of human beings, the bitter "three r's" of human

1. See Claus Westermann's exhaustive three-volume commentary, *Genesis, 1–11, 12–36, 37–50*, for detailed critical analysis of the text demonstrating the salient divisions and sources, plus extensive historical and literary commentary.

history—rivalry, retaliation, regret (cf. Gen 3:22, 6:6, 11:6–7). From chapter 12, however, things take an altogether different turn. The Lord calls Abraham for the sake of a different future, one that he will reveal to him progressively, and in which Abraham's own faithful response will become a blessing for all the peoples of the earth (Gen 12:1–3). The future focuses on a "land (the Lord) will show" Abraham, but effectively a struggle is engaged in the deep geography of the human self.

The source elements of the text, through to chapter 22, are something of a fugue between the Yahwist and priestly authors. But it is always the former (J) which establishes the controlling outline—that of primitive human dysfunction broken open by redemptive Abrahamic blessing. This in itself is a massive achievement, and placing it first in the Bible creates the signature complex of biblical images and themes profoundly seeking an answer to the problem of human existence. The way the material serves to preface and deeply question the subsequent writing, including especially Exodus and the Deuteronomic histories, is a major argument for the Supplementary Hypothesis.[2] In this case, Genesis becomes a deconstructive preface to the rest, reaching forward, in an altogether more radical way, to the fulfilment of Exodus' liberative longing.

Meanwhile, in the course of J's narrative, the P voice intervenes, naming its concerns for order and pattern in midst of the chaos (see the stress on sequence and number in the genealogies, chapters 5, 10, and 11). The E voice announces itself first with a doublet of the J story of Abraham's wife passed off as his sister, then the birth of Isaac, and then, most powerfully, with elements of the story of Jacob. All three sources converge in the great finale of Joseph.[3] The powerful confluence at this point suggests that all authors, especially the final compiler, understood the Joseph story as a climax, a triumph of divine blessing in the face of human potential for death. The sources or strata seem to continue to run through Exodus and subsequent books, but it is easy to see why there is traditionally a division in the books here, at the end of Genesis. There is very definitely a story-end at this point: Joseph remaining in Egypt, embalmed and buried there in a land at peace (Gen 50:26).

As already noted, over the whole arc of Genesis there is a considerable dissonance in the persona of God, in the way this God responds to the human situation. Essentially, there is a contrast of violent reaction

2. See note 20 on page 10–11, above.

3. See Friedman, *Exodus*, and the appendices of *Who Wrote the Bible?* for detailed division of sources.

over against salvific design, or vice versa. This dissonance is by now part of the Christian mindset, the default sensibility which almost any Christian has about God. But Genesis itself does not seek to embed this. Coming to understand the way the codes in Genesis work in this respect will help considerably in getting a handle on the profound meaning the book is giving about "God."

We are used to approaching Genesis morally and legally, and this helps us deal with the sense of dissonance. God has every right to punish people when they go off the rails—after all, he is the sole owner and ruler of everything. When he shows kindness, it is because he is dealing with a few good and pious men and women who deserve his love, or because he simply decides to, as is his right.

But as we are beginning to see, these things can be approached in a quite different way. If we approach the first book of the Bible in broader terms of codes, then we can pick out evolving messages about God spread across the whole of the book. The way in which the codes work is itself oblique and understated, which partly explains why they have not been clearly grasped before. We are distracted by the extreme humanity of the stories and their surface randomness. They appear as raw earthy folklore, or grand proto-cinematic epic. What can they possibly tell us about the spiritual figure of God? The possible hints that are given in the actions of God himself tend to get lost in the passion and drama of these stories. Another angle of approach, therefore, is vital. It will come by paying attention first to the register of human relations, above all in regard to violence, and then observing the larger implied mutations to the character of God. In this way, a profound meditation on the meaning of God is carried forward.

Genesis as Semiosis

If the sagas of the patriarchs make up a broad story of human changes, then God is the indirect protagonist of this change. Because God still appears absolute and self-legitimizing, and sometimes just as reactive as before, does not mean that his role and character are not profoundly in discussion. On the contrary. The underlying code tells us that as human beings change, it is also possible and necessary to understand God differently, and nowhere more critically than in relation to violence. Because violence is not primarily a moral issue, but a structural one, human beings cannot just give it up at the sovereign command of God. This would be effectively for God to wave a magic wand. But neither, in fact, can God give up violence himself so easily, given that God's persona will only be understood out of the human construct, in the terms the latter makes available. So, we see that after Abel's murder by Cain, God does not exact consistent punishment or vengeance; instead, Godself recognizes that it works the other way round, i.e., that Cain has accrued generative value to his own life via his violence. The mark of protection that the Lord places on Cain (Gen 4:15, "sevenfold vengeance") is equivalent to the God of the Bible being recruited by the cultural engine of foundational violence. This is made plain when Cain becomes the founder of the first city (Gen 4:17), the stone-walled space with a warrior garrison that in primitive form is the condensate of human violence. If there is any doubt about this coding, we have the subsequent accumulation in the seven generations from Cain, reaching its terrifying climax in Lamech's hyper-foundational claim: "If Cain is avenged sevenfold, truly Lamech seventy-sevenfold" (Gen 4:24). The unavoidable question is "What has God got himself mixed up in?"—one only answerable in the narrative as it progresses.[4]

Violence can only be given up voluntarily out of the depths of compassion. And it is only as this happens, not just emotionally, but in terms of cultural reflection, that the thought of God can be separated out from its generative origins. There is probably not a single human thought more *implicated* in violence than that of "god," thus it is entirely coherent that the biblical God should be represented by a conflicted struggle in conceptualization. What is remarkable about Genesis is that it more or less demonstrates this struggle thematically. It is only in the transformative power of signs of compassion that humanity changes, and hand in hand, so do its possible thoughts of God. The concept of God first emerged from the fires of violence and sacrifice and this, to begin with, is structurally unnegotiable; it is only by creating an alternative *human* semiosis that God can then feasibly be different. But it is the divinely inspired work of the Bible to display the alternative human semiosis, and thus, completing the circle, begin to challenge the very concept of God. It is God in the depths of the Bible who changes the meaning of God on its surface.

This is the special wonder of the Book of Genesis: it is theology by means of anthropo-semiosis. Genesis is the very first book of the Bible

---

4. It is also worth noting that the Yahwist writer might well be relaying historical memory of the Canaanite small city-state anarchy represented in the list of "kings" in Joshua 12, and analyzed in the work of Norman Gottwald; see *Tribes of Yahweh*.

not because it tells banal stories of a sinful origin with bad legal consequences, but because it announces at the outset that it is only by human
beings and God creating a new narrative about themselves that thoughts
about God can progressively be changed. The very first chapter of the
book—the seven days creation account—is a summary and headline to
the transformative meaning of the rest carrying through until the very
final chapter. It is a wonder in its own right, and personally I cannot conceive it having been added in any period before return from exile, when
the final redaction of Torah was compiled.[5] It tells us that Elohim created
entirely without violence, for the sake of an earth of blessing, i.e., one
that is absent of violence. There is no battle with rival gods, with other
ancient and monstrous forces, as seems the case in every other Ancient
Near Eastern or Mediterranean cosmogony. The God of the first chapter
of Genesis creates effortlessly with the word of speech, subtly underlining
the essential semiosis of creation. Everything comes online in an ordered
progression, but not in any dry or mechanical way. The repetitions of day
and night, and the refrain "God saw that it was good" place the whole
thing within a contemplative, holistic human experience of time and an
unbounded sense of good. At the end of the progression, human beings
are created "in the image of God," situating them somehow on a par with
the creator, participating in God's sovereignty. It is a magnificent writing,
echoing through the nightmare of human history with undimmed hope
and vision of final blessing. It seems impossible that it was composed
before priestly writers were able to forego theological use of violence and
therewith learn dramatically new revelatory meaning. Because the Book
of Genesis has been read in both a legalistic and simplistic folkloric manner, the chapter's whole orchestral movement of codes has been missed.
It was placed at the head of the book because the compiler recognized
that the overall meaning of the stories of Genesis demanded a God of
nonviolence. Nothing less.

It is important to underscore here also that the coding of Genesis
could not be written without the prior founding experience of the Exodus. Unless there was a God who had heard the groaning of his people,
who had pronounced his unfathomable name "I AM," there would not
have been the semiotic opening to see things from the perspective of the
victim, and to begin the long journey toward a sabbath blessing for all.

5. Friedman, *Who Wrote the Bible?*, 221–26. A *terminus ad quem* is supplied by the
deutero-canonical book of Sirach, written at the beginning of the second century BCE,
with its synopsis of stories of the patriarchs (Sir 44:16–23).

And, again, almost equally certain, the headline priestly contribution to Genesis would not be written unless that journey had also first passed by the way of exile and the loss of the national apparatus of force by which self-identity is so often constructed. In short, what comes first in the Bible has none of the naivety of beginnings, but is the sophisticated product of unique and long experience, including the loss of the promised land itself. The whole book is itself a reflection on the origins of Israel "out of Egypt," but not an Egypt of Pharaoh as enemy of the Lord, with his army about to be destroyed in the Red Sea. The Egypt out of which Israel emerges at the end of Genesis is a world-scene brought from economic and social catastrophe to health and well-being by Israel's best Wisdom in the person of Joseph. In which case Israel is Egypt's (or Babylon's) salvation and forgiveness, not its condemnation. In Genesis, Israel finally lives at peace in Egypt, intending its welfare, rather than setting up its kingdom in isolation and over against it.

But now we have given the book its boldest possible (but merited) theme, we should turn back once more to how the story begins, before even the call of Abraham. From the perspective of codes, the prehistories of the first eleven chapters tell us repeatedly that humanity is a native child of desire and rivalry. Rather than hinging the whole meaning of the Bible on chapters 2 and 3 and the so-called "original sin" of our first parents, the five stories—Garden of Eden, Cain and Abel, Sons of God and Daughters of Men, Flood, and Tower of Babel—demonstrate the structural condition of human mimesis. Aristotle told us that humans are "the most imitative of the creatures,"[6] but it is the Bible which shows us that the imitative character of our desire leads seamlessly through rivalry to violence and alienation. To ignore the structure of relationship, in favor of a single parental crime is to give a prosecutor's reading to the text, ignoring Genesis' clear systemic analysis. Again and again conflictual desire is signaled: at 3:6, where it has been caught from the serpent; at 4:7, where Cain is in its most desperate throes, lusting for the Lord's "gaze" directed instead toward Abel's offering; at 6:1–2, where "divine beings" see the beauty of women and break through a cosmic taboo; at 6:5, where it appears at a more psychic level as "every imagination of the thoughts of [the] heart" (KJV); and finally at 11:4, where the builders of the Tower of Babel yearn for something metaphysical, "a tower with its top in the heavens, and . . . a name for ourselves."

6. Aristotle, *Poetics*, 4 (1448b).

Yet it is not just human beings who are to be seen locked in the cage of mimesis. Barring the transcendent writing of the first chapter, the subsequent chapters, 1 to 11, show the creator God as the puppet of mimetic rivalry. For all God's sovereign power, he does not seem able to operate outside of a matrix of rivalry and retaliation. These conditions seem an ontological given, regardless of God's status as God. From the very beginning, he sets up a boundary and prohibition in the garden of Eden. Without the prohibition, the serpent, who is normally blamed for the seduction, would have nothing to direct the human couple's desire toward: mimetic desire simply would not exist. The serpent is in fact a construct of the prohibition. (To say the serpent is "a test" makes no sense, as desire must *first* be mobilized for a test to occur.) The "knowledge of good and evil" is already presupposed in the existence of the eponymous tree (Gen 2:17) placed in the very middle of the garden (Gen 3:3). God has set the scene and named the possibility and so created the preliminary knowledge itself (what Heidegger might call a "pre-understanding") of good and evil. All of which leads to the distinct possibility that the awakening of desire was always already intended as a feature of the human creature. (What indeed would it mean to be "in the image of God" if not to share in the possibility of desire for the other?) But this is to collapse the surface codes into a deeper emerging pattern, the deeper divine meaning which we intuit more and more pervading the text of Genesis.

Remaining for the moment on the surface of the text, we continue to follow the mimetic condition of the divine at the beginning of the human project. After the first parents duly give in to awakened desire, God debates with Godself in terms of his own rivalry (3:22: "See the man has become like one of us . . .") and so moves to an act of retaliation against Adam and Eve, throwing them out of the garden. In respect to Cain, God even more blatantly constructs the object of desire: rather than just announcing a boundary, enticing Adam and Eve's primal glance, he publicly displays his own "gaze" of preference for Abel's offering (Gen 4:4), thus inviting Cain's lethal jealousy. In the episode of the flood, he notes the entrenched mimeticism of the human heart and constant deeds of violence (Gen 6:5, 11) and comes to "regret" his creation. He proceeds to unleash the genocidal waters, oblivious to the irony of his own actions. In the story of the Tower of Babel, he is in direct competition with the builders, saying "this is only the beginning of what they will do; nothing that they propose to do will now be impossible for them" (Gen 11:6). To go on to confuse human language so people will be divided into separate tribes looks more like the actions of a cynical security apparatus, manipulating one ethnic group against another, rather than the work of a loving creator. It seems that the J author, and certainly the final editors, deliberately and ironically present God within the structures of mimesis. For them, mimesis acts as a code which controls the thought of the divine, just as it does the human.

We can state confidently, therefore, that the semiotics of these chapters of Genesis are thematically mimesis and rivalry. The semiotic code controls the sememes of "humans," "God" and "civilization." Genesis intends us to see this, understand it, and ultimately reject it. Effectively, Genesis chapters 2 to 11 have to be read ironically against the background of chapters 1, and then 12 through to the end. There is a double register of the divine: the first self-deconstructs while, at the same time, powerfully outlining the problem against which the second contends. The second is a completely fresh way of conceiving and constructing human existence, based essentially in a move away from violence and its revenges. A new set of signs and sememes arise within a narrative of human actions characterized by compassion and nonviolence. It is only as these show themselves that the possibility of a different understanding of God is intimated or suggested, one that then stretches in a future arc onward from Genesis. A reading like this is immensely more holistic, dynamic, and transformative than the Augustinian cosmic "fall," focused solely in chapter 3, and watched over by a God of unfathomable legal determinations.

A double register is essential if change is going to happen. It is not possible to change the governing set of signifiers at a stroke, especially the most transcendent of them—"God." The source of meaning in violence cannot be displaced all at once, only made weird and problematic. Meanwhile, what is possible is to show a range of compassionately deviated human behaviors which suggest the possibility of new meaning, since they are fully willed and planned by God. Ultimately, the I AM of Exodus evokes and provokes these meanings. But without a human set of signifiers—an actual semiotic code—it is literally impossible for language-based human understanding to express and grasp these meanings. So it is that Genesis begins to build up a file of these signifiers—a new code—in order that we might begin to embrace the possibility of a changed understanding of God and relationship with God.

Abraham and Family, Master Code Makers

Let us look at some of the crucial material illustrating these claims. As already cited, God (Yahweh) calls Abraham for the sake of a new future—in order to make him a blessing for all peoples. He says, "I will make of you a great nation, and I will bless you, and make your name great, so that you will be a blessing. I will bless those who bless you, and the one who curses you I will curse; and in you all the families of the earth shall be blessed" (Gen 12:2–3). This is an immense blessing, carrying well beyond the reactive strategies of the prehistories or, indeed, any simple protective scheme for Abraham. The migrant from Ur is to be a source of blessing to all the families of the earth, an agent not of prohibition or punishment but of sheer life and human welfare. Here is a positive, proactive intention, but how is this to come about?

In chapter 18, the Lord visits Abraham as a part of a larger journey in which he (the Lord) is going to investigate the "outcry" against Sodom and Gomorrah (Gen 18:20). The word "outcry" echoes the "outcry" in Exodus (Exod 3:7, 9),[7] the primal call of the Hebrews that so moved the Yahweh of the E writer to intervene decisively on their behalf. In which case, we are dealing with the oppression of the weak, the dispossessed, the homeless, the hopeless. The specific case against these cities is made in chapter 19, where an attempted gang-rape of visiting strangers is reported. Our moralizing and sexualizing Western viewpoint has centered on the feature of homosexual sex, not on the violent offense to care and hospitality. (Cf. the parallel and even more terrible story at Judges 19:22–26, where it becomes a female rape-murder, brutally perpetrated, demonstrating that the classic offense is indifferent to gender or sexual orientation.) It was Abraham's nephew, Lot, who first offered the strangers shelter. The townspeople accuse him of being himself "an alien" and threaten him in turn, underlining the *Hapiru* experience at the source of these stories. Yahweh is intimately concerned for these immigrants without rights and has come to check on what is happening before carrying out appropriate justice.

But it is exactly in this situation—one of Egypt-style oppression and offense—that Abraham steps forward to be a blessing, even to the city of oppressors. The pivotal story is told in chapter 18, prefacing the actual account of Sodom's crime with a desperate advance calculus of compassion. Abraham attempts to bargain away the Lord's intention to visit vengeance

7. In fact, the Exodus word is an older form of the Genesis word.

on the city, suggesting on a scale of ever-increasing daring that he not destroy Sodom, if only he can find "a few just men" within it. It is a story of earth-shattering power and beauty, with the man Abraham seeking to negotiate away the very principle of divine mimesis, attempting to break the divine from its matrix of reciprocity. But even before Abraham begins his odyssey of intercession, the floor is first given to the reflections of the Lord. Yahweh asks himself,

> Shall I hide from Abraham what I am about to do, seeing that Abraham will become a great and mighty nation, and all the nations of the earth shall be blessed in him. No, for I have chosen him [Hebrew "known"] that he may charge his children and his household after him to keep the way of the Lord by doing righteousness and justice . . . (Gen 18:17–19)

The self-questioning is itself a subtle shift in coding, and in fact not all that subtle. The figure of God is telling us that although he disposes of final retributive power—one that he is about to exercise with extreme prejudice—he is newly sensitive to the role of universal blessing belonging to Abraham, and the possibilities therein of a different response. This places the accent on alternative human emotions, especially human welfare and compassion, not on divine retribution; and it encourages the reader to enter into the path of these emotions. All along, of course, it is God who has set all this up, who has called Abraham and, as the Hebrew expresses, has "known" him, or, in other words, has entered into relation with him. So, what Abraham is about to do—to seek to negotiate a reprieve for Sodom—is already a possibility established by God, in fact engendered in him by God's astonishing promise. God now gives him space to fulfill his appointed role and so to produce a "teachable moment" for his children who likewise are "to keep the way of the Lord." There are thus many reflecting facets of irony here, playing on God's overarching role, on Abraham's promised role, and ultimately on the explicit qualities of compassion and forgiveness. God's words here are basically an audible stage-whisper accompanied by a broad wink, inviting the audience into an emerging persona of God—one that somehow depends on Abraham! It is a prismatic episode of the double register: the God of mimetic violence refracted by Abraham's compassion into a very different possible identity.

Abraham fails in his attempt to dissuade God from destruction. Presumably, God could not find ten just men—the final number agreed on. At the same time, the impression is given that if Abraham had kept going, he could have got the number lower, even down to one! The city could perhaps have been saved for the sake of one righteous person. Even so, an unspoken projection and possibility are set up through the broader matrix of biblical writing, seeking the semiotic possibility of such a figure. I say "semiotic" because, precisely, we are still talking in terms of a bare code: we have yet to discover the actual representational contours of such a figure. In which case, the whole episode at chapter 18 reaches and points forward to further elements of coding. The adjective "righteous" (*saddiq*) is used seven times in the dialogue of Abraham and the Lord, so a natural term of this journey would be the righteous (*saddiq*) servant of Second Isaiah who makes many righteous (*yasdiq*, Isa 53:11). Many specific concrete elements of coding will also be provided by this figure in the actual circumstances of exile, as we shall see below. Meanwhile, the theological architecture of such a development is reinforced by the ongoing semiosis of Genesis. For if Yahweh shifts his coding through Abraham in chapter 18, we have already seen that such a change is also underway for Elohim in chapter 32. And, after that, if there is the projection of one righteous man who saves all in the Sodom episode, that figure is realized archetypally in the story of the last chapters of the book—the saga of Joseph.

Before Joseph, however, first let us conclude the story of Jacob. After Jacob has wrestled with "the man," he refuses to let the mysterious figure go until he grants Jacob a blessing. The man replies that Jacob will no longer be called Jacob, "but Israel, for you have striven with God and humans and have prevailed" (Gen 32:28). Then he blesses him. After this Jacob announces, "I have seen God face to face, and yet my life is preserved" (Gen 32:30). Something about the encounter told Jacob that he had met God/Elohim. There is obviously a coding here, too. It is only via this *man* who loses to Jacob in a wrestling match that Jacob can meet a changed meaning of God. Elohim also gives Jacob a new name: "the one who strives with God and humans and prevails" (Gen 32:28). It is possible to prevail with humans, but who fights God and wins? It is only via a totally alternative meaning of God that this is possible—a meaning mediated by "a man" who surrenders the semiotics of violent victory, allowing himself to be held down by his rival who extorts a blessing from him. Even so, the God whom Israel is in relationship with is a God who does not win by violent means, who in fact loses—and needs "a man" to signify as much!

And we do not have to rely simply on a parsing of the wrestling match for the change of coding. The story continues with a truly remarkable set of linguistic notes, carrying us to an even clearer understanding.[8] To see God face-to-face in the Hebrew is *panim el-panim*. Hence, Jacob names the place Peniel, meaning "face of God." To see God's face is no small thing—it is the goal of all human life, and Jacob achieves it here from the depths of his story of dishonesty and fear of deserved retribution. After all, the place where all this happened is on the far side of the river, away from Esau and his four hundred men, and the imminent threat that they would "come and kill us all, the mothers with the children" (Gen 32:11). Jacob rightly fears revenge from the brother from whom he stole birthright and blessing, and from whom he ran for his life many years prior. But nothing like this happens. Indeed, what occurs is exactly the opposite. In the morning, Jacob "looks up" and sees Esau coming with the four hundred. He hurriedly forms a procession with his wives and their children, putting his favorites, Rachel and Joseph, at the back. He then goes ahead of them all, to meet his brother and his fate, bowing to the ground seven times. But the totally unexpected occurs. Esau "ran to meet him, and embraced him, and fell on his neck and kissed him, and they wept" (Gen 33:4). The picture is one of intense emotion, acceptance, and surrender, and nothing has prepared us for it. Instead, it is Jacob who must give us the clue. Jacob begs Esau to accept his gifts, "for truly to see your face is like seeing the face of God (*pane elohim*)—since you have received me with such favor" (Gen 33:10). Jacob has not slept since seeing God face to face. The experience is still seared palpably in his soul. There can really be no ambiguity—the encounter with Esau awakens exactly the same experience again: Esau's face of love and nonviolence is the very face of God. As James Williams says, Jacob "clearly means that Esau's face is a *reminder* of the divine countenance . . ."[9]

There is no explanation for Esau's complete metamorphosis, from armed threat to gentle love.[10] It is an act of pure grace, unmediated any-

8. The whole passage here has attracted numerous commentaries, including his own style of semiotic reading by Roland Barthes, *Analyse Structurale et Exégèse Biblique*. See Williams, *Bible, Violence and the Sacred*, 48–50, from which I take key details here.

9. Williams, *Bible, Violence and the Sacred*, 53.

10. Earlier Jacob had sent gifts of livestock ahead with the intention of mollifying Esau: "I may appease/atone his face . . . and afterwards I shall see his face, perhaps he will lift up my face" (Gen 32:20, translation from Williams, *Bible, Violence and the Sacred*, 46). Jacob is thinking in terms of exchange and sacrificial offering, but the

where in the text, if not by the theophany at Peniel itself. In short, it is a transformative code at work, one which needs no justification outside itself and its variants. The man who wrestles with Jacob and loses and then becomes God is the same sememe as Esau who loses, who forgives, who is recognized as the face of God. The fact that Jesus, in turn, uses exactly the same motifs employed for Esau to describe the Father, in the parable of the Two Sons (Matt 21:28–32), demonstrates that we are dealing with a transformative semiosis—one which can take centuries to be recognized and suddenly achieve an entirely new use and urgency. In Jesus' story, the younger of two brothers brusquely takes possession of an inheritance, leaving his elder brother to labor, while he departs for a distant country and a life of pleasure and excess. Forced to return, he expects rejection from his father, but instead "while he was still far off his father saw him and was filled with compassion; he ran and put his arms around him [Greek: "fell on his neck"] and kissed him" (Luke 15:20). What Jesus does is shift the Esau story pattern directly to the figure of God, and adds the explicit theme of compassion. So it is that transformative biblical semiotics slowly reaches its goal.

The Triumph of Joseph

However, the semiotics of Genesis are still not finished. Jacob's favorite son, Joseph, becomes the central figure of his own saga: a man who is entirely the victim of collective violence, first in Canaan among his brothers, and then in Egypt in the house of Potiphar. Joseph is one of the paradigm figures of the Hebrew Bible providing Girard with the revelatory pattern of mimetic crisis and scapegoating.[11] In other cultures, Joseph would have met his death at the hands of the mob and been accounted a god and, as such, the source of any deliverance subsequently experienced. The wonder of biblical semiotics is that Joseph is plainly represented as a collective victim, but one saved by God, one who lives and rises to supreme power, becoming the sole ruler under Pharaoh and wearing his signet ring. He efficiently organizes the resources of the Nile according to a real-world, rational plan. He finds a way to feed everyone

---

verse here strongly foreshadows the actual meeting with Esau where he does see his face. Esau's appearance and attitude at that point are heedless of the atoning gifts. He later pointedly asks, "What do you mean by all this company that I met?" (33:8)

11. Girard, *Things Hidden*, 149–54.

during famine, because there was "no one so discerning and wise" as him (Gen 41:39). The blessing promised to Abraham for all the families of the earth at the beginning of the journey is fulfilled now in stunning fashion, at the end, in the figure of Joseph. Genesis completes the arc of its own drama with unarguable éclat. Joseph in this sense is the full completion of the faith journey of the patriarchs. Egypt at the conclusion of the story is the world blessed with peace. It becomes a place of blessed order and stability, a society where all agricultural land is absorbed by a sacred system of Pharaoh and priests. The people work the land, giving a fifth of the produce to the Pharaoh, while living together in cities—a kind of theocratic feudalism and urbanization (47:20–26).[12]

But the truly transformative semiosis belongs to the reconciliation between Joseph and his victim-making brothers. The long game played by Joseph in getting them to bring their youngest to Egypt—Benjamin the only other son of Joseph's mother, Rachel—is a masterpiece of narrative tension and emotion. Eventually, Joseph succeeds in ensnaring Benjamin, rendering him forfeit as his slave, and thus obliging the brothers to remember and recognize their guilt in the earlier enslavement of their brother, Joseph. Judah puts himself forward to take Benjamin's place, finally embracing the point-of-view and experience of the victim. At this point, Joseph can hold out no longer and he reveals himself. There is a scene reminiscent of the encounter of Jacob and Esau: Joseph "fell upon his brother Benjamin's neck and wept, while Benjamin wept upon his neck. And he kissed all his brothers and wept upon them . . ." (Gen 45:14–15). Here Joseph becomes the single righteous individual who forgives and saves all his brothers. However, the other brothers, in abjection, are not able to let go of their retributive thinking There is then a final twist of irony which the text throws before us. After Jacob dies, the brothers come to Joseph with a made-up story of how their father, before his

---

12. There is a difference between the Greek (LXX) and Hebrew wording of this verse, with the latter to be preferred. Some commentators, including Brueggemann (*Old Testament Canon and Christian Imagination*, 49), raise their eyebrows at the picture presented, but I cannot see the text doubting Joseph's wisdom or purpose at this point. What Joseph achieves is social stabilization with the planned storage of surplus grain against future famine. It is a sketch of an earth at peace using theocratic modeling from Egyptian culture. It may even provide a distant foreshadowing of another biblical scene of peace after intense crisis. At the end of the Book of Revelation, the New Jerusalem becomes a final urbanization of all life, a setting of unparalleled beauty in which trees for healing of the nations grow, and human beings dwell together with God and the Lamb.

death, told them to pass on to Joseph his personal entreaty that he forgive their crime. In response, Joseph says something which seems to signal directly a connection to the Peniel story. He says, "Do not be afraid. Am I in the place of God?" (Gen 50:19). The guilty brothers are still servants of a pre-Peniel Elohim—they have not yet wrestled with Jacob's "man," and so cannot meet their Esau. Meanwhile the text hints ironically that Joseph here is in the same role as Esau and is indeed in the place of God—just a very different type of divine from the one the brothers expected. He seeks to assure them. "Even though you intended to do harm to me, God intended it for good . . ." (Gen 50:20). This God that they worship in common might well have a larger purpose and possibility of relationship than they imagine, including the possibility of the forgiving victim. But in any case, they are invited into the human semiosis where Joseph intends no retaliation. The J and E authors, combining their accounts perhaps at the end of the eighth century, brought their antagonist traditions together in triumphant peace. The very fact that these two versions from rival kingdoms were able to be combined in one manuscript is cultural testimony of the truth of Joseph's God. It is certainly no accident that they finish their collective account with his story. If the Supplementary hypothesis is also correct in some measure, then this conciliatory narrative is "front-loaded" before the Exodus sometime in the late-sixth century, thus creating what might be called the neocortex of the Torah.

These semiotic threads are the magnificent legacy of Genesis. Their search for reconciliation over violence becomes the final weight of the first book of the Bible, and neither is it simply a subtext. The overall concern with violence as antithetical to the meaning of Israel is given headline ancestral treatment in Jacob's final blessings to his sons. Simeon and Levi are excluded from blessing and territory in Israel because of their record of violence (especially against Shechem in chapter 34). "Simeon and Levi are brothers; weapons of violence their swords. May I never come into their council; may I not be joined to their company—for in their anger they killed men . . . Cursed be their anger, for it is fierce, and their wrath, for it is cruel" (Gen 49:5–7). Genesis's program of nonviolent meaning for Israel is explicit in these verses, reaching into and through the historical memory and status of the tribes. Once again, it seems evident that the wrapping together of J and E, either at the end of the eighth century BCE or later in the sixth, is an editorial realization of the program of nonviolence and reconciliation.

The movement of codes within the text of Genesis suggests a re-construction of human meaning *in radice*. The blessing of Abraham has *already* transformed the earth, at least in paradigmatic or parabolic fashion. As we continue below to more biblical examples, we can see how these codes continue to proliferate, offering with more and more seminal power a redefinition of both divine and human existence.

3

Job

Once Again, the Blessing of Joseph

READING GENESIS AS WE did makes a purely ancestral narrative explode into theological life. It is true, the text always held a premium theological importance based in the covenant promises to Abraham and his descendants. But in standard Christian thought, this has been understood in a predominantly legal sense, looking forward to the final fulfilment of God's plan through justification by faith in Christ. It allowed commentators largely to overlook and marginalize what was seen often as simply folkloric coloring gathered around a covenantal record. This is especially the case when it comes to the story of Joseph. Although the Joseph saga occupies as many chapters as the massive theological figure of Abraham, it receives scant attention in the commentaries. The common description given to Joseph's story relates to the genre not the content—it is called "a novella"—which has the effect of politely sidelining the material in a purely literary assessment. Almost as if some ancient writer tried their hand at literature and was lucky enough to get their work included in the Bible, while unfortunately missing out on attribution. What is lacking is any sense of the semiotic weight of these chapters, of the amazing transformative code-violation (as Umberto Eco would call it)[1] which shows Abraham's Hebrew great-grandson and designated group victim bringing life and meaning at the heart of a metropolitan culture.

---

1. See Bartlett, *TBM*, 128–29.

Joseph is preeminently a Wisdom figure,[2] and his actions in the overall Genesis story are a fulfillment of a Wisdom project from start to finish. His story accomplishes two immense blessings internal to human existence—forgiveness between brothers and peaceful socio-political order. The concrete transformation at the end of Genesis is, therefore, the fulfillment of the blessing promised to Abraham the Hebrew, and not to see them in this fashion undoes both the textual integrity of Genesis and its unfolding semiosis. It could be countered, perhaps, that the individual source/s that tell most of the Joseph tale, J and E, did not make a break at the end of Genesis and carried straight through into the Exodus narrative. So, our perception is skewed by a later division of the books. But the Joseph story is manifestly a term in its own right, coming to its own climax in the discovery of the awe-inspiring Egyptian official's true identity by the brothers, and the following scenes of fear and reconciliation. Joseph is not a recipient of the earlier promises given to Abraham, Isaac, and Jacob (Gen 12:1–3, 26:3–4, 28:13–15), because, at least to some degree, they are fulfilled through him. Pre-eminently there is the high point of restored relationship between brothers. The narrative in J is the most developed and poignant from 44:1 through 45:28; but E has the climactic scene of conciliation (50:15–21) with its possible play, as we have seen, on the Jacob/Esau "face of God" dialogue in Joseph's loaded question, "Am I in the place of God?" In these words, the text provides a powerful ironic twist, guiding the reader to see the meaning of God not in wrathful condemnation but in fraternal unity and forgiveness. Genesis comes to a natural close at this point; the compositional unity of the Joseph saga gives it a definitive conclusion. The editorial and manuscript history that eventually finishes the first book of the Torah on this note simply recognizes the crucial drama that is already there.[3]

To grasp Genesis this way has a related and essential consequence. It means that the position of Genesis at the front end of the Torah works to demonstrate *in nuce* the whole of God's life-giving Wisdom for his creation. The fact that the plan has to continue to work itself out is of course a given, but, in the meantime, Genesis acts as a parable for the whole enterprise. This means that Genesis contains an implicit critique of the

2. Brueggemann, *Theology of the Old Testament*, 340, 465.

3. The Supplementary hypothesis considerably strengthens the salience of this element. If the J composition is added as a critical "prequel" to Deuteronomy and its histories sometime in the late-sixth century, then the nonviolent theology of Genesis stands out in even greater relief.

violence, hostility, and punishment contained in Exodus and the national epic from thereon through. The scene is set for biblical self-critique continuing in the text from Torah to Ketuvim (the Writings). Moreover, it suggests strongly that the process of redaction of the final Torah came in and after circumstances where a principle of meaning like Genesis could be clearly perceived. A situation of domicile among a non-Israelite nation where Israelite Wisdom for "the blessing of all nations" achieves a powerful narrative value is surely indicated. This makes the exile in Babylon, in the sixth century or later, the ideal setting for the final redaction of the Bible's first book.

These reflections belong properly in the previous chapter, but they also work here, because, as just claimed, they set the scene both chronologically and theologically for all the other deconstructive writings of the Old Testament. At the head of such writings is surely the Book of Job.

Essential Background to Job: Deuteronomy

The poetic vigor and resonance of Job sets it in a league apart, even from the intensity of the prophets or the lyricism of the Song of Songs. Job is the Shakespeare of the Hebrew Bible, its power of language linked genetically to its depth of insight. Job is a Wisdom figure as great, if not greater than Joseph. Where the light of Joseph shines softly forward on the plagues of Exodus, the flame of Job is directed back on the writing of Deuteronomy with a solar flare of criticism.

In order to appreciate this fully, we have first to take a step backward to understand this default setting against which Job's poetry is struggling. This setting may be named as the "Deuteronomic worldview," because it belongs centrally to the Book of Deuteronomy and then to the historical narrative which flows on through Joshua, and especially in Kings.[4] We've already had cause to mention that the end of this Deuteronomic history shows a huge appreciation for King Josiah and his religious reforms, and then, directly after, a greatly reduced interest in any of the following monarchs, apart from brief formulaic statements. Josiah was a hero of reform (destroying the high places, centralizing the Yahwist cult, burning the Asherah, smashing the pagan altars, cf. 2 Kings 22–23), but he was killed in a battle against King Necho II of Egypt at Megiddo in 609 BCE.

---

4. Martin Noth is the primary scholar associated with this literary understanding. See his *Deuteronomistic History* and *History of Pentateuchal Traditions*.

Thereafter, the religious role of kings is overwhelmed by the onrushing doom and destruction of Jerusalem in 587. But the writer has to give some explanation for the horrendous collapse directly after the virtues of Josiah would seem to warrant their opposite. So he turns to the sins of a *prior* king, Manasseh, grandfather to Josiah, as the inexorable cause, no matter anything that Josiah did. When Nebuchadnezzar of Babylon sends the first forays of mercenary troops to harass Judah, the Deuteronomist comments: "Surely this came upon Judah at the command of the Lord, to remove them out of his sight, for the sins of Manasseh, for all that had committed, and also for the innocent blood that he had shed . . ." (2 Kgs 24:3–4). Put another way, the fate of Jerusalem had *already* been decided, despite the qualities of Josiah: Manasseh had been so bad, the destruction was foreordained. Earlier, the same writer wrote, "[because of the crimes of Manasseh] I will wipe Jerusalem as one wipes a dish, wiping it and turning it upside down" (2 Kgs 21:13). And again, conclusively: despite there never being a king like Josiah, "[s]till the Lord did not turn from the fierceness of his great wrath, by which his anger was kindled against Judah, because of all the provocation with which Manasseh had provoked him" (2 Kgs 23:26).[5]

The Deuteronomistic writer has created an exact calculus, between suffering and sin, between bad things happening and causative crime. There can be no avoiding the organic connection, the mathematical logic. Even the greatest of kings, who instituted all the wished-for reforms, could not prevent the catastrophic consequences of a *previous* monarch's misdeeds. So, history takes on a meaning and a shape, one that could be exactly analyzed and understood. The rise of the Mesopotamian empires of Assyria and Babylon, and their relentless expansion against Israel and Judah, were never simply accidents of geography and history. They were God's unstoppable hand, reaching out to punish the wayward nation.

Roots of this thinking go back at least as far as Amos, as we have seen. Speaking in the eighth century BCE, Amos says things like this:

> Hear this word, you cows of Bashan who are on Mount Samaria, who oppress the poor, who crush the needy, who say to their husbands, "Bring something to drink!" the Lord God has sworn by his holiness: The time is surely coming upon you, when they shall take you away with hooks, even the last of you with fish-hooks. Through breaches in the wall you shall leave, each one

5. Cf. Friedman, *Who Wrote the Bible?*, 140–141.

straight ahead; and you shall be flung out into Harmon, says the Lord. (4:1–3)

These are fearfully exact images of a conquering nation overrunning the city capital of Northern Israel and dragging its inhabitants into exile. The prophet announces it as the imminent judgment of God declared in the present. The ferocity of the image—the women dragged along like fish on a hook—strongly suggests the prophet was not a stranger to an invading force and the ruthless treatment they handed out. In any case, his prophecy came true: around the year of 720, after previous deportations from Israel's territory, the Assyrians besieged the capital, Samaria, destroying the city and carrying off the bulk of its inhabitants to far-flung regions of their empire. This is the basis of the "lost tribes" of Israel, a catastrophic event in which the political entity of Northern Israel disappeared forever.

Once again, we are dealing with semiotics—a set of signifiers that become embedded as revelatory writing and continue powerfully to exert meaning. They tell us that God makes use of the imperial nations of the time to severely, or even terminally, reprove and punish his people. "The eyes of the Lord God are upon the sinful kingdom, and I will destroy it from the face of the earth" (Amos 9:8). It is a terrible and terrifying thought, and here we recognize again the role of primal mimeticism. If something bad happens, it is because a hostile force—an evil spirit, an enemy's curse, the wrath of a god—has done it. Such is the impact of mimeticism—the experience of the "other" as rival—it is extremely difficult, if not impossible, for the human mind to conceive negative events as purely objective occurrences, rather than, reactively, as a personal attack.

The situation in the Bible is made more intense, and by orders of magnitude, by reason of its covenantal-sacrificial structure. We have signaled the parallels between biblical covenants and ancient treaty formulae, but we did not yet underscore the function of sacrifice in establishing and reinforcing covenant. Chapters 19 to 24 in Exodus represent material generally agreed to be among the earliest strata giving Israel its identity and norms of life. Because so many of the ordinances are designed to protect the poor, it is not hard to grasp here Israel's Hebrew (*Hapiru*) origins; and, at the same time, we see the covenantal-sacrificial origins of Amos' demand for "social justice." The way of life described is established and structured as a covenant sealed by sacrifice. In chapter 24, after Moses tells the people "all the words of the Lord," the people answer "with one voice," saying "All the words that the Lord has spoken we will do" (Exod 24:3). Moses then proceeds to makes sacrifices of oxen, gathering the blood in basins. Half of the blood is dashed on the altar he has constructed, and half is splashed on the people. He says, "See the blood of the covenant that the Lord has made with you in accordance with all these words" (24:8).

The agreement to another way of life is ritualized by an animal sacrifice. The structure of the sacrifice is broken open so that the violence discharged into the victim is "sprayed" out onto the participants in its sacred or "inert" form. This has the effect of invoking the activated violence on the parties should they ever break apart the sacred bond and agreement. The sacrifice becomes a covenant ritual and indeed part of the covenant itself. It adds a significant layer of violent ritual sanction to a relationship with the divine already marked by mimetic potential. Otherwise stated, should bad things happen, the people have an added cultic reason to understand this as the unleashing of their God's personal violence upon them. The fact that this is represented in a text, rather than an actual ritual, does not make it any less impactful. If anything, the semiotic rendering of this relationship makes it ever more internalized and terrible. This is especially and crucially true of the Book of Deuteronomy. In Deuteronomy, there is a mutual oath-giving in the middle of the book (Deut 26:16–19), establishing the sacred bond. Walter Brueggemann believes this represents the residue of a ritual performance. He says "[T] he literature of Deuteronomy replicates liturgical practice and, in a literary mode, is a tradition that *enacts* Israel as YHWH's covenant people."[6] What this suggests is that the kind of covenant ritual we have described stands behind the text, and the text reproduces its dynamic semiotically. It places the devout reader into a ritual covenant situation expressed and fulfilled by words.

Deuteronomy's imaginative scene-setting has Moses and the people on the far side of the Jordan just before entry into Canaan. Moses gives three speeches which hinge on the people's imminent possession of the land. The speeches narrate the prior events leading up to the dramatic moment and then shift largely to the present and future tenses plus imperative mood. The effect is to make the historical scene an ever-present semiotic event and, as underlined, one structured by and as covenant. Throughout their history, Moses continually addresses the people via

---

6. Brueggemann, *Introduction to the Old Testament*, 89.

Deuteronomy and continually instills in them the relationship of covenant. The first speech is a broad introduction, the third navigates a transition to the military figure of Joshua and the actual occupation of the land. The middle provides by far the longest commentary.

It is comprised of a proclamation of God's gifts, an extended legal segment (again with significant accent on protection of the poor), the declaration of oaths, and, finally, announcement of blessings and curses. The speech builds to a devastating climax. It establishes a closely reciprocal contractual scene: "Today you have obtained the Lord's agreement: to be your God, and for you to walk in his ways . . ." and "Today the Lord has obtained your agreement: to be his treasured people . . . and for you to be a people holy to the Lord . . ." (Deut 26:17–19). There then emerges the potent declaratory voice of retributive justice. If the people keep the laws and ordinances, they will be given a series of blessings, including fruitfulness, prosperity, defeat of enemies and eminent political success. These blessings occupy twelve verses (Deut 28:3–14). However, if the people do not obey the Lord and his commandments, they will be cursed. The volley of curses occupies fifty-four verses (Deut 28:15–68), a terrifying litany of physical, social, and political harm.

It seems beyond dispute that the descriptions reflect the post-factum experience of the Southern Kingdom's (Judah's) defeat at the hands of the Babylonians in the first decades of the sixth century BCE.

> The Lord will bring you, and the king whom you set over you, to a nation that neither you nor your ancestors have known . . . The Lord will bring a nation from far away, from the end of the earth, to swoop down on you like an eagle, a nation whose language you do not understand . . . The Lord will bring you back in ships to Egypt, by a route that I promised you would never see again. (Deut 28:36, 49, 68)

The book even goes on to state that

> [w]hen all these things have happened to you, the blessings and the curses . . . if you call them to mind among all the nations where the Lord your God has driven you, and return to the Lord your God, and you and your children obey him . . . then the Lord your God will restore your fortunes . . . gathering you again from all the peoples among whom the Lord your God has scattered you. (Deut 30:1–3)

In sum, the intended actual readers of the final text are those who are in exile and who have even returned. This strongly suggests that the urgent core of meaning—the source code, we might say—which created Deuteronomy was the terrible experience surrounding exile forcefully understood as retribution. All this happened because of our sins! We must now be totally vigilant lest the same thing happen again! The structuring semiosis of Moses' speeches then makes this experience present, pressing, and normative for succeeding generations. We can, therefore, justly speak of a Deuteronomic viewpoint or worldview. Deuteronomy becomes the great prevailing voice of the biblical text, creating a master understanding of God's relationship with his people.

The retributive viewpoint becomes enshrined as the root code shaping any relationship with the God of Israel, the Lord who first called Abraham and, finally, in the Christian faith, sent his Son Jesus. It is an enormously powerful semiosis, mobilizing both mimetic projection, sacral covenant form and ritual, and the brutal *realpolitik* circumstances of the ancient Near East. We do have to underline that the Deuteronomic viewpoint does not exhaust the Deuteronomic text. The clear implication of Deuteronomy is that the Lord has not abandoned his relationship with Israel, that the code of retribution is there to uphold the radical demands and reality of the relationship, and that the final name for the relationship is love (Deut 7:7–8, 10:15). Nevertheless, there is obvious tension between this aspect and the fierce retribution described in chapter 28. In a way, the tension is unbearable and the two aspects together—love and punishment—create a condition aligned to the philosopher Hegel's unhappy consciousness, where the self is both free and in fetters. In Bible studies I have led on the subject, it has often been remarked that the God of Deuteronomy is like an alcoholic and abusive father: someone we tiptoe around in order to avoid a crisis while striving to hold on to the sense that he really does love us. Meanwhile, the voice of Deuteronomy is probably the most distinct and distinctive in the Bible, and, for many in fact, the representative voice of the Bible itself.

Job and the Crowd

But this cannot be upheld as the final truth of the matter. Other voices cut across, question, and contradict this voice, and they too are the Bible. The Bible in fact is exactly this clamor of voices, and that is surely why it retains its fascination. A parliament of voices and inflections produces the Bible and generates its singular dynamic of meaning, and perhaps none is more striking and singular in the mix than Job. Job takes the semiotic hints of Genesis and the massive semiosis of Deuteronomy and makes them the case to be tried at court, a proceeding second to none.

At first Job does not seem so—the book's character is so different that it seems to belong in a weird class of its own, a tale relevant only to itself. It is the work of René Girard that suddenly raises the creator of Job to the level of a critical giant where, before, he was perhaps just a writer of wondrous but obscure poetry![7] Job says there is something wrong with the Deuteronomic math, something off in its calculations. Yes, the Book of Job deals with a single individual, the uniquely righteous, famously defiant son of Uz. Job's situation is not that of a whole nation with its aberrant religious practices and power-hungry kings. And the political history of such a structural whole cannot be compared with the drama of a single unfortunate man. And yet Job deals with the logic of retribution, and once he blew a book-of-poetry hole in that logic—one that cannot be patched over—it became impossible completely to trust the Deuteronomic worldview. If there is an unbreakable bond between morality and history, between religion and history, Job puts it on record that the bond itself is deeply suspect and has to be revised.

Girard showed that Job is the paradigm of the scapegoat, surrounded by the monstrous forces of the crowd seeking to destroy him. Among the crowd, "God" functions as persecutor-in-chief. "God" in this sense is nothing other than the sum-total of human violence seeking its resolution in a victim. Job brings to a clear term all the free-floating suspicions of Genesis that the signifier "God" is all too easily a fiction of mimesis and violence. The labor of Genesis, to illustrate human compassion and forgiveness as the possible-yet-still-to-come lens for understanding God, finds an absolute affirmation in Job. It happens because this masterpiece of Old Testament Wisdom exposes the systematic opposites of those virtues—i.e., blame and accusation—in a culturally definitive way.

Girard's analysis of the text is compelling, consistently linking divine and human violence. The so-called friends of Job continue to harp on a non-specific wicked man, describing his terrifying fate. God functions as the final force of justice bringing down terrible violence on the hateful individual. This is the "God" whose meaning is validated by tens of

7. Girard, *Job*.

thousands of years of human culture. "He" is also inevitably tied up in the doctrine of Deuteronomy: at some point, the curses unleashed because of the people's wickedness were bound to find expression in this kind of biblical fever dream.

> On him God looses all his burning wrath,
> hurling against his flesh a hail of arrows.
> No use to run away from the iron armoury,
> for the bow of bronze will shoot him through.
> Out through his back an arrow sticks,
> from his gall a shining point.
> An arsenal of terrors falls on him,
> and all that is dark lies in ambush for him.
> A fire unlit by man devours him,
> and consumes what is left in his tent.
> The heavens lay bare his iniquity,
> the earth takes its stand against him.
> A flood sweeps his house away,
> and carries it off in the Day of Wrath.
> Such is the fate God allots to the wicked,
> such is his inheritance assigned by God. (Job 20:22–29 JB)

But, as Girard underlines, there is no distinction between this metaphysical figure and the much more concrete, anthropological understanding of the persecutory crowd asserted by Job. "And now ill will drives me to distraction, and a whole host molests me, rising, like some witness for the prosecution, to utter slander to my very face. In tearing fury, it pursues me, with gnashing teeth. My enemies whet their eyes on me, and open gaping jaws. Their insults like slaps in the face, and all set on me together" (Job 16:7–10 JB).

The continual juxtaposition of the two accounts—the "celestial armies" invoked by the friends and the steadfast complaint of human enmity and persecution by Job—constitutes one of the revelatory contrasts of the book. It is a systematic, revelatory code violation. But the hostile dance can only continue so long. The friend's circling threat of divine fury must at some moment translate into direct accusation. Necessarily, they come to point the finger directly at Job. First Zophar comments archly: "Know that God exacts of you less than your guilt deserves" (Job 11:6). Later, Eliphaz declares it directly. Asking why God has turned against him, he answers his own question: "Would he punish you for your piety, and hale you off to judgment? No, rather for your manifold wickednesses, for your unending iniquities!" (Job 22:4 JB).

As far as the friends are concerned, the equation is complete, the case closed. And so has been the broad decision of the Christian tradition. The standard opinion has understood Job as a model of virtue (*beatus Job*, according to Aquinas), but has also demurred that in some minor regards he is still guilty ("venial sins," sins of his youth, or, in Evangelical mode, his own "self-righteous" claim of righteousness). In his final speech, Job appears to give grounds for this, seeming ultimately to repent and accept that the God of the persecutors has been right all along. We shall comment on this in detail below. But we need first to establish the principle that the Book of Job uses indirection and suggestion to reach its goal, where a more frontal declaration would meet with anathema, or, at the very least, incomprehension. A deity who too easily gives up its functions of violence could not be one "translated" from past orthodoxies of the divine. In parallel, the declaration of an entirely "new god" would not do justice to the hints of trans-semiosis already present in past writing, for example, in Genesis. So, the writing of Job works to make the concept of God collapse from its own weight, revealing the new in the very same process. The code violation of Job, therefore, masks itself under various ironies and disguises in order more effectively to bring about its final revelation.

Refiguring God

Nowhere is this more evident than in the frame story which sets up the whole series of speeches between Job and his interlocutors. This consists of prologue in Job 1:1—2:10 and epilogue at Job 42:7–17. The opening scene especially is well known and, in many ways, constitutes the classic Job story—the one where God decides, in God's inscrutable counsels, to subject Job to testing and torment. In Girard's opinion, this "should not be taken seriously" because it belongs to a more banal or popularist stage of textual composition, not part of the genius of the dialogues.[8] A different assessment is possible. The links between the prologue and the rest of the text are subtle but very real and need to be understood in order to appreciate fully the semiotic movement brought about by the whole book.[9]

8. Girard, *Job*, 3.

9. A serious difficulty with taking the frame as independent/later addition is the

After an initial description of Job, of his wealth and scrupulous virtue, the scene shifts. The Lord is in his heavenly court, in the presence of the *bene ha'elohim*, the "sons of God." These are probably a deliberate anachronism from early Canaanite mythology, here providing the essential drama of a king in the presence of his royal court, a classic scene of systemic mimesis and rivalry.[10] Into their company comes *ha-satan* (the *satan* or "accuser"), who is not the horned evil of Christian imagination, but a court official with a role likely taken from Persian imperial organization and practice.[11] He is basically a police spy with powers to coerce and torture. The Lord sets up an idle banter with this satan, suggesting that his servant Job is completely above reproach, too good for satan's kind. The satan replies—exactly according to type—that it is not "for nothing" that Job is so virtuous; that Job is only good and righteous because he has everything he could possibly want. The Lord is impelled thus to wager a bet on Job, allowing his cruel official to take everything from Job, bar

---

way the satan completely disappears after the prologue. If the prologue and epilogue are independent, then the traditional dynamic of the storytelling surely demands that this crucial antagonist reappear, at the end, in order to be answered and bested? The way it stands, however, the satan is effortlessly absorbed by the friends, and the God of the friends, in the text of the dialogues. And, as we shall see, the epilogue subverts the prologue in a subtly pointed way, and yet one profoundly connected to the speeches. Moreover, the incorporation of the "modern" Persian motif of secret police/satan would speak against an ancient tale. It seems much more likely that a brilliant writer has composed his own archaicized setting in which to introduce his dramatic poetry.

10. See Ps 89:6–8 and Deut 32:8–9 for other references to such heavenly beings.

11. See Pope, *Job*, 10: "[T]he figure and role of the Satan derives from the Persian secret service . . . [T]he vast Persian Empire, as organized by the genius of Darius the Great, depended in great measure for its security on the well-developed system of highways and communications which linked the provincial capitals, and on an efficient intelligence agency which kept the powerful governors under surveillance to detect and prevent sedition and rebellion. Some of these inspectors or master spies were known as "The King's Eye" and "The King's Ear." "The Eye of the King" appears to have been an officer in constant attendance on the king." Also Austin, *Re-reading Job*, 36: "Given the strong likelihood that 1) the original Job frame tale came from a Persian or other Near Eastern source, and 2) the composition of the Job poem occurred after the Persians had conquered Babylon and freed the Jews, it is extremely likely that the author imagines the satan, who comes to the court of heaven after 'roaming all over the earth' (Job 1:7), as something like a shadowy member of the great Persian secret police—a political spy with a charge to root out sedition and accuse disloyal officials before the king." Meanwhile, placing Job in the Persian period helps us see Job as a relatively late writing—contemporary with (or not long after) the final editing of the Torah—and thus an inspired Wisdom reaction against Deuteronomy's retributive logic.

his life, with the implication that Job will surely maintain his righteous character. There then unfolds the series of misfortunes which shatter Job's world—the loss of livestock, servants, children, followed by destruction of Job's health and wellbeing. Girard objects to this scenario because it has nothing to do with Job's actual complaint in the dialogues, which is his persecution by the mob.[12]

But the frame's setting up of the story in this way tells us forcefully that the book is about the identity of God and his collusion with the satan or accuser. To dismiss it as simply an additional layer loses the acute drama of a God who has abandoned Job to arbitrary persecution, and the *consequent* justice of all Job's complaints. Because of the frame, the reader is much more inclined to take Job's side in his biting protests, seeing his suffering as the result of a casual bet between the heavenly Lord and one of his less-savory courtiers. Further, if we read the overall story in this way, then the door has to be opened to an epochal critique of the Deuteronomic worldview. This in itself is a plausible rationale for its inclusion in the biblical corpus—as a "Genesis-style" riposte to Deuteronomy. It becomes possible then to see Job both as a representative individual (a human being who suffers unfairly) and a symbol of members of Israel subjected to unwarranted punishment. By stripping the prologue away from Job's speeches, Girard effectively cuts the latter off from an internal biblical discussion about the true nature of the biblical "God." It deprives the revelation of the victim (in the dialogues) of its essential connection to revelatory theology.[13]

A strong hint that this is about the identity of God is given in the prologue and epilogue's use of the Exodus and Deuteronomy revealed name for God, something avoided in the speeches. In the first chapter, at verse six, the divine being is introduced as "the Lord," i.e., Yahweh. It is the Lord who spars with the satan and who makes the deal allowing Job to be tested. Then after 2:7, the name of Yahweh is avoided, in favor

12. Girard, *Job*, 3, 142–43. According to Girard, the effect of the prologue and epilogue "is to eliminate the essential and make the dialogues unreadable, to transform the Book of Job into a ludicrous anecdote recited mechanically to everyone" (*Job*, 142). See Pope, *Anchor Bible Job*, xxiii–xxx, for critical overview regarding secondary additions: "The Book of Job in its present form can hardly be regarded as a consistent and unified composition by a single author. Nevertheless, there is a considerable degree of organic unity despite the incongruities" (xxx).

13. The characteristic approach in Girard is to see the revelation of the victim as a discrete conceptual event rather than a semiotic one. This has the effect of closing off any consistent change in overall meaning, including the meaning of God.

of *el* or *elohim*, not returning again until the end of the book when the Lord answers Job directly "from the whirlwind," at 38:1.[14] From there on, it is always the Lord who is the divine protagonist, forced ultimately, if obliquely, to answer to Job.

What would this mean? As a series of code-markers, the names of God may tell us, first, that the frame story is very deliberately looking toward the Exodus and Deuteronomic revelatory tradition, while also invoking the Genesis stories where Yahweh presents with the unreliable persona he very much has here. In parallel, Job's personal devotion to the Lord is marked at 1:21 in what could be heard as a confessional phrase: "The Lord gave, and the Lord has taken away; blessed be the name of the Lord." Thus, in broad terms, we are in the world of Torah faith, but what seems very much in question is the character of its Lord. The general sequence through the book—the Lord, then God, then back to the Lord— reinforces this sense that the meaning and character of Yahweh are being subject to inquiry. Job is a foreigner (his name is not typical Israelite, and he comes from the obscure land of Uz), so it would be appropriate for him to speak of and to God in generic terms in his speeches. To have him then dealing so clearly with "the Lord," first at the beginning and then in the final chapters, seems to suggest deliberate Israelite inquiry and comment. Especially after the intervening dominance of *el* or *elohim*, the last focus on Yahweh seems to announce clearly that we are actually concerned with the identity and character of Israel's God.

There can be no doubt that at the start of the story, Yahweh does the unspeakable in Deuteronomic terms. He colludes with the satan in bringing Job's unmerited downfall, flying directly in the face of any calculus of retribution. How could this scandal not be noticed; or rather, on the contrary, very deliberately be endorsed by the inclusion of Job in the biblical Writings? The very fact of the frame story's existence, together with its arbitrary narrative, are testimony of its critical theological character.

After the second assault by the satan, Job still does not open his mouth. But then something happens. The narrative shifts the scene fully from the heavenly court to earth. The three "friends" arrive and sit with Job on the ground for seven days and nights, saying nothing "for they saw that his suffering was very great" (2:13). It is one of the many ambiguities of the text: the friends deafening silence can be interpreted as some

14. There are two exceptions, at 12:9, and then in the Wisdom hymn at 28:28. The latter is almost universally regarded as an interpolation, and the former seems to be carried over or quoted from Isa 41:20.

kind of piety, or as cold complacence at Job's suffering. In any case, it is then that Job can bear it no longer. He begins his long and bitter protest which certainly holds "God" accountable and charges him with violence ("he will kill me . . ." at 13:15). By this point, the satan has completely disappeared from the story, not to be heard of again: in effect, he has been replaced by the friends and their God. Thus, we have migrated from the heavenly accuser and torturer to the victim-making mob. By the same token, the Deuteronomic figure of the Lord has also migrated from the heavenly court into the universal figure of "God" completely at home in the voices and actions of the lynchers.

By connecting thus with the "metaphysics" of the frame, we see how the progression is a complete inversion of the Deuteronomic doctrine. In effect, the text has translated "the Lord" into the satan, the prosecuting officer, and thereafter into the mob. The Lord here does not discriminate, blessing righteousness and punishing wickedness as he is supposed to. As Job sums it up: "It is all one . . . he destroys both the blameless and the wicked" (9:22). There is nothing strict or special about the justice of Israel's God, there is only its fell and arbitrary violence. Girard says on plural occasions that there is an identity between God and the satan in the Book of Job.[15] What he fails to say is that this identity is also pinned on Yahweh and, by implication, on the Deuteronomic economy of retribution. If Deuteronomy says for crime there must be a punishment involving terrible suffering, the underlying human logic also believes the converse: if there is terrible suffering, then there must first be crime. Job responds with a resounding "No" to both. Suffering is arbitrary and unjust, because everyone (including God) gangs up to blame the one who is suffering.

But the story does not end there. As we pointed out, at the end the text shifts back to the Lord. There is a very careful quality to the shift and its deft irony—one of the many layered ironies of Job—should not be missed. After the three friends have failed to quell Job's protest, a fourth apologist for God is suddenly introduced—Elihu, whose name literally means, "He is my God."[16] Elihu is young and zealous, angry with the friends because they cannot answer Job. He launches into a long, religiously pompous speech, distinguished only perhaps by its dialing down the threats of celestial violence, while accenting the Wisdom motif of God's sovereign management of the physical earth. He gives an extended

15. Girard, *Job*. 64, 139.
16. Pope, *Job*, 242.

account of what we might call meteorology, of thunder, rain, and ice. The impossible challenge then to Job is whether he can replicate any of this: "Can you, like him, spread out the skies . . .?" (37:18). The obvious answer is "no," and so mortals should fear God who "does not regard any who are wise in their own conceit" (37:24).

It is at the point where Elihu concludes that Yahweh leaps into action: "Then the Lord answered Job out of the whirlwind" (38:1). It's as if the Almighty, who so far has been unwilling or unable to give Job an answer, is suddenly inspired by Elihu's defense. Where Elihu talks about the mysteries of meteorology, the Lord expands the disciplines to include cosmogony, astronomy, more meteorology, and a great deal of zoology. But the resulting rhetorical question is always a variation of the same: "Where were you?"; "Do you know?"; "Can you?" The exegetes and interpreters seem to have missed this. Girard says again: "[I]t is difficult to take this farce seriously."[17] But is that not in fact the point? The text is telling us that the Lord here is really just another version of Elihu, whose name so easily refers back to God himself.[18] It tells us that this version of God is simply another pious fiasco and that we are still on the journey of translating the meaning of God. However, with this in view, there is perhaps one substantive change which does give pause. The Lord of the whirlwind is less violent than the God of the speeches. He has recourse not to threat but to awestruck wonder. Girard insists this is mere sleight of hand and God here is just "less openly ferocious,"[19] succeeding on the textual level while still rooted in the scapegoat mechanism. No doubt that is true, but to make it simply a dialectical opposition is to miss the semiotic transformation at work. The theatrical but peaceful display of the Lord's creational wisdom is *not* the celestial armies: it holds a space open while preparing the ground for the total reversal to come. We are dealing here with a pedagogy of transformation, not an academic thesis at a conference. If we consider how deeply rooted the Deuteronomic viewpoint was (and is), and that the author of Job sought a hearing within that tradition, was there in fact any better way?

17. Girard, *Job*, 142.

18. The four speeches of Elihu and two from God add up to a multiple of three (3 x 2), which collectively would mimic the three speeches by each friend. God is perhaps covertly recognized as just another "friend."

19. Girard, *Job*, 142.

A Redeemer Lives

Because all along something much more radical is being brought to light. At a couple of points in the speeches of Job, there arises a sudden anomaly in the relentless language of protest. It introduces a third party between Job and God, which out of nowhere suggests another way. How this figure could establish any agency does not seem to be explained. It is the very abruptness of the interruption which draws attention and somehow gives authority to the topic:

> Even now, in fact, my witness is in heaven,
> and he that vouches for me is on high.
> My friends scorn me;
> my eye pours out tears to God,
> that he would maintain the right of a mortal with God
> as one does for a neighbor. (Job 16:19–21)

It appears that a duality is introduced into God—that somehow God should intercede with God. The duality is something in the pattern of the satan infecting God with his character in the opening scene of the book. But this time the infecting figure is a witness for the defense, an ally, an advocate. Just before these verses, the text says, "O earth, do not cover my blood; let my outcry find no resting place." It's as if the ancient biblical *topos* of Abel's blood crying out to the Lord from the ground has leaped in the mind of the author and produced a second iteration of God, one who listens to victims. If this is the case, then it is a semiotic connection, not a dogmatic one. It is the powerful recoding effect of this tradition that brings the author to produce a dramatic new element—a redemptive *secondness* in God.

The possibility of a generative semiotics is strengthened by the next instance, one of those set of verses that have become the common lore of religious culture. The way the passage starts, calling for words to be written down in a book, or on a rock, suggest that these words are themselves somehow productive of new, transformative reality:

> O that my words were written down!
> O that they were inscribed in a book!
> O that with an iron pen and with lead
> they were engraved in a rock forever!
> For I know that my Redeemer lives,
> and that at the last he will stand upon the earth;

> and after my skin has been thus destroyed
> then in my flesh I shall see God,
> whom I shall see on my side,
> and my eyes shall behold, and not another. (Job 19:23–27)

There is a quantum jump from written-down words to the knowledge that a Redeemer/Vindicator lives. The name is from the Hebrew verb *gaal*, which means "to act as a kinsman/avenger" and has a rich history in the tradition. It refers to the duty of next of kin to avenge/restore the victim of violence (Lev 25:25–26, 47–49; Num 35:9–34; Deut 19:1–13). It also includes the revelatory identification of the name with the Lord at Isa 43:14, 44:24, 49:7. Here, in the text of Job, we may ask if the poet is claiming that his words—the overall semiosis of the book—will themselves serve to transform the meaning of God, so that one day that meaning will be established on earth? And, moreover, that the very anticipation of this meaning can act to transform the final story of Job itself? The verses are an announcement of immense confidence. They suggest that the author not only protested the retributive theology of Deuteronomy, but believed there was an entirely different dynamic at work deep in the relationship between Israel and its God.

It is possible to suggest this because the book has something enormous yet to give us as the dialogues appear to wind down to a dismally anticlimactic end. After the Lord's second speech, Job makes his supposed recantation. "Therefore I despise myself, and repent in dust and ashes" (42:6). Ah, so there it is! Job was wrong all along, and now confesses his crime!

"This certainly cannot be attributed to the author of the Dialogues."[20] Girard is assured that the critical judgment of separate and separable stages of composition saves us from what looks like a banal surrender of poetic integrity. Some other reflex hand of orthodoxy wrote this. But a judgment like this does not sense the long, fraught struggle of the Bible's semiotic shifts which brought us to this point. Whatever stages the text possibly went through, it is the final canonical form that really interests us, because it is there that the semiotic tensions and contrasts can most clearly be seen.

And, wait! Perhaps precisely we have been misled by the traditional order-supporting reading? Here is the *New Interpreter's Study Bible* comment:

---

20. Girard, *Job*, 143.

> The Hebrew . . . allows for a variety of translations, most of
> which render Job's words as anything but a confession. The verb
> rendered as "I despise myself" (Heb. *'emas*) is not a reflexive
> form. Its other occurrences are all rendered as a simple verb "I
> hate/reject" (see Jer 31:37 and 33:26). The second Hebrew verb,
> *nikhanti*, has been rendered as "repent" but other uses of the
> verb argue for a meaning of "rue/regret" (see also Gen 6:7; 1
> Sam 15:11; Jer 4:28, 18:8). Thus, a more accurate rendering of
> the verse might read: "I reject and regret dust and ashes."[21]

So the pious translation has been imposed in order to satisfy theological
appearances, making Job beat his breast, and avoiding the radical possibility of the original Hebrew: which is that, to the very end, Job maintains
his innocence and rejects his condition.

In English translation (interpretation), we lose all the ambiguous
inflection of Job's words, the way he cannot directly answer the Lord's
magnificent demonstration of superior power and knowledge, and yet he
remains essentially faithful to the truth of his human condition. This is
what Heidegger would call "authenticity" or human "ownership" of existential truth, and, really, how much of the seedbed of existential thought
lies in the rich ground of Job and its writing? If Job actually "repents," as
the tradition has it, then it's perfectly understandable how Girard could
doubt the connection to the passionate argument of the dialogues. But
if the words of Job's reply leave sufficient ambiguity and verbal slippage
to allow final endorsement of his speeches, then we have a semiotic shift
of world-historical proportions sneaking in under the battlements of
violent orthodoxy. Job dodges the intellectual and technocratic superiority of the Lord's words with an evasive formula which preserves his
human integrity. In which case, we are still dealing with the same author
(or at least the same essential argument) and the text has a complexity
and sophistication that the critics have seriously underestimated. Even
more significantly, such a supposed repentance runs counter to perhaps
the most crucial verse of the whole book, coming directly after in the

---

21. *New Interpreter's Study Bible*, 745. See also Gutiérrez, *On Job*, which translates
the phrase "I repudiate and abandon (change my mind about) dust and ashes" (86).
For Gutiérrez, this includes the sustained refusal by Job of retributive theology while
retaining an aspect of repentance regarding his personal attitude (82–87). So, a traditional element of pious submission is preserved while the rolling ambiguity of the
phrase is recognized. The writer of Job clearly leaves a gaping hole for interpretation
in the hero's final cryptic words. See also, for example, Greenstein's moody, ambivalent
wording: "That is why I am fed up, I take pity on dust and ashes" (*Job*, 185).

epilogue. Immediately after Job's words the narrative picks up again, telling us that the Lord addresses one of the friends, Eliphaz. Astonishingly, he announces, "My wrath is kindled against you and against your two friends, for you have not spoken of me what is right, as my servant Job has" (42:7). Girard calls this "one remarkable sentence" which stands as a truth apart from the rest of the conclusion.[22] But really it fits entirely once we accept the alternative possibilities of 42:6. The epilogue becomes completely coherent and just as powerful as the most radical insights of the dialogues.

When it is connected with the whole sequence of the text, the epilogue gains its formidable power of meaning. Indeed, unless the whole text had prepared for this statement, it must become a surd, something without sense or meaning. Only when the overall struggle and drama of the text, including the frame story, is kept in mind do these words attain their full power as revelation. They tell us that this apparent volte-face on the part of the Lord is what the Book of Job has been working toward all along, *a complete and intentional dissociation of the Lord from the Deuteronomic calculus.*

It is the same biblical technique of challenging and changing the character of God that we already found in Abraham's intercession for the inhabitants of Sodom, in Esau reflecting the face of God, or Joseph modeling divine forgiveness and life for his brothers and the Egyptians. Except this time, the Lord confesses in first person to the semiotic transformation effected. The Lord has been moved explicitly in the story from a colluder or alter-ego with the satan, to an ally of the victim, Job. And just like Abraham, Esau, or Joseph, it is Job who by his words and existential truth has brought about this new reality.

Job has shown forth the true meaning of God in the world, and God's final remark gives this astonishing corroboration. But the story is still not finished. God tells the three friends to go to Job and ask him to pray for them, and to do so within the context of a ritual sacrifice. Even so, within the religious lifeworld of the time, his prayer will have an atoning value. "Now therefore takes seven bulls and seven rams, and go to my servant Job, and offer up for yourselves a burnt offering, and my servant Job shall pray for you, for I will accept his prayer not to deal with you according to your folly; for you have not spoken of me what is right, as my

---

22. Girard, *Job*, 144.

servant Job has done." The three friends do as instructed, "and the Lord accepted Job's prayer" (42:8–9).

Far from being the outcast and pariah, Job is now the Lord's appointed intercessor, priest, and intermediary. Job is even the Redeemer that he sought in his own case, standing at the side of men on earth threatened by the God (anthropology) of violence. Even thus the poetry of the book brought about its own desired outcome, producing the redemptive effect of the disclosed and forgiving victim that the revelatory labor of the Bible is always looking toward.

This final scene alone should make the epilogue a central component of the book's theology. It connects both with Job's words in the instances we have mentioned and also with the final speeches, so quickly dismissed by critics. At one point in his blustering performance, Elihu suddenly launches off at a tangent relating to those who find themselves near death burdened by their evil deeds:

> Then, if there should be for one of them an angel, a mediator, one of a thousand, one who declares a person upright, and he is gracious to that person, and says, "Deliver him from going down into the Pit; I have found a ransom; let his flesh become fresh with youth; let him return to his days of youthful vigor"; then he prays to God and is accepted by him, and he comes into his presence with joy, and God repays him for his righteousness. (33:23–26)

This sounds so remarkably like what Job does for the friends that it must act as a foreshadowing in that earlier chapter. Otherwise, what the passage is doing in Elihu's speech is not clear—who is he suggesting might do this for Job? Is it Elihu himself? Hardly, because he does not declare Job upright and is not gracious to him. But if it is there as an abrupt foreshadowing, it sets up exactly the role that Job takes on at the end.[23]

In which case, this is where the book has always been bending, toward Job as mediator for and with God, the one who has "found a ransom." The sevenfold sacrificial offering of the bulls and rams is a costly ritual of atonement, but it is not the bloody death of the animals that counts. It is a displacement or metaphor for the effective role and words of Job. It represents implicit knowledge that Job has carried through the very thing that sacrificial ritual aimed for all along: the revelation and

---

23. This understanding may also tie the Elihu speeches into the epilogue as part of a coherent theology. Elihu is not blamed in the epilogue, as the three friends are.

forgiveness of and by the victim. Job's declared innocence, without retaliation or revenge, now becomes the point at which new human meaning is made. The unmasked human suffering of Job, surrounded by the God-authorized mob, created an entirely new reference point for the meaning of God itself. The Lord himself endorses this and directs the three friends accordingly to find redemption in relation to it, by means of Job's non-vengeful prayer. Their own prayer, in relation to this reference, saves human beings from the wrath of the God they themselves previously engineered. As such, Job is semiotically the presence of this other God, this reconfigured Lord, on earth. And all this has been achieved by a stunning sequence of written, semiotic shifts, carefully intertwined and navigated in the midst of the biblical tradition.

The final scene of the epilogue sets us up for the next study, on Second Isaiah. In the end, the two share a remarkably similar message in respect of one-who-makes-others-righteous. In his final assessment, Marvin Pope relates the figure of Job making intercession for his friends to the figure of the Suffering Servant in Isa 53:10–12, without being able to draw a clear direction of influence between them.[24] We can be confident that they both emerged from the same raw experiences of nonviolent human suffering and of theology re-forged in its flames. But where Job is unidentifiable in precise historical context, Second Isaiah is clearly discoverable

24. Pope, *Job*, lxxxi–lxxxii.

4

The Servant

Jeremiah's Meaning

MASS DEPORTATION OF A community will concentrate its thoughts like nothing else.

When we are thrown in jail, we reflect on our existence, the flame of selfhood inside our heads flickering against a sea of darkness. If we are thrown into jail together, the pain is not just inside our heads but on every ravaged face looking back at us.

Destruction of my people, of sisters and brothers, of mothers, fathers, and children! For the gods have turned against us and the worth of our lives is no more!

In these circumstances, anything that offers an expedient for survival—including accepting fate and abandoning past identity—will always beckon to human beings so they may save their lives and the lives of those dear to them.

Today, it is possible to retain your identity as victim and seek a reversal by the power of your case. Back in the first millennium BCE, it was vastly different. "Woe to the victims," the Romans would certainly have said. It is hard now to put ourselves exactly in the circumstances of that ancient time. But we can try. In the case of the inhabitants of Jerusalem and surrounding territory, the effort is both helped and hindered by the record of the Bible itself.

To think of the situation of the Judeans carried off into exile in Babylon is to navigate back through the narrative of the Bible itself, back through the layers of restorative meaning in the return, back through the grim Deuteronomic judgment of divine punishment in the final chapters of Second Kings. We have to get behind these layers, back to the starved, beaten, and bewildered citizens of Jerusalem dragged along unforgiving highways, until finally they are dumped in some abandoned area around the imperial city, pathetic trophies of war never to regain their former dignity. It is a moment of abject horror.

> The Lord will bring you, and the king whom you set over you, to a nation that neither you nor your ancestors have known, where you shall serve other gods, of wood and stone. You shall become an object of horror, a proverb, and a byword among all the peoples where the Lord will lead you. (Deut 28:36–7)

Deuteronomy's prophecy-after-the-fact must reflect the abyss of alienation and contempt that those far-flung deportees ended up in. Once they had to some degree familiarized themselves with the language and the functioning of the city, it would certainly be a temptation to forget everything and turn themselves into opportunist second-class Babylonians. Surely some did just that, just as some of them in the siege of Jerusalem defected to the enemy (2 Kgs 25:11). But the fact is that a significant number of them did not take the survival path of assimilation, especially astonishing as the people passed into second and third generations.

It is very possible that the trope of punishment itself helped them survive. Invasion and conquest by Babylon were not, and never would be, the random impacts of imperial history. Paradoxically and uniquely, it was evidence of God's ultimate fidelity to his covenant, reproving and disciplining those he has chosen out of all the rest. If this is true, it tells us a great deal about the code structure that the experience of exile produced. Here the prophet Jeremiah takes on a huge importance. He had warned the people in explicit terms. He said,

> Because you have not obeyed my words, I am going to send for all the tribes of the north, says the Lord, even for king Nebuchadrezzar of Babylon, my servant, and will bring them against the land and its inhabitants, and against all these nations around; I will utterly destroy them, and make them an object of horror and of hissing, and an everlasting disgrace. (Jer 25.8–9)

In a third-person preface to these words, the prophecy is precisely dated to "the fourth year of King Jehoiakim son of Josiah (that was the first year of King Nebuchadrezzar of Babylon)," i.e., the year 605 BCE. The prophet places the coming events in broad political context, demonstrating his grasp of the menacing violence of current history. He goes on to use the metaphor of the "cup of the wine of wrath." The prophet takes the toxic cup directly from the Lord's hand and makes the nations drink, but he begins with "Jerusalem and the towns of Judah, its kings and officials, to make them a desolation and a waste, an object of hissing and of cursing" (Jer 25:18).

We see then how Jeremiah uses the military-political facts of his time and makes them actions of the Lord. More than anyone perhaps it was Jeremiah who embedded the code of wrath in the biblical meaning of God. Deuteronomy used it to understand and write past history, but Jeremiah presented it psychologically and in the present tense in his poetry. God through Jeremiah hands the cup of wrath directly to the Judeans, and in the very same moment he loves them. In the slightly earlier prophet Habakkuk, the figure of the cup is a kind of distributive justice administered impartially and neutrally by God—the nations which inflict violence will themselves become the victims of it (Hab 2:12–17). Jeremiah makes it personal and conflictive within Israel's sense of God himself. The same God who unabashedly claims his program of violence against his people is the God who loves them. Violence becomes an upside-down version of love, as the prophet goes from one to the other without pausing for breath.

> [F]or I have dealt you the blow of an enemy,
> the punishment of a merciless foe,
> because your guilt is great,
> because your sins are so numerous.
> Why do you cry out over your hurt?
> Your pain is incurable.
> Because your guilt is great,
> because your sins are so numerous,
> I have done these things to you.
> Therefore all who devour you shall be devoured,
> and all your foes, everyone of them, shall go into captivity;
> Those who plunder you shall be plundered,
> and all who prey on you I will make a prey.
> For I will restore health to you,
> and your wounds I will heal, says the Lord,
> because they have called you an outcast:
> "It is Zion, no one cares for her!"
> Thus says the Lord:
> I am going to restore the fortunes of the tents of Jacob,

and have compassion on his dwellings. (Jer 30:12–18)

Or see the even more directly conflicted emotions of the following.

> Is Ephraim my dear son?
> Is he the child I delight in?
> As often as I speak against him,
> I still remember him.
> Therefore I am deeply moved for him;
> I will surely have mercy on him. (Jer 31:20)

It is an unbearable tension being fought out in an anthropomorphic heart attributed to God, and as such can only be a partial revelation.

Jeremiah also famously advised the exiles to get ready for a long stay. He told them to put down roots.

> Build houses and live in them; plant gardens . . . take wives and have sons and daughters . . . multiply there, and do not decrease. But seek the welfare of the city where I have sent you into exile . . . Only when Babylon's seventy years are completed will I visit you, and I will fulfill to you my promise and bring you back to this place. (Jer 29:5–10)

Together with the two-sided, push-pull sense of the relationship, there can be little doubt this constructive image of a foreign sojourn proved a sustaining identity in the midst of exile. Indeed, the constructive vision was so successful that when the return eventually happened, a vigorous community remained behind in the region, one ultimately responsible for a version of the Talmud.[1] But what is of fundamental interest for us is how those who did return brought with them the push-pull structure of relationship as a master theological coding. We will see this clearly illustrated when we come to examine the books of Ezra and Nehemiah in the next essay.

A Sixth-Century Messiah

This theological coding has to be taken at its full weight in the constitution of Second Temple Judaism. However, the event of return by no means exhausted itself in this retributive theological response. Far to the contrary, a voice arose in this juncture of history that found a completely different telling of the story, one that amounts to a genuinely new code formation

---

1. See Neusner, *History of the Jews in Babylonia.*

and a transformed understanding of God. It emerged from the fires of the punishment model, from their collapse, under their own weight, into something other, something that we can now call a transcendence of nonviolence. The historical circumstances helped produce a definitive breakthrough, one that effectively separated out the compassion of God from the violent frequencies of mimesis. It is against the background of Jeremiah's vivid, tortured message we can clearly hear this beautiful new counter melody. The contrast is not to belittle the magnificent author of the original biblical "confessions"—a thousand years before Augustine— but to see how, through an astonishingly realized experience of suffering, the calculus of both Deuteronomy and Jeremiah is undermined. Where Job uses protest, hints, irony, and ambiguity, this new voice is situated, direct and bold. Of all the code violations and semiotic shifts we will study in the Old Testament, this is the one that is both historically most identifiable and stands most evidently as the watershed of the Gospels.

In the year 539 BCE, Babylon threw open its city gates to Cyrus, king of Persia. The charismatic general was well on his way to establishing the largest empire the world had yet known. He would be styled "King of the Four Corners of the World" and two centuries later would inspire Alexander of Macedonia in his own quest both to emulate and outdo him. Cyrus fought many battles, but not all his conquests were by force. Stories tell us that Cyrus won two armies of Medes to his cause without a drop of blood shed, and that the people of Babylon opened their gates to him without a battle. Although it is impossible to draw a sharp line between historical fact and imperial propaganda, it is clear that Cyrus desired and built a reputation for conciliation and religious piety.

In 1879 of the present era, archeologists working in the ruins of ancient Babylon discovered the "Cyrus Cylinder." It was a small clay barrel about the length and thickness of an adult forearm, inscribed with Akkadian cuneiform and dating from the sixth century BCE. Its forty-five lines describe Cyrus' peaceful entry into Babylon and his restoration of the traditional worship of the Babylonian god, Marduk. They also tell how the king returned images of other gods which had been taken from subjugated cities and their temples, also sending back some of the cities' inhabitants who likewise had been forcibly transferred to Babylon.[2] Marduk's approval of Cyrus is underlined and celebrated. The god is said to have sought out an upright king who would be to his liking. "He took

2. Anderson et al., *Understanding the Old Testament*, 428.

the hand of Cyrus . . . and called him by his name, proclaiming him aloud for the kingship over all of everything."[3]

It is of exceptional significance that the Bible announces Cyrus in almost identical terms of divine election and righteous behavior, but in relation to the only God, Yahweh, and his special people, Israel. It does so in the prophecy known as "Second Isaiah," a figure recognized as a second author within the Isaiah corpus (covering chapters 40–55). Not only is Cyrus God's chosen, he is even given the title of the Lord's "Anointed" or "Messiah," the sole non-Jewish person in the Bible to be so named.

> Thus says the LORD to his anointed, to Cyrus, whose right hand I have grasped to subdue nations before him, and strip kings of their robes, to open doors before him—and the gates shall not be closed. I will go before you . . . so that you may know it is I, the Lord, the God of Israel, who call you by your name. For the sake of my servant Jacob, and Israel my chosen, I call you by your name, I surname you, though you do not know me . . . (Isa 45:1–4)

According to the beginning of the Book of Ezra, Cyrus decreed the return of the Judeans to Jerusalem, in very much the same mode as we hear the citizens of the subjugated cities were repatriated in the Cylinder (Ezra 1:2–4). The Ezra note echoes the universal kingship of the Persian ruler, but declares, by Cyrus' own mouth, that it was the Lord God who had given him this power. If there is any historical validity to this, it is no more than a kind of diplomatic ecumenism on Cyrus' part. However, the writer of Second Isaiah is fully persuaded, effortlessly transferring the theology of election by Marduk, the god of Babylon, to Yahweh, the god of the Hebrews. But what is now at stake is something much greater than simply changing the name of the divinity responsible for Cyrus' world-making achievements. Assuring the city of Babylon that their long-standing god Marduk gave his divine seal of approval to their new king is purely a matter of shifting an imperial deity to another regime. In contrast, Second Isaiah amounts to a full-scale redefinition of divinity itself. The Lord is now the only God there is—beside him "there is no god" (Isa 44:6, 45:5). This declaration by the prophet has long been celebrated as the breakthrough to true monotheism in the religion of Israel.[4] But the abstract concept is removed from its context: the God of the Hebrews is

---

3. Simonin, "Cyrus Cylander."

4. Friedman, *Exodus*, 153–55. See also Brueggemann, *Isaiah 40–66*, 26–27.

the sole God because the prophet understands his writ runs for all the nations, not just Israel. The Lord is able to raise up a foreign ruler to bring about his purposes for his special people. And, even more crucially, what has also not been fully appreciated is how this claim goes hand in hand with an organic separation of God from violence.

Cyrus' conquests are not for the sake of Babylon or of Persia, but *for the sake of Israel and her relationship with her God*. Cyrus is named the Lord's Anointed/Messiah because his actions and their astonishing success shows forth the historical action and meaning of Israel's God. This would have a natural implication of monotheism. But it is the character of this singularity which is the true nature of the breakthrough. We do not know exactly how and why Cyrus added the Judeans to the list of peoples to be restored to their native cities, but his doing so means that the redemptive story of Exodus is now repeated *without God exercising any violence to achieve it*. Instead, the story of Cyrus' apparently effortless conquests are part of the Lord's sovereign, irresistible, but non-military action to bring about his purpose.

> Thus says the Lord to his anointed, to Cyrus
>   whose right hand I have grasped
> to subdue nations before him—
>   and strip kings of their robes,
> to open doors before him—
>   and the gates shall not be closed:
> I will go before you
>   and level the mountains,
> I will break in pieces the doors of bronze
>   and cut through the bars of iron. (Isa 45:1–2)

Physical objects are leveled, broken, and split apart; kings are stripped of their robes; because the Lord's sovereign power is engaged. But there is no talk of killing. The will of Yahweh is carried out on earth, but without plagues or battles or armies, and the immediate sense of Yahweh God is thus detached from human aggression. The closest parallel in semiotic terms is perhaps the nonviolence of the act of creation described in Genesis 1. Cyrus' decree, therefore, becomes a part of a theology which appropriates it and transcends it completely. This is an extraordinary achievement by the prophet, mining the shape of historical events to create a new mood and meaning, going from a tone of despair to one of joy, from provincial disaster to universal blessing, from a meaning of violence to one of compassion. The prophecy becomes a semiotic shift of world-historical proportions.

Divine Nonviolence

Because—as we continue in Second Isaiah—the role of Cyrus is really only a subplot. The major protagonist is not at all the Persian, but the Lord and the emerging truth of his nonviolence and compassion. "Comfort, O comfort my people, says your God. Speak tenderly to Jerusalem, and cry to her that she has served her term, that her penalty is paid, that she has received from the Lord's hand double for her sins." These are the first words of the main prophecy, at Isa 40:1–2, and they address at once the Deuteronomic principle. The prophet does not reject it outright. Rather, the prophetic voice renders it empty, redundant: Israel has done her time—her sentence is over, and in point of fact she has served twice the just sentence. Meanwhile, the new tone of consolation and compassion is set in its place. Very shortly, the ancient image of God as shepherd of his people is given, but developed poetically and in the real-time conditions of a return of the exiles to Jerusalem, making the emotion present-tense and alive.

> Get you up to a high mountain, O Zion . . . See the Lord comes with might and his arm rules for him . . . He will feed his flock like a shepherd; he will gather the lambs in his arms, and carry them in his bosom, and gently lead the mother sheep. (Isa 40:9–11)

The Lord is effectively more of a mother to the sheep than their own mothers!

In between these passages comes the echoing self-introduction of the prophetic voice: "A voice cries out: 'In the wilderness prepare the way of the Lord, make straight in the desert a highway for our God'" (40:3). The same introduction, of course, is used in the four Gospels, in relation to John the Baptist, linking the return and its transformation of meaning to the story of Jesus. This is an enormously important genetic line of descent in terms of biblical semiotics. It helps us grasp that there is an intentionally changed set of signs at work in the Gospels, and they derive so much of their impetus from the non-retributive voice of Second Isaiah.

The weakness of Israel is another essential element of code in Second Isaiah, consistent with the absence of divine violence. Only when

Israel is reduced to the status of nonentity in the world is it possible truly to introduce a God entirely of compassion. So long as the people have a national force of arms at their back, then they will necessarily interpret their God with fragments of generative violence mixed in with feelings of love and goodness. The push-pull God of Deuteronomy will then promptly make its return. (And, of course, the God of Constantinian-Augustinian theology is easily recognizable in the same frame.) But now the returning exiles had no military power or identity, and before the nations they could only have felt fear. It is these very conditions which reveal and celebrate a new mode of relationship with their God. "Do not fear, you worm Jacob, you insect Israel! I will help you, says the Lord; your Redeemer is the Holy One of Israel" (41:14). And again, at 43:1–2, "But now thus says the Lord, he who created you, O Jacob, he who formed you, O Israel: Do not fear, for I have redeemed you; I have called you by name, you are mine. When you pass through the waters I will be with you . . . and when you walk through fire you shall not be burned . . ." Redemption (deliverance) only truly occurs in conditions of helplessness, and what Second Isaiah does is stress these conditions in order to heighten and purify the answering note of nurturing, restorative care. Nevertheless, as I mentioned, the past image of God is not simply rejected. The prophet is no pre-Christian Marcion, setting up a metaphysical opposition between an old God and a new one. Indeed, the theology of punishment is referenced in Second Isaiah more than once.

> Who gave up Jacob to the spoiler, and Israel to the robbers? Was it not the Lord, against whom we have sinned, in whose ways they would not walk, and whose law they would not obey? So he poured upon him the heat of his anger and the fury of war . . . (42:24–25)

And yet this passage is followed immediately by the one just quoted from the beginning of chapter 43. The statement of past punishment is succeeded in virtually the same breath by a statement of active compassion. Moreover, this is no push-pull, because the latter voice is by far the dominant one, leaving the old one terminally behind. What is happing is semiotic transformation, rather than dialectical opposition, a new emotional tone and meaning that stretch away from the old framework like a tide carrying us off to a new shore. At one point, the movement becomes irreversible, but in an emotional code, not a metaphysical one:

> For a brief moment I abandoned you, but with great compassion
> I will gather you. In overflowing wrath for a moment I hid my
> face from you, but with everlasting love I will have compassion
> on you, says the Lord, your Redeemer. (54:7–8)

The phenomenon of wrath is seen as an aberration or mistake, like a
bucket of water carelessly carried and its contents slopping over; hardly
intentional. Now instead, the Lord's loving kindness will be an uninter-
rupted source of compassion for the people. The face of the Lord which
Jacob saw and recognized in Esau, the face of forgiveness, will now be the
imprinted features continually present to the people.

> Can a woman forget her nursing child, or show no compassion
> for the child of her womb? Even these may forget, yet I will not
> forget you. See I have inscribed you on the palms of my hands;
> your walls are continually before me. (49:15–16)

Again and again, the prophet opens up a horizon of gentleness and compassion, offering a transformed future of relationship, one based entirely
in nonviolent love. The unique conditions of the return—without political power and totally reliant on the political supernova of Cyrus—gave
the prophet a window of opportunity to express a revolutionary new
coding made up of open-ended compassion and nonviolence. But the
possibilities of the conditions were not exhausted by the new horizon.
The genius of the prophecy understood something more, something also
rooted in powerlessness, but looking now to human relationships, rather
than the divine persona. Surely the two things went hand in hand at the
level of generative coding; the startling anthropological breakthrough of
the "servant" grounds the note of divine nonviolence in a way that nothing else could.

The Pedagogy of the Servant

The figure of "servant" is a central element in the prophecy, and it applies initially to the people as such. The title is applied in previous biblical
writing to King David, and also in the Isaiah prophetic tradition to the
original prophet, Isaiah of Jerusalem (Isa 20:3). In Second Isaiah, the figure first appears identified with the people, in an unusual style of address.

> But you, Israel, my servant, Jacob, whom I have chosen, the off-
> spring of Abraham, my friend; you whom I took from the ends

of the earth, and called from its farthest corners, saying to you,
"You are my servant, I have chosen you and not cast you off": do
not fear, for I am with you. (41:8–10)

A title that before was given to a prestigious individual in the biblical
story is now given to the whole of the people considered as a unit. Again,
it must be the conditions of exile and return that make this shift intelligible. Something immense has happened to the whole people together,
welding them into a single experience and identity. It also happens when
the institutional leadership figures of king and priest have disappeared,
or at least lost their traditional role and status. What emerges, therefore,
is the sudden new coding of the people as a single entity and selfhood in
the particular conditions of national distress: a semiotic event of huge
importance. The titular sense of "servant" is then applied to this singularity, signifying both privileged relationship and, as the name implies, a
special task, or set of tasks, to be carried out.

What could the task possibly be, given that Israel seems stripped of
all agency? To answer this question, we have to turn to an exceptional literary feature of Second Isaiah, something known as the "Servant Songs."
These four distinctive poems (42:1–4, 49:1–6, 50:4–9, 51:13—53:12)
were first put in relief and identified separately from the rest of the text
by nineteenth-century scholarship. They stand as a unit because of a
number of distinct elements tying them together: for example, teaching
or instruction, suffering, contempt, shock or surprise to the nations, and
of course the name and figure of "servant." However, a problem arises
from detaching the songs from the surrounding text in this way: standing
alone, they can seem to apply to a distinct, historical individual, not the
corporate character of the people as proposed above. And a rigid distinction between a symbolic or representative individual and the people is
not elsewhere adhered to in the Bible—for example, Jacob as "Israel," or
the people's identity and destiny tied up with their kings. At the same
time, the profile of the servant is so intensely and powerfully realized, it is
difficult not to conceive the prophet/writer (or a member of their school
or community) as a model for the figure and a first point of reference.
Thus, it is much better to hold the songs as both set apart *and* integral to
the overall prophecy. In semiotic terms, it is inevitable that "the servant"
may perform as a sign which can apply equally to the people or a distinct
individual—semiosis is free, it can flow in many directions at once! But
what is the role of this servant?

> And now the Lord says,
> who formed me in the womb to be his servant,
> to bring Jacob back to him,
> and that Israel might be gathered to him,
> for I am honored in the sight of the Lord,
> and my God has become my strength—
> he says, "It is too light a thing that you should be my servant
> to raise up the tribes of Jacob
> and to restore the survivors of Israel;
> I will give you a light to the nations,
> that my salvation my reach to the end of the earth. (49:5–6)

The servant's job is a matter of the restoration of the people's existence and wellbeing. Not only that, the servant is to be a light to all the nations, in order that the Lord's life and goodness might reach to the ends of the earth. The passage clearly treats the servant in individual terms: the address of the Lord echoes passages of election spoken to a prophet, like Jeremiah or First Isaiah (e.g., Isa 6:8–10). Even if this may be read as a literary effect, treating a certain corporate Israel (e.g., returnees from exile) in the role of an individual prophet, it is impossible not also to see it in fully restrictive terms: i.e., as individual election and vocation for the sake of Israel.

But what would the proclaimed salvation look like? Because dominant Christian atonement theories focused on the sacrificial, compensatory death of Jesus, not only has the role of Israel been overlooked, but the singular import of the servant has been almost erased. The servant is the crown jewels of transformative semiotics in the Old Testament, the single most startling piece of code violation and creation in the entire Bible. But it has been very easy to misread, perhaps because—precisely—it is dealing with the root code of human meaning, and this has a built-in or genetic power continually to reboot and restore itself in the face of anything contrary.

The first thing, therefore, to underline is the servant's nonviolence. This nonviolence has been named always as "suffering" and seen as expiatory. But the first poem or song is explicit. I give the whole passage to relay its full impact:

> Here is my servant, whom I uphold,
> my chosen, in whom my soul delights;
> I have put my spirit upon him;
> he will bring forth justice to the nations.

He will not cry of lift up his voice,
or make it heard in the street;
a bruised reed he will not break,
and a dimly burning wick he will not quench;
he will faithfully bring forth justice.
He will not grow faint of be crushed
until he has established justice in the earth;
and the coastlands wait for his teaching. (42:1–4)

The issue is justice (*mispat*—generally the act of just judgment). The servant is to be a figure of judgment for the whole earth, but the method of achieving this is an extraordinary gentleness and nonaggression in relation to what is broken and close to extinction. Such gentleness stands in stark contrast to the penal and violent response normally associated with a judge. What is coded here, therefore, relates to the heart of social order and meaning, and very much to the current situation of Israel. Where the judgment against Israel was harsh and brutal—because of its sins, God gave up Israel to the spoilers and the robbers—the attitude of the servant is entirely the reverse. Instead of a pitiless *quid pro quo,* there is a compelling attitude of compassion and nonviolence. It's hard, if not impossible, to find parallel biblical references for shouting out in the street, or refraining from snapping a reed or snuffing a wick, but it's almost as if these tropes do not need it. They gather their own atmosphere and theme: an essential nonviolence.

An amazing transformation in social modeling has taken place through the servant. It is not explained or developed, and so remains vulnerable to misrepresentation or simply being ignored, but we can be sure that the manner of existence of the servant constitutes a profound shock to the rulers of the nations who have relied always on violence. The first three poems of the servant (42:1–4, 49:1–6, 50:4–9) are followed by short responses or comments directly related to the poems. The second response includes the following: "Thus says the Lord, the Redeemer of Israel and his Holy One, to one deeply despised, abhorred by the nations, the slave of rulers, 'Kings shall see and stand up, princes, and they shall prostrate themselves, because of the Lord, who is faithful, the Holy One of Israel, who has chosen you'" (49:7; cf. 52:14–15). The weakness which is disgusting and abhorrent to the violent of the earth somehow is turned around and becomes a revolutionary new authority and truth. The weakness of Israel, of the "worm Jacob," becomes by the attitude of the servant the source of an entirely new framing of human existence, one which the whole earth awaits.

But, once again, how can this work? Does the prophet simply state these things and expect his audience to believe them? At 52:13 to 53:12, we have the fourth and longest of the poems, the most detailed account of what happened to this figure. If the poems were movements of a concerto, the fourth would be the final and most profound, the one where the woodwind, strings, and percussion are set loose, giving the theme its fullest, most memorable treatment. It is a music that has been taken up and played again and again by Christian interpreters. Some of the phrases are better known than passages from the Gospels themselves.

> He was despised and rejected of men, a man of sorrows, and acquainted with grief. (53:3 KJV)

> He was wounded for our transgressions, he was bruised for our iniquities: the chastisement of our peace was upon Him. And with His stripes we are healed. (53:5 ASV)

But this language is so deeply inflected by Christian era transactional thinking—Jesus paid the price of our sins—that it is extremely difficult to hear in its place a transformative meaning. In the fourth poem, the crucial meanings of inflicted suffering (together with the prepositional "for" or "because of" iniquities/transgression) seem automatically to produce the dynamic of an exchange—punishment in exchange for salvation. The code of paying a price is embedded in the Deuteronomic worldview, but it is in distributive form—the offender did the crime and so they must suffer for it. In the fourth poem, however, it is now not the offender, but one who is in fact innocent who is seen to suffer. To turn this into a kind of logic, of one man taking the punishment from God in the place of others, is not only antithetical to Deuteronomy; it goes against the whole fabric of compassion in Second Isaiah. It establishes violence at a "higher" yet more primitive level in God. What happens is no longer a matter of a reforming discipline for one who broke the law, but simply a "pound of flesh" for the offended lawgiver. "Someone has to take the fall!" This kind of vicarious suffering is a long, long way from Deuteronomy and all the codes of justice it (and Exodus) establish. It is even further from the nonviolence of Second Isaiah, amounting to a crassly deliberate mechanism of scapegoating, formally at work for the lucky people who benefit from its arrangement. How could the letting-go-of-violence message of Second Isaiah institute this "primitivizing" meaning in place of Deuteronomy, stepping deeper into the dynamics of violence after asserting its break from them?

To get out of the bind of this interpretation, we have to stick to the text, accepting its work of changing the codes radically, rather than imposing a regressive style of codes upon it. The other poems reinforce the servant's refusal to retaliate. This is all important in strengthening the core theme of nonviolence.

> The Lord God has opened my ear,
> and I was not rebellious,
> I did not turn backward.
> I gave my back to those who struck me,
> and my cheeks to those who pulled out the beard;
> I did not hide my face,
> from insult and spitting. (50:5–6)

The attitude is reaffirmed in the fourth poem in another famous line: "He was oppressed, and he was afflicted, yet he did not open his mouth; like a lamb that is led to the slaughter, and like a sheep that before its shearers is silent, so he did not open his mouth" (53:7). In the past, this would be conceived as simply the pathos-filled submission of the object-victim. Reading it for itself, we see it as transformative nonviolence.

To understand why and how this is the case, we must realize that beginning at 53:1, a new voice is introduced in the fourth poem. Up to this point (52:13–15) it has been the Lord who is speaking, proclaiming the virtue of his servant and the way kings shall be struck dumb before him. But from there on (until verse 7) it becomes a plural "we," a community of some kind which very pointedly takes up the narrative:

> Who has believed what we have heard?
> And to whom has the arm of the Lord been revealed? . . .
> He was despised and rejected by others;
> a man of suffering and acquainted with infirmity;
> and as one from whom others hide their faces
> he was despised, and we held him of no account.
> Surely he has borne our infirmities
> and carried our diseases;
> yet we accounted him stricken,
> struck down by God and afflicted.
> But he was wounded for our transgressions,
> crushed for our iniquities;
> upon him was the punishment that made us whole,
> and by his bruises we are healed. (53:1–5)

Who are these plural speakers? If, as sometimes suggested, the group speakers are the nations, talking about Israel, it produces two quite difficult consequences. First, the nations are speaking in revelatory and confessional terms, coming to understand that the action of God in the servant has been for their sake. This must imply some degree of repentance which is of course completely ideal and non-historical. Second, and at the same time, the conversion of the nations must be by reason of a vicarious "othering"—Israel suffering in place of the nations—because the nations are nowhere shown to learn from the servant by renouncing their violence. They appear simply to take him as their "get-out-of-jail-free" card, in precisely the version of atonement so popular in the age of Christendom. But, again, this is so far from the justice of Deuteronomy, and the compassion of Second Isaiah as to be completely implausible.

Much more coherent, therefore, the "we" is the writer and prophetic community, or a gathered, representative community of Israel, of which the servant was part. In this instance, they really are witnessing a single individual who did seem to them to be struck down by God, for that is what they say: "we accounted him . . . struck down by God." At this point, they are exactly the same as the "friends" in Job, who righteously conclude that Job must have done something wrong, so severe are his sufferings.

However, something occurred which showed this group a new and revolutionary truth. They conclude, in the present tense, "Surely he has borne our infirmities and carried our diseases," and this conclusion comes *subsequently* to their previous, now-seen-as-incorrect penal and retributive conclusion. They understand, therefore, that the way the servant bears their infirmities and diseases is *not* by othering, by scapegoating, but by a totally unheralded *novum* in the human scene. It depends on *the revolutionary empathy of nonviolence.*

The servant gives his back and his cheeks to the aggressor and does not hide his face. Learning from his open ear to his Lord, the servant makes his body a nonretaliatory receptacle of violence. An individual who in this way refuses to imitate the violence of the aggressor, but rather uses his own body as a non-reciprocating mirror of the violence, will necessarily detonate in the enemy a revolutionary awareness: a complex mixture of provocation, perception, pity, and peace. This is the case because violence is mimetic and in the context of actual violence the antagonist is in a state of hyper mimesis. When the other does not retaliate but actively models his own vulnerability, the aggressor will helplessly—neurally—imitate his condition at the deepest level. In that moment, he sees his own violence for itself, declared and highlighted against the disjunctive nonviolence of the other. It becomes a theme and a motif he had never seen before and which he cannot now unlearn. There is certainly no guarantee that the aggressor will fully accept his lesson: he may in fact double down on his violence, to try and get this unwelcome revelation disappear; but in his soul, an indelible perception has been implanted. *How much more so* for any witnesses who already have some feeling for the one attacked, who are already neurally engaged in watching the violence against him? Initially, they may well have been tempted to think this person brought his suffering on himself; but observing his sustained revelation of the aggressor's violence—an attitude that is also patently a faithfulness to God, for how else could the servant have done it?—suddenly, there's a completely transformed experience and understanding. The companions of the servant undergo their own imitation of God-initiated nonviolence. The community grasps the nonretaliation as a true revelation of God-self, and its new, liberating, non-penal righteousness at once enters their souls. Seemingly out of nowhere, a new human coding is achieved, an anthropological and religious breakthrough of world-historical dimensions. "Who has believed what we have heard? And to whom has the arm of the Lord been revealed?" (53:1). It is so absolutely subversive that almost inevitably it is swallowed up in a twisted construct of vicarious sacrificial atonement. But today it depends very much on us on how we decide to read it.

We can read the words of the speakers—"he was wounded for our transgressions, crushed for our iniquities"—in compensatory sacrificial terms, or we can see the writer and his community struggling to find adequate expression for what they had experienced. They knew that what the servant had done is not just a private event; it is a transformation of public human meaning and to be understood as happening for their sake. Thus, the servant was wounded on account of others' transgressions in order to turn them effectively to the same root innocence as the servant. But how was the prophet or writer to express this seismic shift. The text says he was wounded "because" of our transgressions, crushed "because of" our iniquities. If we take this in the original sense, "by cause of," we see that the efficient cause of the wounding is us! It is then to be understood as the action of God only in the sense of final cause—the willing and bringing of this about for the sake of an organic human change. This interpretation is pivotal at 53:10, "It was the will of the Lord to crush him with pain."

The choice of words in translation accents a sense of brutality ("crush" may be rendered less harshly as "bruise" or "bring down," and "pain" as "grief"), but the real point is to step back and see the providential will of God, not a vindictive and punitive will. God wills this suffering in order to bring about the religious experience of nonviolence. It is still possible that the writer made use of some sacrificial tropes to invoke an effect found in sacrifice, while nevertheless not envisaging any kind of transactional mechanism. This seems pretty clearly the case in the continuation of verse 10: "When you make his life an offering for sin." It seems to be God who is being addressed as agent, so it is God (not humans) who sets forth what is understood as a sin or guilt offering (using the technical term, *asham*; cf. Lev 5:6–7). If we take this literally (which of course the Christian tradition has) it involves the religious monstrosity of God offering a sacrifice to himself. But the writer is not thinking about the mechanism, but the effect. This death brought about by human violence is yet willed by God because astonishingly it produces a transforming human-religious impact, the only semiotic parallel to which is found in temple practice. It does not mean that the servant is the "perfect sacrifice." Far from it: it tells us that something has happened by other means entirely from temple ritual, and yet it brings about an effect which can only be described by pressing into service the ancient religious terminology. It is "the sacrifice to end sacrifice," taking those words in their full contradictory, paradoxical, deconstructive value.

The most critical question of translation, however, comes in relation to the word "punishment" in 53:5 (the last verse in the excerpt bottom p. 77). This word seems to give the game away all in one go—the servant is punished in our place, just as the penal substitution theory tells it. The word (Hebrew *musar*) is also given in the translations as "chastisement," but more often than not in the Old Testament, it is translated as "instruction" or "discipline." A good example is in Proverbs 23 where it is used three times, twice as instruction paralleled with teaching and wisdom (23:12, 23), and one time as discipline applied with corporal punishment (23:13)! In other words, this is a tough and possibly painful teaching, but it is a *teaching*, the administering of a lesson intended for change of behavior, rather than any kind of sacrificial compensation. When we add this to the role of the servant as teacher (50:4; cf. 49:2), it is inescapable that the servant's job is both to undergo and communicate a challenging pedagogy. That word is the best translation I can think of for the overall text of servant songs—the *pedagogy of the servant*. It is indeed the servant's anthropological pedagogy—experienced and given in the heart of violence—"that [has] made us whole."

At 53:11, another choice of reading made by translators underlines what is at stake. The NRSV says, "Out of his anguish he shall see light; he shall find satisfaction through his knowledge. The righteous one, my servant, shall make many righteous . . ." Others render the phrasing and meaning differently. For example, the KJV says, "He shall see of the travail of his soul, and be satisfied, by his knowledge shall my servant justify many . . ."

What does the servant see through his travail and so find satisfaction? The NRSV makes his knowledge the source of his satisfaction, but then the knowledge remains vague, esoteric. If with the KJV we make the knowledge govern the work of justifying, then we are back with the work of the servant-teacher. It is what the servant learned and then imparted that justifies many, and this indeed is what he sees! He has shown to human beings an astonishing new way of dealing with human sinfulness—by demonstrating the coding of nonviolence that comes from God, simultaneously removing the hostility both from God and from humankind. Out of his anguish, he sees the impact it has had, and so he is consoled.

Once we have established this reading of the prophet describing the change of a root anthropological code, it is possible to flip the whole thing once again and find a secondary interpretation in the space that I earlier dismissed. I said the nations could not be the speakers at 53:1 because they show no sign of transformation and thus, automatically, if the servant suffers for them, we must revert to an extrinsic, penal atonement. But if the prophetic community were the first ones to undergo the "software" revolution created by the servant, then it is possible that the writer might have, at a second moment, projected it on the nations. In which case, the "we" passage does double duty and develops a prophetic scenario where the nations do genuinely receive the remarkable new coding. By that token, Israel has been given a deep prophetic identity, occupying the role of the nonviolent servant and standing in an ideal historical sense as "light to the nations." It is a play of mirrors where Israel mirrors the servant, just as the servant mirrors Israel, and the nations mirror the prophetic community, just as the community mirrored the nations in their first reaction to suffering.

What an amazing project of this Hebrew prophet of the Babylonian deportation! To turn the experience of imperial violence around and make it work for the sake of universal humanization! Philosophers have carried through dazzling redefinitions of the nature of things, allowing us to see the question of "what is as such" in profoundly new and insightful ways, but has anyone ever attempted to give us the source code to a new humanity? This is what was achieved by the prophecy of Second Isaiah, following in the path of Exodus and Genesis, and, in all likelihood, inspiring the devastating critique of "merited suffering" in Job. It arrives at a higher intensity of revelation than any of these works because it explicitly relates God's personal righteousness to nonviolence. The fact that this was swallowed up historically in sacrificial reading does nothing to alter the radical power of the breakthrough.

A philosophy of semiotics, of signs, has developed progressively throughout the Christian era. We are now in a position to see how the roots of this thinking are located in the biblical text, with a movement of signs running from the oppressed in Exodus, through the overcoming of violence in Genesis, to the question of the scapegoat in Job, and, at the vertex of the sequence, the emergence of the nonviolent servant in Second Isaiah. As suggested before, the end of Job reaches a conclusion parallel to Second Isaiah—the innocent victim is the source of righteousness—strongly indicating its composition came at least under shared influences, if not directly from that of the Isaiah prophecy. In which case, the sign value of these stories clearly works progressively to change our relationship to human violence. This, neither more nor less, is the heart of semiotic transformation, shifting the core of our sign systems from the hidden victim to the victim revealed in nonviolence and forgiveness. During the metaphysical-dogmatic ages of Christianity, it was almost impossible to see the transformative coding for itself. But this did not mean it did not have an impact—beginning with Augustine who realized that the Scripture did in fact have a sign value, equal and parallel to ordinary instrumental signs in the world.[5] We are now well on our way clearly to understand this massive impact for itself; to understand and embrace the possibility of seeing the Bible as God-inspired transformative semiotics.

5. See Bartlett, *TBM*, 80–81.

5

Ruth

First Read Ezra and Nehemiah

AFTER THE NUCLEAR FISSION of Second Isaiah, to turn to the simple tinder of the Book of Ruth might seem anticlimactic. But all fire is equal in giving energy, and if the story of Ruth lights a different path, more local than the great crossroads of the sixth century, it is nonetheless an essential part of the journey for the pilgrim nation of Israel.

Just as to understand Job we had to look at the thought of Deuteronomy, to understand Ruth we have to come to grips with the world of Ezra and Nehemiah, allowing ourselves to be introduced to their worldview. Why do we put these works together? Isn't it anachronistic to link Ruth, whose story is situated somewhere in the eleventh century BCE, before the rise of David, with these two historical books straddling the fifth and fourth centuries BCE? The answer lies with the creative energy of biblical writers, always able to see their whole national story as one of continuous meaning, regardless of which exact niche of time they find themselves in.

The historical sequence of the two figures, Ezra and Nehemiah, is much debated, but the overall themes and shared concerns are evident. Initially (in the Hebrew manuscripts), the two writings constituted a single book, and the narrative has the titular figures overlapping in time and place, suggesting why it would be seen as one volume. Ezra was a priest and scribe who was commissioned by a Persian king, Artaxerxes, to return from Babylon to Jerusalem, appoint magistrates, and teach the laws of God to any who did not know them. Nehemiah was an official in Artaxerxes' court who received the mission to go to Jerusalem and rebuild its fallen walls. These two tasks complement each other—the walls represent a bounded space in which the divine laws of Israel can be maintained, the laws themselves are a boundary around the people. Thus, the two leaders underpin each other's project. The historical problem is that there were two Artaxerxes, I and II, and the biblical text nowhere specifies which one is being considered at a time. Ezra 7:8 says that Ezra arrived in Jerusalem in the seventh year of King Artaxerxes, while Neh 2:1–9 has Nehemiah arriving in Artaxerxes' twentieth year. This would be 458 and 445 BCE, respectively—Ezra first, Nehemiah next—if we are dealing with Artaxerxes I. However, Ezra 9:9 suggests that when the priest arrived, the walls were already in a sound state, which indicates Ezra could have arrived much later in the reign of Artaxerxes II, with a date of 398 BCE.[1]

Why this is important is that it (and other factors) suggest a process of composition and editing of the text sources, going through into the fourth century and creating a coherent narrative unit involving these two prestigious figures. To what point? The answer lies in the religious and semiotic activity of the two men. In the Book of Ezra there is first a long description of the earlier rebuilding of the temple, followed by an account of the edict of Artaxerxes commissioning Ezra, the king's gifts of silver and gold, followed by the return of Ezra with a considerable company of named families. Then we come to the nub of the story in chapter 9. Here Ezra is speaking in the first person, part of the so-called "Ezra memoir" that makes up some of the text:

> After these things had been done, the officials approached me and said, "The people of Israel, the priests and the Levites have not separated themselves from the peoples of the lands with their abominations, from the Canaanites, the Hittites, the Perizzites, the Jebusites, the Ammonites, the Moabites, the Egyptians and the Amorites. For they have taken some of their daughters as wives for themselves and their sons. Thus the holy seed has mixed itself with the peoples of the lands and in this faithlessness the officials and leaders have led the way." (Ezra 9:1–2)

---

1. For possible dating and historical order of text of Ezra-Nehemiah, see Myers, *Ezra-Nehemiah*, xxx–xlviii.

This is startling information. It means that Ezra and the people with him—arriving in Jerusalem and Judah either in the middle of the fifth century or the beginning of the fourth century BCE—found the original returnees in a state of ethnic mixing of which they heartily disapproved. The "holy seed" of Israel was faithlessly mixed with the "peoples of the land." The list of alien nations, with whom the Judeans are intermarrying, is partially copied from a list of nations in Deuteronomy, those that the Hebrews of the Exodus had to destroy at their entry into the land (Deut 7:1–2). However, it now also includes the Moabites, the Egyptians, and the Ammonites. The forbidden group also certainly implies the Samaritans who considered themselves true Israelites and had in fact offered help (Ezra 4:1–2) in rebuilding the temple, but were roundly rebuffed and alienated (cf. Neh 2:10, 19, 4:1–2). It also likely overlaps with "the poor of the land" who were left behind in the original deportation (2 Kgs 25:12; cf. Ezra 4:4).

In short, Ezra and the group with him have brought with them a critical sense of identity, one to be preserved by strict endogamy among the families who returned from exile. This is not ethnic identity as such, i.e., one defined by strong geographical and cultural continuity, with resulting physical aspects in common. This is something different. It is a matter of a "holy seed," a group born out of a highly particular historical-religious experience in which a dispossessed, exiled people preserved a relationship with their God and, as such, have discovered their existence as holy.[2] The group defined themselves in an absolutely unique way. A term applied normally to the temple, its contents, and its city is now transferred to the people who have undergone the loss of all these things and yet in the process taken that quality to themselves. The physical marker for this quality is not the precincts of the temple; it is, instead, endogamous marriage. It is an unparalleled religio-ethnic revolution, one with huge historical impact and consequence. The thing to underline here is that it comes from a returning group which seems to have successfully nurtured this distinct identity in Babylonia over the course of two centuries.

---

2. See Blenkinsopp, *Judaism*, 229: "[T]he arrival of Ezra and Nehemiah in the province of Judah represented not so much a 'return to Zion' but a kind of diaspora in reverse from the parent body in southern Mesopotamia, a religious colonization with a definite religious agenda, namely, the creation of a self-segregated, ritually pure society inspired by the new temple and new society profiled in Ezekiel's vision and elaborated by his disciples in the diaspora."

The previous returnees did not seem to have had held this concept, intermarrying freely with the surrounding population, something which occasioned Ezra's horror. It seems in fact that the prophet known as Third Isaiah, working soon after the first return from Babylon at the end of the sixth century, nourished an entirely opposite opinion about foreigners.[3] The author talks approvingly of "foreigners who join themselves to the Lord" (56:6) and makes the epochal announcement, "My house shall be called a house of prayer for all peoples" (56:7). It's possible that this attitude had influenced the earlier returnees, but later became offensive to Ezra and the self-definition of Israelite tradition he brought with him.[4] At all events, Ezra's prayers show us clearly the fundamental coding at work in the strict policy:

> After all that has come upon us for our evil deeds and for our great guilt, seeing that you, our God, have punished us less than our iniquities deserved and have given us such a remnant as this, shall we break your commandments again and intermarry with the peoples who practice these abomination? Would you not be angry with us until you destroy us without remnant or survivor? (Ezra 9:13–14)

The semiotic labor of Second Isaiah to establish a relationship free of wrath has disappeared. The coding has reverted to the much more direct and visceral Deuteronomic formula, now powerfully endorsed by the Babylonian remnant. When it came down to it, after Ezra's intervention, 110 men divorced their wives and sent them away with their children, according to the list in chapter 10. This is considerably less than 1 percent of the number of initial returnees given in chapter 2. Again, we can only guess at what it means. If we surmise the first returnees were a majority of males willing to risk the hardships of the journey and encounter the threats of opposition, would they have not looked to local women for wives? This would have (partly) explained Third Isaiah's positive attitude. As it stands, the number of divorcees is a comparatively low number. It could be there was resistance, and the words of Third Isaiah were invoked in effective opposition. Semiotically, however, the number is not paramount. The sacrificial animal is only one out of the herd: the fraction of

---

3. The name "Third Isaiah" is used to represent the set of oracles subsequent to Second Isaiah, chapters 56–66.

4. See Cohen, *From the Maccabees to the Mishnah*, 141–42.

1 percent was the effective sacrifice necessary to make the people holy according to the vision of the Book of Ezra.

The Book of Nehemiah describes the work of Nehemiah, appointed, probably before Ezra, by King Artaxerxes I, as royal commissioner to rebuild the walls of Jerusalem. Ezra also appears in the middle of the story, conducting a reading of the Law before an assembly of the people, representative of all the original returnees, followed by an agreement on their part to be faithful to the Law (chapters 8–10). This episode would make a lot of sense placed *before* Ezra's polemic against mixed marriages in the earlier Book of Ezra, chapter 9. It may very well have been moved to its present location to indicate that the population of newly walled Jerusalem (many transferred there from the surrounding countryside, Neh 11:1) consisted of a faithful Israel, or, in Ezra's term, "the holy seed." In fact, a key part of the Nehemiah narrative, following the reading of the Law, is the crucial impact: "[T]hose of Israelite descent separated themselves from all foreigners, and stood and confessed their sins, and the iniquities of their ancestors" (Neh 9:2). The outcome to the reading of the Law clearly links with the Book of Ezra's policy of divorce and its list of divorcees.

The overall effect is to unite the efforts of Nehemiah and Ezra, political governor and priest, demonstrating a joint authority and effect (cf. Neh 8:9). The walls and the populace within them form together a sacred perimeter, separating off from the non-holiness of the other nations. Nevertheless, this ideal image of Jerusalem is balanced by quite large hints of a longer and more conflicted effort to achieve it. Chapter 5 of Nehemiah describes how wealthy families among the Jewish population operated debt servitude against the Jewish peasantry during a time of famine when, on top of that, the smallholders had to pay the Persian royal tax. Nehemiah insisted that these "nobles" stop taking interest and restore the peasantry's seized properties (Neh 5:6–13).

Here is a human constant—oppression of the poor, something the prophets railed about since the earliest days of Israel. The fact that Nehemiah is so urgently concerned shows that he belongs to that core tradition, the one that said not to take interest on a loan nor a poor man's property when it's essential for survival (Deut 24:12). But Nehemiah's concern is also political—he needs to ensure the cohesion of the Judeans both in and around Jerusalem. The final chapter of the book turns away from the editorial suturing with Ezra and has the feeling of a vivid first-hand report by the governor. It is perhaps used as a conclusion to show finally the real-world struggle in which these policies work themselves out. The governor is dealing with resistant human habits and he does not hesitate to record his militancy against them. Once again, the central issue is the exclusive identity of the returnees.

In chapter 13, Nehemiah notices that people were working on the sabbath and traders were bringing produce into the city for sale. These included foreigners, "Tyrians"; but the leaders of the Judeans were also complicit (Neh 13:15–18). He locks the gates at night the keep the traders out, and when they camp outside waiting for morning, he threatens them with violence. After that, it seems the sabbath traders did not come back. The strict sabbath rest represented an indispenable marker of Jewish identity—something not practiced by any other culture—and Nehemiah's struggle to defend it demonstrates its pivotal character.

And then, suddenly, there is also this:

> In those days also I saw Jews who had married women of Ashdod, Ammon and Moab; and half of their children spoke the language of Ashdod, and they could not speak the language of Judah, but spoke the language of various peoples. And I contended with them and cursed them and beat some of them and pulled out their hair; and I made them take an oath in the name of God, saying, "You shall not give your daughters to their sons, or take their daughters for your sons or for yourselves . . . Shall we then listen to you and do this great evil and act treacherously against our God by marrying foreign women?" (Neh 13:23–27)

This is a much rawer version of Ezra's "mixing of the holy seed." Nehemiah can literally hear in the speech of the children the ebbing away of the Hebrew language and the people's identity with it. Language is a prime repository of the semiotic register of any group, and when that goes, much that is vital in that register will go with it. At the very least, the people's assured self-concept will erode among the collective markers of another linguistic community. Even at this distance, we can feel Nehemiah's militant zeal, his authority as governor physically demonstrated on the bodies of those he governed. And at the heart of the militancy is the same fearful rationale that Ezra spoke of—God's anger that might destroy the community entirely. When he answered the leaders earlier in the chapter, defending his strict enforcement of the sabbath, Nehemiah invokes the theme of wrath, the unarguable sememe of divine violence:

What is this evil thing that you are doing, profaning the sabbath day? Did not your ancestors act in this way, and did not our God bring all this disaster on us and on this city. Yet you bring more wrath on Israel by profaning the sabbath. (Neh 13:17b–18)

Nehemiah and Ezra are two sides of the same coin, one political, the other liturgical. Wherever Ezra stands historically, it does not really matter. In sign terms, he represents the religious majesty of the priestly and scribal office while Nehemiah belongs to the complex affairs of politics. Ezra's presence throughout the two books ensures the central "holiness" of the program which they both share. Ezra is the sacred in its unanswerable authority, while Nehemiah is the fury of the sacred within a plural world where other worldviews resist. Behind each man stands the authority of the exilic community in Babylon, able to send emissaries to Jerusalem backed by the power of the king and an interpretation of Jewish identity that is newly purist and confident. What unites the activity of both men is the will to effect the boundaries through exclusion. Nehemiah concludes his report with more than a hint of official satisfaction: "Thus I cleansed them from everything foreign [*nekar*] . . . Remember me, O my God, for good" (Neh 13:30–31).

But the enormous thing about the Bible is that it is not a single book! It is a collection of books with different voices and different points of view, and probably this is no more clearly the case than when the Book of Ruth is held up in comparison to Ezra and Nehemiah. Having understood something of the thinking represented by these men, we are in a position to grasp the electric freedom generated by Ruth. The name "Ruth" is from a Hebrew root meaning to "keep company" or "to friend," and, as the eponym of the biblical story, the heroine's name is synonymous with loyalty, courage, and compassion. The drama of Ruth's story turns on her central status as "foreigner" outside the household of Israel, while at the same time manifesting classic covenant virtue.

Ruth, the Moabite Redeemer

Whatever the general attitude among Judeans to foreign wives, an unknown writer decided to give a contrasting view to the ideology of "holy seed" by creating one of the most beautiful pieces of the Hebrew literary canon. Ruth is an amazingly modern figure. Not only is she a migrant coming from beyond the borders, without rights or standing—the *arrivant*, as Derrida would tell it—but as a woman she produces dynam- ics impossible for men, and makes those dynamics triumphant. She thus achieves one of the Bible's most concussive code transformations.

We know the Book of Ruth is written around the same time as Ezra and Nehemiah because it is not part of the "former prophets" in the Jew- ish Tanakh—a place it occupies in the Christian Bible between Judges and First Samuel. Ruth in the Tanakh comes in the Ketuvim, the addi- tional writings, after the Torah and Prophets. It belongs there to the "five scrolls" (*Hamesh Megillot*)—together with Song of Songs, Lamentations, Ecclesiastes, and Esther—which include some of the very latest elements in the Hebrew Bible.[5]

More to the point even, it is the whole narrative scene-setting which tells us the exact nature of the argument this story is making. The open- ing of the book elaborately and artificially places Ruth's mother-in-law, Naomi, in the foreign territory of Moab, thus setting the plot engine in motion. We remember that both Ezra and Nehemiah finger Moab as the source of unwanted foreign women—Ezra includes the Moabites among the list of Deuteronomic nations to be expelled from Israel; Nehemiah fumes that he found "Jews who had married women of Ashdod, Am- mon and Moab" (Neh 13:23), and he proceeds to curse and beat them. We remember also that the Book of Deuteronomy decreed that Moabites should be banned from the assembly of the Lord, down to the tenth generation, because they refused to give help to the Hebrews on their way into Canaan—instead, they hired a prophet (Balaam) to curse them (Deut 23:3). There was an ancient, bitter, and now topical grievance be- tween Israelites and the Moabites. It can't be any accident, therefore, that the plot device of the book ensures its central character is from Moab.

The artificiality of the plot is underlined by the names of Naomi's sons, Mahlon and Chilion, sounding like the Hebrew words for "dis- eased" and "perishing." Fulfilling their denotation, these men promptly die, leaving Naomi and her two Moabite daughters-in-law, Orpah and Ruth, without economic or social standing. Naomi sets out to return to Judah, giving permission to the two young women to remain in Moab to seek new husbands. Ruth refuses to leave her mother-in-law and so begins to unfold the story of Ruth's "kindness." This quality has already been invoked by Naomi, speaking to both Orpah and Ruth: "May the

5. Note the Book of Esther is set in a semi-fictional court of king Ahasuerus, com- monly identified with the fifth-century Persian king, Xerxes I. Ahasuerus is also men- tioned in Ezra 4:6 as part of its historical context.

Lord deal kindly with you, as you have dealt kindly with the dead and with me" (1:8b).

The word in Hebrew is *hesed*, with a rich range of meaning, beyond simple kindness: from loving kindness, to mercy, steadfast love, loyalty, and faithfulness. It is one of the great central concepts and qualities of the God of Israel, echoed again and again throughout the Old Testament. We hear it twice in the Lord's lapidary personal revelation to Moses in Exodus: "The Lord, the Lord, a God merciful and gracious, slow to anger, and abounding in steadfast love (*hesed*) and faithfulness, keeping steadfast love (*hesed*) for the thousandth generation . . ." (Exod 34:6–7). When Naomi speaks it in blessing on her daughters-in-law ("May the Lord do *hesed* . . .") and in the same breath says that they have practiced the same thing ("as you have done *hesed*"), she is telling us in no uncertain terms that these Moabite women are capable of the core Israelite covenant virtue. Ruth, in refusing to leave Naomi, goes beyond Orpah and begins to manifest the deep radicalism and generative power of divine *hesed*.

The migrants arrive in Judah and Ruth the Moabite (2:2) asks Naomi if she can go and glean in the fields. The writer thus introduces another core piece of biblical coding, the concern for the poor central to the Exodus experience. Leviticus and Deuteronomy both tell us that the poor must be allowed to take whatever of the harvest is growing at the very edge of the field or accidentally left behind by the workers (Lev 23:22). Deuteronomy specifies categories of the poor who are to be accorded this right—the fatherless, the widow, and the migrant/stranger (Hebrew *ger*, Deut 24:19). We are here fully in the world of meaning of the *Hapiru*/Hebrews, of Friedman's Levites, the dispossessed of the earth called by God to build a society where the poor should never be likewise abandoned. The writer puts Ruth squarely in that frame, evoking the formative experience and perspective of the Exodus Hebrews. The fact that this perspective is also enshrined in the Deuteronomic legislation demonstrates the way the Book of Ruth signals toward the spiritual-cultural revival represented in that writing. But it does so at an entirely different, more primitive level than Deuteronomy's harsh meta-history of Israel. That is why the story is set before the time of the kings, before the sedimentation of power brought national identity, and then, ultimately, military and political loss, and, with that, the need to explain everything as God's retribution.

Instead, the Book of Ruth talks only of personal life-relationships and the way God's kindness is worked out directly in this framework.

The Book of Ruth is the story of Ruth, and Ruth is *Hapiru*; but Naomi not quite. Naomi belongs to the community of Israel without centralized power, but nevertheless with cultural institutions designed to preserve justice among its members. A crucial institution in this sense is that of the *go'el*, the next-of-kin who has the duty to redeem the life of an individual should it in some manner be taken away. The writer gracefully leads us to this classic figure and so interjects a third vital element of early biblical coding, now essential to telling the story of a foreign woman, Ruth the Moabite.

The near relative of Naomi is a man named Boaz who is introduced at the beginning of chapter 2, but left hanging there without clear connection to the plot until the chapter develops. Ruth goes to glean after the harvesters, and "as it happened" (2:3) she does so in the portion of fields owned by this man. Not only that, but he shows her special favor: he introduces himself to the Moabite (her origin stated twice at 2:6), and she speaks with him. There are the first glimmers of a romance here, as Boaz shows particular interest in this woman, although at the moment it is simply because he knows everything she has done for her mother-in-law (2:8–13). Later, when Ruth returns to Naomi and tells her the day's events and about the actions of Boaz, her mother-in-law cries out, connecting the key motifs of the narrative: "Blessed be he by the Lord, whose kindness (*hesed*) has not forsaken the living or the dead . . . The man is a relative of ours, one of our nearest kin [whose job is to redeem]" (2:20).

Naomi knows that an absolutely key element has now presented itself. She is referring explicitly to the *go'el* (the noun form from the verb *gaal*), the one who "recovers" or "redeems" a relative's property that has been alienated or the relative themselves when sold into slavery (Lev 25:25, 48–9). In the case of the worst alienation—the murder of a person—the *go'el* "redeems" the life by covering it with the lifeblood of the murderer (Num 35:9–21). Finally, in the case of a man who dies without offspring, his brother takes the widow in marriage to raise up heirs for him (Deut 25:5–6), in order that his name "may not be cut off from his kindred" (Ruth 4:10). It is important to understand this legislation in the way it reflects a "primitive" situation without centralized state power or the guarantees of courts, etc. It demonstrates the imperative of maintaining the "existence" of the covenant people in their concrete economic and social situations. Life and all it involves are a fundamental concern, including in the situation of a murder victim whose life is given back its value by a reciprocal killing. In every case, the possibility of annihilation is overcome—for the sake of the value of life itself. But there is one thing to note. Exchange governs the "redemption" in all except in one case: the sexual genesis of life by the dead man's widow and his brother. Buying back property requires the exchange of money, and the avenging of a murder is a death for a death, but conceiving a child is an act of creation. It is this last function that is operative in the story of Ruth and to see this brings us close to the full, rich range of signs at play. It is a story of covenant kindness bringing new life, effected by the life of a woman who is a Moabite.

The critical role of the woman will become progressively clear, but first we need to underline her situation as foreigner. After Boaz first speaks to her and gives her his support and protection, she falls prostrate before him "with her face to the ground" (2:10). The power differential is emphatic, demonstrating Ruth's helplessness as an outsider. She says, "Why have I found favor in your sight, that you should take notice of me, when I am a foreigner" (2:10). The word used for foreigner here is *nokri*, from a root shared with *nekar* (used at Neh 13:30, as quoted above). But in this form, it can double as "harlot" or "adulterous woman." This is the sense it has in the Book of Proverbs where the "adulterous woman" is paralleled by the "strange," "other," or "evil" woman (Prov 2:16, 5:20, 6:24, 7:5). Proverbs gives a sustained lecture on the dangers of the "other woman," an urgent symbol of the life of folly tempting young men away from the practice of Wisdom. Ezra and Nehemiah had a sense of identity forged in the socio-religious experience of exile in Babylon, while Proverbs belongs to a wider timespan, but it is no less exclusive. Proverbs is another example of Israel seeking to draw a boundary around its existence and life, and the trope of the outsider woman is key in constructing this inside. If Proverbs, or its thinking, provides a further background to the novella of the Moabite, then Ruth can be heard protesting: "Why have I found favor in your sight, that you should take notice of me, when I am the corrupting other?" The whole Book of Ruth swings around this phrase, gradually overturning it completely. The irony could not be more marked: the very figure dreaded for her power to adulterate Israel in every sense, until it is no longer Israel, becomes an unsubstitutable source of Israel's life.

Boaz has the role of *go'el*, but before that can happen someone has to take the initiative, and it is not Boaz. Whether because he is relatively advanced in years, has a diffident personality, or is unwilling at this point to risk his own family, etc., Boaz does nothing to develop the situation. In contrast, the women do everything, and it is straightforwardly a matter of sex—an agency over which the women have some measure of control where in other respects they are completely dependent.

It appears little short of shocking how sexually aware and expressive the Book of Ruth is; chapter 3 fairly fizzes with sex. Here is part of the note in the New Interpreter's Study Bible:

> The Hebrew *shakab*, "lie down," is used eight times in 3:4–14. *Shakab* can simply mean "sleep," but the word is frequently used in biblical texts to imply sexual intercourse (e.g., Gen 19:33–35, 30:15–16, 38:26). Similarly, the word *galah* ("uncover") is frequently found in texts prohibiting incest (Lev 18:6–19); *regalim* ("feet" or "lower body") is a common euphemism for the genitals (Deut 28:57; Isa 7:20; Ezek 16:25); and "threshing floors" were traditionally associated with sex for hire (Hos 9:1). The verb *yada'* ("make known" in 3:3; "observe" in 3:4; "know" in 3:11; and "known" in 3:14) is also used in OT texts as a euphemism for sexual activity. When Ruth asks Boaz "to spread your cloak over your servant," she uses a phrase that has sexual overtones in Deut 27:20 and Ezek 16:8. Thus while the narrator does not spell out for us what happened between midnight and morning, the language used throughout the chapter is both ambiguous and playfully suggestive.[6]

It's more than playful, if playful means trivial. Were the Book of Ruth a movie, it would come with a bolded warning of "Multiple suggestive content and strong sexual images." But why is the content there? It seems clearly to be a sub-code in the writing adding a vital layer of meaning, and specifically in relation to the women, Naomi and Ruth. To illustrate sexuality as a code, I could reference a fantasy novel I authored, *Pascale's Wager*, in which a group of powerful people engineered a life of immortality for themselves.[7] These "immortals" participated in endless sexual adventures with countless serial partners. I wrote it this way to create a sign of acute privilege and transcendence (somewhat in the manner of the Greek gods) among a self-selected elite. It did not matter whether such a thing would actually work in practice. What was important was the fiction of interest and imbroglio provided by the multiple possibilities of sex among a privileged caste of beautiful people. In the Book of Ruth, the sex is much more realistic and grounded but it is still very much a

---

6. *New Interpreter's Study Bible*, 387–88.
7. Bartlett, *Pascale's Wager*.

code. Naomi and Ruth are the opposite of "immortals"; they are desperately poor women seeking the slim possibility of life where death is all around. Sex for them represents not transcendence but sheer possibility at hand, a single chance to fling the dice in a male-dominated world. The text gives us hints and cues of seduction as a way of opening a dramatic sense of this possibility in the narrative. Such cues are full of transgression and risk. In the Book of Ruth, however, the transgression and risk are in service of survival and life, and every time they occur, they signal to the reader a pathway through a world dominated by death, toward a future of life. This is the point of the code.

As such, Naomi and Ruth's use of sex is not to be misread for a conventional male-exploited role. They *can* be read in these ways, but it would be false to the revelatory tenor of the story to do so. Naomi's directions are remarkably plain and bold:

> Now wash and anoint yourself, and put on your best clothes and
> go down to the threshing floor; but do not make yourself known
> to the man until he has finished eating and drinking. When he
> lies down, observe the place where he lies; then, go and uncover
> his feet and lie down; and he will tell you what to do. (3:3–4)

Reading the code, we understand exactly what this means—just imagine how it would look in a movie! But the "seduction manual" gets its authenticity from being taught by a woman who has lost everything and is doing whatever she can to find a positive outcome. Naomi thus also plays a woman's part in the story of redemption; but it is Ruth who carries it through. Ruth retains vital agency throughout the story, deciding to accompany Naomi, gleaning in the fields, and then corresponding vigorously to Naomi's plan that she seduce Boaz. Ruth's sexuality, while carried through in the shadows, is powerful and direct. Essentially, she waits until Boaz is pleasantly drunk and then lies down next to him, overwhelming him with the pleasure of her touch (3:7–8). But even at the moment of climax, the text makes clear that the coding of sex is always in service of the code of life, of redemption. It is an electric pathway which opens to an unbounded horizon.

In verse 9, Boaz asks who she is, and Ruth declares he is her next of kin (go'el). Then Boaz cries out (presumably in a hoarse whisper),

> May you be blessed by the Lord, my daughter; this last instance
> of your loyalty [hesed] is better than the first; you have not gone
> after young men, whether poor or rich. And now, my daughter,

do not be afraid, I will do for you all that you ask, for all the assembly of my people know that you are a worthy woman. But now, though it is true that I am a near kinsman [redeemer, go'el], there is another kinsman [go'el] more closely related than I. Remain this night, and in the morning, if he will act as next of kin [gaal] for you, good; let him do it. If he is not willing to act as next of kin [gaal] for you, then as the Lord lives, I will act as next-of-kin [gaal twice] for you. Lie down until the morning. (3:10–13)

In the moment of his delight, Boaz recognizes its intense theology. He knows that she could have carried out the same seduction with a younger man, even possibly a rich young man. In other words, her *hesed*, her covenant faithfulness, has brought her to him alone. He recognizes, therefore, that her sexual presence is a request that he act as *go'el* or redeemer *through* her *for* the line of Naomi's husband, Elimelech. He is not strictly obliged to do this (he is not a brother to Elimelech—possibly the other kinsman was), but he voluntarily chooses to do so. Thus, Ruth acts as an intermediary for the sake of her mother-in-law, Naomi, and her heirless deceased husband, Elimelech. Ruth the Moabite's sexuality is freely enacted for the sake of the life corresponding fully to this extraordinary intervention.

The threshing floor encounter finishes with Ruth "lay(ing) at his feet until morning" (there is no mention of sleep), then continues: "but (she) got up before one person could recognize another, for he said, 'It must not be known that the woman came to the threshing floor'" (3:14). Ruth's action retains its early morning risk of a "walk of shame," telling us again that the drama of redemption is ultimately hers. Although Boaz is the technical *go'el*, it is really her *hesed* in the face of all risk, of poverty, danger, rejection, shame, that has motivated him to take on that male-specified role. In which case, the true *go'el* of the story is Ruth. And it is as *a Moabite woman* that she has progressively achieved that status through the story.

Chapter 4 gives us the negotiation between Boaz and the other relative, concluding with the closer relative forfeiting his right and Boaz redeeming the property while taking Ruth as his wife. (It seems the other relative did not want to take the land because of the risk of future disputes over his own property. In which case, the romance between Ruth and Boaz is again vindicated.) There is then a delightful bit of "period detail": the handing over of a sandal as a sign of sealing the deal. The author describes it in a storyteller's aside, addressing the audience directly in the present moment. "Now this was the custom in former times in Israel concerning redeeming and exchanging: to confirm a transaction the one took off a sandal and gave it to the other; this was the manner of attesting in Israel. So when the next-of-kin said to Boaz, 'Acquire it for yourself,' he took off his sandal" (4:7–8). The aside seems to be an arch bit of authorial commentary, a broad hint signaling that the story is set in "olden times" but written in the "modern" period. By virtue of which, the entire narrative is at once given a clear literary genre—not an ancient bit of folklore amazingly preserved, but a brilliant feat of archaizing writing producing a deliberate and compelling parable. At this moment, the semiotics explicitly trump the facts, even as they claim a "just so" account of the facts!

The scene is then set for a final triumphant celebration of the two women in the context of all Israel. The last to be mentioned by name is Naomi, after the birth of Boaz and Ruth's son, Obed. The women of Israel say, "Blessed be the Lord, who has not left you today without next-of-kin [go'el]; and may his name be renowned in Israel. He shall be to you a restorer of life and a nourisher of your old age, for your daughter-in-law who loves you, who is more to you than seven sons, has borne him" (4:14–15). Obed is to become effectively Naomi's son, and so her final named go'el. But Ruth is explicitly valued at seven times his worth, and thus again the real go'el of the story. The text goes on to establish Obed's lineage—he becomes the grandfather of David. The parable connects itself to royal and messianic history: David, the ideal king of Israel, turns out to be part Moabite! This becomes itself a generative hint, broadening the meaning of the messianic horizon at a stroke.

Just before the women's prayer of praise in relation to Naomi there is a blessing for Ruth, one which establishes her on a par with the mothers of the twelve tribes and links her explicitly with another "scandalous woman" in Israel's story:

> Then all the people who were at the gate, along with the elders, said, "We are witnesses. May the Lord make the woman who is coming into your house like Rachel and Leah, who together built up the house of Israel. May you produce children in Ephrathah and bestow a name in Bethlehem; and through the children that the Lord will give you by this young woman, may your house be like the house of Perez, whom Tamar bore to Judah." (4:11–12)

Ruth is given a status beside the matriarchs of Israel, but she is also modeled according to the Canaanite, Tamar, the wife of two of Judah's sons who both died without producing heirs. Tamar took the role of a prostitute in order to get her father-in-law, Judah, to carry out the same task of redemption here fulfilled by Boaz (Genesis 38). Not only is Ruth a crucial mother within Israel, she represents the strand of the outsider and strange woman in its semiotic DNA: the woman who in these cases "seduces" the man to provide a service to life, and thus is more of a redeemer than he ever was. The point is driven home: Israel has never had totally pure origins, neither in terms of narrative, nor ethnically, nor morally. The revisionist attempt to construct those pure origins is a defensive sacrificial gesture, not a reflection of reality. The story of Ruth drives a semiotic coach and horses through that construct. Its code invention of *migrant-hesed-poor-foreign-woman-go'el-Israel* deeply transforms our perception and understanding. Ruth is a generative woman who creates possibility for those around her. She is a mother of Israel precisely in her situation of outsider and contaminant, because in this situation she is able both to reproduce Israel's origins and give the purest—the most selfless and generous—version of *hesed*. The signs she composes out of her situation generate a code of something entirely new. And yet it is the code the Bible is always striving for, the deep code of *hesed*, achieving freely given compassion, love, and life, for those who have no claim on these things beyond their being given.

The fact that the Book of Ruth is in the Bible demonstrates that the ideology of Ezra and Nehemiah was never definitive. Ruth's diametrically opposite view shows that what is canonical is a live discussion between two positions (as so often is the case in biblical writings). The point of Christian interpretation is to see which option of generative meaning Jesus chose and set out to represent in his life and ministry. We glean a big hint from Matthew's Gospel. In recounting Jesus' genealogy, the evangelist names five women as part of his ancestry: Ruth and Tamar, along with Rahab, Bathsheba, and, of course, Mary, his mother. It is pretty clear which semiotics this Gospel is headlining as it sets out to tell the story of Ruth's Galilean *go'el* descendant.

6

Daniel

Greeks and the Maccabees

WHAT HAPPENS WHEN YOU have nowhere to turn? When everything that is most precious to you can only be defended by corrupt institutions, bodies which have come to represent something so different from your values that you'd rather forsake them completely?

A situation like this was almost bound to come to Israel, or elements within it, as time wound on and the imperial nations and their influence began to multiply and strengthen around the tiny sliver of a nation. The spectacular rise of the Macedonian empire at the end of the fourth century BCE changed the face of the ancient world, not only bringing into being new geopolitical forces and dynasties, but introducing new constructs of human life, its relationships and meaning. Alexander the Great, son of Philip II of Macedon and pupil of Aristotle, carried through a devastating military campaign in the space of ten years, destroying Persia and going on to conquer the known world from the Adriatic to the Indus valley. Alexander set the bar for military prowess ever after. Not only that, he brought in his wake the Greek worldview, its philosophy, architecture, urban planning, and lifestyle. Even today the mythic value of both Alexander and Hellenistic culture remains alive and vigorous. We live in the backwash of Mediterranean dynasties, armies, Plato, temples, gymnasia, and the baths. How much of a raw tsunami would it have appeared there and then when it was crashing on every shore? It must have seemed the gods woke up one morning and decided to move *en masse* to

Olympus. An event of such mythic proportions would seem inevitably to require a response with its own answering mythos. On cue, enter the Book of Daniel.

But before we come to examine the history-defying semiotics of Daniel, we need to attend in more detail to the desperate fix that faithful Jews were in. As the imperial worlds grew, collided, and spilled their shrapnel all over the ancient Near East, the traditional lifeworld of Israel came under critical pressure. The two-millennia-old political geography of Egypt and Mesopotamia had held Israel like a handful of fruit between two giant millstones. But the millstones were just far enough away never to be able to completely crush the fruit, and sometimes, when they momentarily stopped grinding, they allowed Israel to flourish and grow into a rich and powerful realm in its own right (viz., the kingdom of Solomon). Even the sixth-century new-kid-on-the-block, Persia, from the Iranian Plateau, did not threaten to overwhelm Israel's self-concept. As we have seen, Cyrus the Great allowed the Judeans to return to Jerusalem to rebuild their temple, witnessing still to a world of shared religious values. But the rise of the Hellenistic empire brought something qualitatively new. The new power that came from the outland west—effectively from the sea itself—brought with it a material and aesthetic culture that had been nourished on much less recognizable elements. At the same time, they held great allure, because they seemed to establish human life on a much more exciting basis than the grim laws of Yahweh. To see this, we need to turn to a deuterocanonical/apocryphal writing rejected in the Reformation but included in Roman Catholic Bibles and in many study Bibles. The Books of Maccabees, from the second century BCE, are an invaluable resource. They provide essential background to the Book of Daniel because Daniel is evidently written in the same period and context, as will be confirmed below. But, even more to the point, without the militancy of the Maccabees, we would not be able to grasp the profoundly different, generative response of Daniel. We need to follow the accounts in First and Second Maccabees in order to prepare the ground for an accurate uptake of Daniel.

To begin with, the books of the Maccabees provide their own independent story, one related to a particular family that became a dynasty known as the Hasmoneans. The family did not have Davidic credentials but nevertheless took on royal power and profoundly shaped Jewish history all the way through until the time of Jesus. Book 1 of Maccabees is written as an apologia for the Maccabean rulers, absent prophetic or

Davidic warrant for their rule.[1] Book 2 is not the same propaganda for the new rulers, but a broader argument for the validity of Jewish religion, and, once again, from a Deuteronomistic perspective.[2] Nevertheless, the military exploits of the Maccabean leader, Judas, feature centrally and provide a core part of the book's traditionalist theology and politics.

So, what do you do when you are occupied by a foreign power, one with a patina of cultural superiority that flaunts itself right at the heart of your nation? You light the fires of nationalism with the lightning strike of religion! This is certainly what happened with the Maccabees. However, in Judea things are never quite that simple, and in more ways than one. First, we remember the culturally accommodationist leaders in Jerusalem that Nehemiah found it necessary to confront. It seems they were still very much around in the second century; in fact, at this point some of them had become out-and-out cultural renegades, abetting the assault of the foreign regime and its ways.

One of the most notable offenders was a certain Jason, the brother of the high priest Onias III, and a rival for his job. At this point in time, Jerusalem was under the control of a foreign dynasty called Seleucids, named from one of the generals of Alexander who together took control of the conqueror's far-flung territories after his death. The Seleucids were one of the most important of the successor regimes. Based in Antioch in Syria, they ruled an area broadly from Anatolia to Persia; and at the end of the third century, Jerusalem and Judea fell within their orbit. The Seleucid empire was a major Hellenizing force and not only did Jerusalem come under its political control, but the city also fell prey to its cultural seduction. In 175 BCE, someone with the grand name of Antiochus Epiphanes IV took the Seleucid throne. Jason bribed the new ruler to appoint him high priest in place of his brother, and when the king granted his wish, Jason promptly set about making reforms. The description in the Second Book of Maccabees gives as good a set of notes for what is meant by "Hellenization" as we are likely to find (2 Macc 4:7–22). First, Jason sought permission to establish a gymnasium and a cohort of youths to attend it, and "to enroll the people of Jerusalem as citizens of Antioch" (2 Macc 4:9). The latter seems to mean that families in Jerusalem would gain Antiochene status and identity, much as prominent urban centers in

---

1. Silva, *Introducing the Apocrypha*, 257–60.

2. The Second Book of Maccabees is a defense of traditional Jewish religion with a connected "Deuteronomic" interpretation of history (Silva, *Introducing the Apocrypha*, 271–75).

the Roman empire were granted privileges of Roman citizenship. Things continued from there:

> When the king assented and Jason came to office, he at once shifted his compatriots over to the Greek way of life. He set aside the existing royal concessions to the Jews . . . and he destroyed the lawful ways of living and he introduced new customs contrary to the law. He took delight in establishing a gymnasium right under the citadel, and he induced the noblest of the young men to wear the Greek hat. There was such an extreme of Hellenization and increase in the adoption of foreign ways because of the surprising wickedness of Jason who was ungodly and no true high priest, that the priests were no longer intent upon their service at the altar. Despising the sanctuary and neglecting the sacrifices, they hurried to take part in the unlawful proceedings in the wrestling arena after the signal for the discus-throwing, disdaining the honors prized by their ancestors and putting the highest value upon Greek forms of prestige. (2 Macc 4:10–15)

The story continues with the fluctuating political fortunes of the Hellenizers. Jason in turn lost the office of high priest to someone named Menelaus, of the tribe of Benjamin (2 Macc 3:4, 4:23–24). The adopted Greek names of the protagonists is another indication of the dramatic cultural shift going on, as is the usurping of the office of priest by an individual not of the tribe of Levi and a line going back to Zadok (cf. Ezra 3:2 with 1 Chr 6:15). The upshot in the account is that Antiochus Epiphanes comes to restore order in Jerusalem, pillaging and violating the temple in the process, and installing a Greek military governor. Meanwhile, these events are given an interpretive theological framework by the writer: he sees them in Deuteronomic mode as divine punishment for the sinful acts of Hellenization (2 Macc 5:17). Finally, the whole thing sets the scene for the righteous—and brilliantly successful—revolt of Judas Maccabeus (5:27, and chapters 8–15).[3]

A parallel but different account is given in the First Book of Maccabees. This other rendering delivers a partisan and consciously epic narrative of the family of "hammerers" and leads us, in fairly short order, to the point of all this material in the present inquiry. We are able to see that the propaganda for the military revolt of the Maccabees, and the subsequent establishment of their royal and priestly dynasty, contains within it hints

---

3. "Maccabeus" is a nickname for Judas meaning "hammerer," hence "the Maccabees" applied to him and the rest of his warrior brothers.

of an entirely different response, one with crucial links to the Book of Daniel. The biblical and revelatory value of the books of the Maccabees is how they prepare the canvas for Daniel, and by a pointed contrast show us the profound meaning of nonviolence emerging in that seminal work of prophecy.

The First Book of Maccabees commences with the figure of Mattathias, the father of Judas and four other sons. But before Mattathias is introduced, it gives a recap of the exploits of Alexander, placing us squarely in the presence of this world-historical evil. "He advanced to the ends of the earth, and plundered many nations" (1 Macc 1:3). "Then his officers began to rule, each in his own place. They all put on crowns after his death, and so did their descendants after them for many years; and they caused many evils on the earth" (1 Macc 1:8–9). Directly after, we are introduced to the local instance of the catastrophe, the notorious Antiochus: "And from them came forth a sinful root, Antiochus Epiphanes . . ." (1:10).

The traumatic impact Alexander and his successors had on Judea is evident and clearly connects the two writings (Maccabees and Daniel); but if we dig deeper, we will find clues to even more substantive links.

First Maccabees has its own account of Antiochus' actions. It avoids the chaotic rivalries between claimants for the high-priesthood in Jerusalem, presenting Antiochus as much more the direct source of Judea's harsh suffering. However, we are given a quick summary of the situation among the Jews that fully endorses the Second Maccabees picture. In a way, this brief description gives an even more acute sense of the cultural prestige of Hellenism and its powerful assault on Judaism:

> In those days certain renegades came out from Israel and misled many, saying, "Let us go and make a covenant with the Gentiles around us, for since we separated from them many disasters have come upon us." This proposal pleased them, and some of the people eagerly went to the king, who authorized them to observe the ordinances of the Gentiles. So they built a gymnasium in Jerusalem, according to Gentile custom, and removed the marks of circumcision, and abandoned the holy covenant. They joined with the Gentiles and sold themselves to do evil. (1 Macc 1:11–15)

The account then proceeds swiftly to Antiochus' attack on the temple and his installation of a foreign garrison in Jerusalem (168–67 BCE), followed by a concerted attempt to stamp out the Jewish religion through all Judea. It demonstrates a full-scale and bitter religious persecution and is perhaps the first historical example of the kind. The head-on clash of ideological Hellenism and conservative Judaism represents a "culture war" of signature nature; it has a distinctly modern feel to it:

> Then the king wrote to his whole kingdom that all should be one people, and that all should give up their particular customs. All the Gentiles accepted the command of the king. Many even from Israel gladly adopted his religion; they sacrificed to idols and profaned the sabbath. And the king sent letters by messengers to Jerusalem and the towns of Judah; he directed them to follow customs strange to the land, to forbid burnt offerings and sacrifices and drink offerings in the sanctuary, to profane sabbaths and festivals, to defile the sanctuary and the priests, to build altars and sacred precincts and shrines for idols, to sacrifice swine and other unclean animals, and to leave their sons uncircumcised. They were to make themselves abominable by everything unclean and profane, so that they would forget the law and change all the ordinances. He added, "And whosoever does not obey the command of the king shall die." (1 Macc 1:41–50)

Alongside the forces of accommodation and assimilation—the many in Israel who "gladly adopted" the king's religion—there was inevitably the opposite reaction among those who identified with Israel's ancestral tradition (we surely think here of cultural heirs of the policies of Ezra and Nehemiah). Mattathias was a priest of Israel, of a line of priests, entitled to serve and offer sacrifice in the temple. He seems to have left Jerusalem when the profanation instigated by Antiochus, and the likes of Jason, became too much to bear, settling in a small town by the name of Modein (1 Macc 2:1). He laments, "Alas! Why was I born to see this, the ruin of my people, the ruin of the holy city, and to live there when it was given over to the enemy, the sanctuary given over to aliens?" (1 Macc 2:7).

The scene is set for a showdown. After a further description of brutal violence against Jews, including the killing of babies which had been circumcised, there is no room left for maneuver.

Officers of the king arrive in Modein, assembling the populace, including Mattathias and his sons. They demand they offer sacrifice to the Greek gods. Mattathias refuses, proclaiming his and his sons' faithfulness to Israel's covenant. When an apostate Jew comes to the altar to offer incense, Mattathias "burned with zeal and his heart was stirred. He gave vent to his righteous anger; he ran and killed him on the altar" (1 Macc 2:24). Mattathias is a priest. His act of open killing of a man on the altar is a deliberate unleashing of all the violence that is meant to be held in check by the ordered cult of the altar itself. It is a code for unleashing war, and the priest had no doubt about what he was doing. He at once issues the summons: "Let everyone who is zealous for the law and supports the covenant come out with me" (1 Macc 2:27). They head for the hills, and the guerilla resistance is begun.

The Nonviolent Resistance

The story goes on to describe a hugely successful military campaign by Mattathias' sons, especially Judas, issuing quickly in the purification and rededication of the temple. But before the story develops, before the very first battles, there is an episode inserted which signals something else happening in Israel—something which shows us that Mattathias' generative violence is not the only possibility emerging from Israel's covenant of holiness:

> At that time many who were seeking righteousness and justice went down to the wilderness to live there, they, their sons, their wives, and their livestock, because troubles pressed heavily upon them. (1 Macc 2:29–30)

It seems that before Mattathias killed his man and took to the hills, a significant body of Jews had chosen internal exile, finding a home in the wilderness rather than continue to associate with the horrible cultural and religious offense going on in Jerusalem. Mattathias and his followers clearly share in the same deep alienation,[4] but this other group had taken a step beyond violence. It seems that their sense of holiness has precluded it, at least in one circumstance. We learn that the king's troops pursued the group, then on the sabbath challenged them to surrender or do battle. The result is as striking as it is full of desperate pathos.

> [T]hey said, "We will not come out, nor will we do what the king commands and so profane the sabbath day." Then the enemy quickly attacked them. But they did not answer them or hurl a stone at them or block up their hiding places, for they said, "Let us all die in our innocence; heaven and earth testify for us that you are killing us unjustly." So they attacked them on the

---

4. See 2 Macc 5:27, where the Maccabees' life in the wilderness is also described.

> sabbath, and they died, with their wives and children and live-
> stock, to the number of a thousand persons. (1 Macc 2:34–38)

Sabbath observance, which in Nehemiah we saw as a marker of identity, had so entered their souls that they would die without retaliation in order to preserve it. Mattathias and his followers immediately draw from this the lesson that they must fight, including on the sabbath, lest the Gentiles "quickly destroy us from the earth" (1 Macc 2:40). This is the evergreen existential challenge to nonviolence and the Maccabees follow the standard option, but the very inclusion of the question demonstrates an alternative space of possibility had been opened up. It means that somehow a practice of radical sabbath nonviolence had become a critical issue in circles to which the Maccabees owed some recognition, and its adherents had enough prestige for its practice and principle to be mentioned, if only to be set aside.

The internal and symbolic content of sabbath is an earth of peace and blessing, where a fullness of life overtakes and displaces the need to work. To be prepared to maintain this even to the point of death—including that of your children—has to signify an inner vision that goes beyond all mimetic reciprocities. In sum, there is a contemplative content to the martyrs' actions. Their language suggests this. The Greek for "innocence" is from *haplous*,[5] meaning "single," "without folds," indicating a single-minded dedication to the spiritual meaning of sabbath without defensive or aggressive reference to the enemy. The fact that they call to witness heaven and earth suggests also they see the universe ultimately on their side. It's also noteworthy that they do not hail down vengeance, as in the much more frequently commented-on martyr narrative of Second Maccabees—the story of the seven sons and their mother tortured and put to death for refusal to eat swine's flesh. While acting with great courage and nobility, the brothers and mother curse and promise vengeance on their afflicters (2 Macc 7:9, 17, 19, 31–36). It's possible in fact that the seven brothers account in Second Maccabees is written as an intentional, militant counter-story to the nonviolent practice of the First Maccabees wilderness martyrs. (This possibility becomes more focused when the mother and brother's astonishing Daniel-style belief in resurrection is factored in, as we will have cause to remark below.) Meanwhile, Mattathias and his followers have the normal "complicated" view of reality,

---

5. Jesus in fact uses the same expression as 1 Macc 2:37 when he says, "Let your eye be single" (Matt 6:22; cf. Luke 11:34).

with their glance over the shoulder to normal human mimesis and the need to take up arms.

They use the group that is wiped out as a lesson, not one of contempt, but out of respect for the dedication shown, and yet determination not to suffer the same fate. Even so, the theme of radical dedication to the meaning of the law is shifted in a trice to zealous violence on its behalf, from nonviolent death to Maccabeean rebellion and slaughter. But what happened then to the nonviolent ethos represented by this group? Did everyone die? Who were the witnesses? Were there no supporters who honored them and cherished their testimony? It is to the Book of Daniel that we need to turn to answer these questions. Indeed, the Book of Daniel is very likely the authentic spiritual voice of this group, at least spiritually connected to it, if not issuing directly from survivors. Let us see how this could be the case.

Daniel's Authentic Apocalypse

The Book of Daniel is structured in an amazing way, one which may alert us to its deeply semiotic character. It has two distinct halves. The first, chapters 1–6, comprises six stories about a sage named Daniel told against the background of Babylonian, Median, and Persian royal courts (with the hint of a fourth Greek regime). Then, there are chapters 7–12, consisting of four apocalyptic visions, still centered on the figure of Daniel and moving again through the four regimes, but with a stress on the last. It is definitely a unity, but at the same time it goes from fairly standard dream interpretations and popular stories of the miraculous to astonishing visions which disclose the final outworking of history. It is like a series of Russian dolls, each nesting in the other, while the design of the last four differ in color and intensity from that of the first six.

In chapter 1, Daniel is introduced along with three companions who are to be educated as royal servants and courtiers. "To these four young men God gave knowledge and skill in every aspect of literature and wisdom. Daniel also had insight into all visions and dreams" (Dan 1:17).

We know immediately that in the figure of Daniel we are dealing with a hero of literature (Hebrew *seper*, "books," "writings") and a source of wisdom: he is someone with supernatural insight together with the ability to write his visions down. The stories then unfold with an alternating pattern of risk to the lives of Daniel and his companions, and then dreams and experiences of loss by succeeding monarchs. Thus: (1) Daniel submits to a restricted diet, but he and his companions are unharmed; (2) there is an interpretation by Daniel of Nebuchadnezzar's dream of a four-part statue as four succeeding kingdoms; (3) Daniel and his companions refuse to worship a golden statue and are thrown into a furnace, but unharmed; (4) there is an interpretation by Daniel of Nebuchadnezzar's dream in which the king is reduced to sub-human condition but ultimately restored. Following on, the order (risk to companions and danger to kings) is reversed in order to keep the historical sequence of kingdoms; thus (5) the interpretation by Daniel of the writing finger at Belshazzar's feast—the Babylonian empire is to be handed over to the Medes and the Persians; and (6) Daniel refuses to pray to Darius the king and is thrown into the lions' den, but is unharmed.

Throughout, Daniel and the various kings inhabit the same visionary and supernatural world. It is a world of immense earthly power and yet God's sovereignty over that power, both in terms of protection of his faithful ones and the eventual fate of kings. There is a repeated formula, "[T]he Most High has sovereignty over the kingdom of mortals and gives it to whom he will" (Dan 4:25, 5:21). The alternating motifs—repeated vignettes of risk to the Jews and loss for the kings—compose an explicit code for the reader's understanding. We are not dealing with a random court narrative for our amusement. This is an intentional binary alternation intended to convey as deeply as possible God's disruption of violent history. Meager food, fire, and wild beasts are the ever-present violence of the kingdoms surrounding the faithful Jews, who at the same time continue to serve while the power of kings hinges ultimately on God's say-so. We feel the heat of the furnace and the fire of the lions' breath, but we know these phenomena are themselves hemmed in by the might of God and his ultimate rule on earth.

Some of this material may be rooted in traditional stories going back to the end of the sixth century, the Babylonian period, but the way it is connected to the rest of the book belongs certainly to the second century, to the period of the Maccabees. We know this because chapter 7 suddenly shifts to that point in time and its crisis, offering an up-to-the-moment emphasis on the fourth kingdom. We are still in the same dreamscape world, but the figure of Daniel changes from the one interpreting the dreams and visions of kings, to the one himself having dreams and visions of kings and their kingdoms. This tells us that we are at the fulcrum point of the writing, the moment when a traditional lore of the Wisdom-figure Daniel merges into the revelatory insight of a first-person writer. You would think that this shift might run in parallel to another curious feature of the book, the otherwise unexplained mixture of languages, Hebrew and Aramaic. Daniel 2:4b—7:28 is written in Aramaic, inserted between the rest in Hebrew. Aramaic was the *lingua franca* of the Babylonian and Persian empires, and its written form was adopted by their scribes for trade, governmental, and literary writing. However, the more urgent second-century setting of chapter 7 does not change idiom, but has the same language as the older court stories, emphasizing, thereby, the single prophetic experience of the Wisdom hero. It is then all embedded within a Hebrew text, in the first chapter on one side and then stretching through the visionary material to the end. The different languages straddle both sections, encapsulating, in this way perhaps, the fraught lifeworld of the alien empires within the overall revelatory language of the Bible,

But what of that urgent moment of the second century? Chapter 7 bursts on the page with enormous energy, announcing Daniel's "dreams and visions in his head" and seeing him writing them down in the first person (Dan 7:1–2). The prestige of the storied Daniel is poured into a terrifying "I, Daniel" account of empire and cruelty, while making everything appear against the backlight of ongoing divine sovereignty. The four-kingdom scheme from the composite statue in chapter 2 is repeated, but in much more fearful terms. There are few other literary images as nightmarish as this. The four winds of heaven stir up the great sea and four great beasts come up out of the sea, each different, possessing various features of the most savage animals, but the last the worst of all (Dan 7:2–7). While the first three are associated with actual animals, the last is closest to a dragon or dinosaur. It is a picture of primeval chaos and violence, an anti-creation creature, the inverse of Genesis 1. Whoever wrote this was possessed of a horrifying vision of violence on the earth, and he or she boldly overturned the vision of Genesis in order to bring both the reader and biblical revelation to crisis. Taking our cues from the succession of kingdoms through the book, we see that the four beasts are respectively the Babylonian, Mede, Persian, and Greek empires. The Greek empire is not named as such until Dan 10:20, but it is evident both from its terrible violence, devouring everything and breaking it to pieces, and from the imagery which immediately follows and details the successive regimes following on from Alexander's conquests. This is clearly not classical prophecy with its broad, pregnant allusions: it is a detailed, after-the-fact coding, allowing us to see the present historical situation from an otherworldly, transcendent perspective. The standard name for this style of revelatory writing is "apocalyptic."

We are told the fourth beast was

> terrifying and dreadful and exceedingly strong. It had great iron teeth and was devouring, breaking in pieces, and stamping what was left with its feet. It was different from all the beasts that preceded it, and it had ten horns. I was considering the horns, when another horn appeared, a little one coming up among them; to make room for it, three of the earlier horns were plucked up by the roots. There were eyes like human eyes in this horn, and a mouth speaking arrogantly. (Dan 7:7–8)

The three earlier horns which are plucked up refer to inter-dynastic struggles resulting in a single "little horn" coming out on top. This is confirmed later in chapter eleven (v.21) where the same basic story is told again beginning from Alexander "the warrior king" (Dan 11:3). Meanwhile in chapter seven the identity of the victorious horn becomes unmistakable in a further explanation.

> As for the ten horns, out of this kingdom ten kings shall arise, and another shall arise after them. This one shall be different from the former ones, and shall put down three kings. He shall speak words against the Most High, shall wear out the holy ones of the Most High, and shall attempt to change the sacred seasons and the law, and they shall be given into his power for a time, two times and half a time. (Dan 7:24–25)

We are evidently in the real-time context of persecution by Antiochus Epiphanes IV, exactly the same historical setting as the Books of the Maccabees. The timescale of his assault on the holy ones—three and a half years—matches the historical period from Antiochus' attack on Jerusalem and its temple until its recapture and rededication by Judas Maccabeus (168/7–164 BCE). It seems in fact the Book of Daniel was written in precisely this period. Antiochus died in 164 in Persia, but the Book of Daniel seems ignorant of the exact circumstances of his death (Dan 11:45).

But what else does Daniel see? What is the divine response to these monstrous happenings? Does the Lord raise up a David to defeat the invader? Or does the prophet see Judas Maccabeus as God's anointed agent? The answer to these questions is startling. If the Book of Daniel is written in the same period as the Maccabeean revolt, there is absolutely no reference to it. Instead, a very different response is proposed. Rather than endorsing a military solution—one certainly already underway in Judea—the writer produces a nonviolent answer, amounting to a fully transformative code in the place of reciprocating war. Out of the fiery furnace, out of the lions' den, the writer conjures a miracle of code invention. This is so different, so new, so daring, that I can only conceive it came from profound, religious trauma, something like the slaughter of those who refused to fight on the sabbath. The passage from Dan 7:25 quoted above makes no mention of the profanation of the temple—a matter that is of great concern to the writer elsewhere (cf. 9:27, 11:31). Rather, it centers here on the persecution of the "holy ones," a distinctive group of persons who are entirely the focus. We remember from Ezra the term "holy seed" coined well before the Greek crisis. The Daniel expression in Aramaic corresponds to Hebrew *qodesh* in the verse from Ezra. Sometimes commentary makes the "holy ones" into "angels" (cf. the *qadoshim* of Ps 89:7; see Dan 4:17). But as Ezra shows, the word is also used of priests and the whole people of God (cf. Deut 7:6). Anyway, here, in this setting, how could angels be given into Antiochus' power? Much more naturally the reference here is to current events that have set the people apart as visibly and experientially holy.

As André Lacocque declares, the Israel of Daniel 7 is "the eschatological community already existing in the heavens." More precisely, the Book of Daniel witnesses "the merging of the cosmic and the historical" taking place in the people's lives, and it is this which brings the association with angels.[6] It is in fact because the people (or a representative group of them) has breached the separation between earth and heaven that angels/*qadoshim* so readily become part of the narrative. What I would add, and underline, is that it cannot simply be a rhetorical flight which brings about this language. It is a decisive perception arising from the nonviolent surrender of the "single-intentioned" men and women, an act of human meaning that most powerfully breached the wall between earth and heaven. Through their nonviolent death, they have opened a

6. See Lacocque, *Book of Daniel*, 156, 158–59.

dramatically new sense of what is "holy," and by this firsthand revelation they become equivalent in meaning and identity to God's heavenly
companions.[7]

But before these hints as to Daniel's source community are developed, there is the heart of the code. The holy ones have their status as part
of another figure first mentioned in chapter 7, verses 9–14. The passage
comes just after the scene of the beasts rising from the sea and is among
the most famous in the Old Testament. To begin with, a scene of divine
judgment is set up:

> As I watched thrones were set in place, and an Ancient One took
> his throne, his clothing was white as snow, and the hair of his
> head like pure wool; his throne was fiery flames and its wheels
> were burning fire. A stream of fire issued and flowed from out
> his presence . . . (Dan 7:9–10a)

The name for the deity is literally "an Ancient of Days" or "Enduring
One," a being of immense antiquity. It has been frequently noted that
this description harks back to descriptions of the grey-headed supreme
God *El* found in Ugarit literature (mythological texts from the second
millennium BCE).[8] The writer of Daniel has dug down in Israel's cultural
subsoil for a scene-setting which will allow the expression of something
dramatically new. The court sits in judgment and then the beast is simply
put to death, its body given over to be burned without any mention of
direct agency. The scene is a divine passive—something happening by divine power without any instrumental description given. It is this together
with what happens next that is crucial:

> As I watched in the night visions
> I saw one like a human being [a son of man]
> coming with the clouds of heaven
> and he came to the Ancient One

7. Others have argued for the identification of "holy ones" as a group within Israel.
A favorite candidate is the *hasidim* of First Maccabees, but these ancient *hasidim* are
identified as willing to fight: "a company of Hasideans, mighty warriors of Israel" who
joined themselves to the Maccabees (1 Macc 2:42); cf. Towner, *Daniel*, 105–6. Continue below for a much more persuasive group.

8. See Lacocque, *Book of Daniel*, 157; and Collins, *Apocalyptic Vision of the Book
of Daniel*, 99–101: "The clustering of images which we find in Dan 7:9–14 can only be
understood directly against a background of Canaanite myth . . . In all, the imagery of
Dan 7:9–14 is unmistakable. It derives from a Canaanite enthronement scene in which
Baal, rider of the clouds, approaches El, the whitehaired father of years who confers
kingship on him."

and was presented before him.
To him was given dominion
and glory and kingship,
that all peoples, nations, and languages
should serve him.
His dominion is an everlasting dominion
that shall not pass away,
and his kingship is one
that shall never be destroyed. (Dan 7:13–14)

Here is an enthronement scene, one in which a particular figure—"like a son of man"—is given universal and everlasting dominion, a breath-taking scope of power. But who is this figure? Frank Moore Cross highlights the connection to the Ugarit literature but stresses the reinterpretation to which it has been submitted:

> The text of Daniel 7 is of particular interest. The apocalypticist utilized for his eschatological theme: El sitting in judgment in his court. The identity of the Ancient One is transparent. The manlike Being ("like a son of man") who comes to receive kingship is evidently young Ba'l reinterpreted and democratized by the apocalypticist as the Jewish nation.[9]

The god, Baal, is known in the Ugarit "Baal cycle" as a hero god among whose battles is a brutal conflict with Yam, god of the sea.[10] The technical name given to mythic representations of this type is *Chaoskampf* (battle with primordial chaos), and the beasts arising from the sea earlier in chapter 7 is often noted as a scene of such chaos. Clearly, however, Daniel has made the chaos historical, identifying it not mythically but as the successive forces of historical empire. And yet there is absolutely no mention of counter force or violence on the part of the "human being." The victory over the forces of violence is, again, by divine passive. But there *is* an instrumentality hinted at: the figure of humanity is presented *by contrast* with the hyper-armed and terrible beasts, especially the last. "One like a son of man" is, therefore, one *without* claws, horns, huge teeth: it is a figure characterized, in comparison, by defenselessness. The divine passive attached, therefore, to this figure is attached to its nonviolence. This, assuredly, is the root of the "democratization" that Cross speaks of. Violence always seeks its brutal mythos, while nonviolence is

9. Cross, *Canaanite Myth and Hebrew Epic*, 17.
10. Cross, *Canaanite Myth and Hebrew Epic*, 113–16.

simply human—people-like! The only adjustment necessary here, therefore, would be that the "democratic" association is not with the Jewish
nation as such (then currently led by the warlike Maccabees), but with
the *holy ones*, something like the wilderness sabbath martyrs and their
allies. Meanwhile, the historical-critical search for mythopoetic origins
for Daniel 7 is useful only as far as it goes. What it lacks is an answer
to the question of why should the writer cast so deep into pre-Israelite
mythology and then, within the picture he found, insert the distinctly
nonviolent, deconstructive figure of "one like a son of man." Why, moreover, would the writer risk in this image an impression of duality in God?
There has to be a profound, and, as I say, traumatic spiritual event behind
it, something that called out for a powerful code invention in order to
be expressed. This is a scriptural phenomenon which almost goes back
behind Genesis 1 in order to present its own meaning. What conceivable
spiritual event could provide the motivation for this if not catastrophic
violence confronted by humanly helpless, but experientially transcendent
nonviolence? In a moment of unprecedented spiritual suffering there is
the breakthrough of history's miraculously transforming "other."

The writer of Daniel has turned the Baal cycle upside down. Against
the ancient Canaanite background, the reversal of code could not be
clearer. The hero does not fight. Indeed, it is the very nonviolence of his
presence before God which brings the end of empire. The writer has created a new semiosis which has dug back into the most "ancient" figure
of God (El) and at the same time introduced an entirely new transcendent figure, one simultaneously human and divine.[11] What made this
astonishing theological synapse possible has to be an event of revelatory

11. This is the most profound reason why Margaret Barker's reading of First
Temple Israel and its "two gods" has to be historically inadequate. The belief that there
were always two deities in Israel leaves no room for Daniel's revelatory breakthrough,
reducing it simply to "more of the same." It is only by a progressive and scrupulous
identification of El and Yahweh during that early period that Israel's theological separation from original violence could be built up and understood. For normal humanity
there cannot be a duality without rivalry and/or scapegoting—Baal and El are united
essentially against the background of the victory over Yam. Biblical duality without
rivalry can only happen when it arises progressively from the most profound experiences of nonviolence. There has to be the event of the nonviolent martyrs—and the
experience of this as identity with the divine—in order for there to be a "son of man"
presented to the Ancient of Days. There has to be the cross of Christ for there to be
the Son's being of one substance with the Father. Barker's "two gods" robs the bank of
Daniel and Christianity's martyrological history in order to trade on a putative "eternal" narrative.

nonviolence; and the one thousand slaughtered Judeans in First Mac-cabees are the best candidates we know able to offer this. The "apocalyp-ticist" has broken the wall between the divine and the human via their witness; that is, because their witness demolished it first. From now on, because of this broken wall, it is possible to speak of Israel's singular God and the human person in the same breath: they are "on the clouds of heaven," in the same semio-ontological frame, since the meaning they share is infinitely one of nonviolence. The "one like a son of man" is a corporate figure representative of (generated by) the nonviolent martyrs. It is logical that the universal authority granted to this figure is also the destiny of all those who associate with the "holy ones": "The kingship and dominion and the greatness of the kingdoms under the whole heaven shall be given to the people of the holy ones of the Most High; their king-dom shall be an everlasting kingdom, and all dominions shall serve and obey them" (Dan 7:27).

It is also true that because that space has now also been opened semiotically, it means any individual can choose to occupy it person-ally. Indeed, someone could decide to repeat it in a paradigmatic way, as seems to be the case with Jesus. "One like a son of man" becomes "*the* son of man" (*the* human one) because the meaning of the code has become so clear and urgent that someone finally opts to fulfill it in a singular, personal way. A certain juncture in history will make this radical code invention the *one* thing necessary to repeat and realize.

But we are jumping ahead here. Returning to our main argument, we can say that any other interpretation of these passages risks a violent re-mythologization. We either make the "holy ones" divine beings who carry on fighting because that is their very nature/being, or focusing on "one like a son of man" as a stand-in purely for the nation of Israel, we make it part of a simple nation-history with all its attendant risks. It is true that the Book of Daniel appears to contribute to these possibilities. It seems in chapter 10, verses 10–21, there is a conflict engaged at the cosmic level between angelic forces (Michael and the "princes" of Persia and Greece). But we have to remind ourselves this picture is rooted in the phenomenology of nonviolence. The apocalyptic genre looks toward the triumph of the holy ones and it is not unwilling to spell out the process of that triumph in terms of a cosmic conflict. Part of the function of the genre is to provide the consolation that such "battles" and their ultimate outcome supply for persecuted groups seeking to survive emotionally. But we have to continue to remind ourselves that the very displacement to the "cosmic" level means, essentially, we do not know how this battle works. Of course, for human imagination it will default quickly to violent means and outcomes, but Daniel provides no substance for such thinking. Meanwhile, the displacement itself cannot happen without the transformative trauma of the martyrs, i.e., through the perceptual opening of nonviolence. The cosmic battle is in fact happening at the level of human semiosis, of a constitutive change in the very structures of human perception and meaning.

Community of Code Breakers

We do not have to rely simply on the explanatory power of the hypothesis so far to arrive at these conclusions. The text of Daniel gives us further clues as to the identity of the community that produced the text, and thus a further pointer to the nature of the "holy ones." We find the clues in the final chapters, where we are also led to the climax and most dramatic point of the whole book. The four-empire scheme followed by the events surrounding Antiochus Epiphanes IV is repeated twice more, first in another vision of violent animals (8:1–26), and then in an extended vision-narrative of the Seleucid kingdom (10:1—11:45). In the middle there is the third vision, amounting to the use of previous prophecy as a code. "[T]he man Gabriel" comes "in swift flight" and tells Daniel that Jeremiah's very specific announcement that the Babylonian exile would last for seventy years (Jer 25:11–12) is in fact a numerical code for seventy *weeks* of years, i.e., four hundred and ninety in total (9:2, 21–7).

The sudden elasticity of time allows the book to concertina together the experience of the exile and the crisis of the second century, awakening the present moment in a new light and looking toward a definite "end time" to all these sufferings. In one stroke, the writer gives birth to a compression of time toward a definitive end, a temporal phenomenon which will resonate through the New Testament all the way to our own contemporary Christian reading of history. This is another impact of Daniel's extraordinary recoding—pressing history up against a profound transformation to come. Lamentably, this has been understood in a near-exclusively violent key. In fact, however, any violence is the resistance of the old world-order doubling down and trying to reassert itself, not the transcendent nonviolence that is urgent to be revealed.

At all events in chapter 11, we are given vital information about the community which produced the Book of Daniel. It comes right after we are told (once more) of Antiochus Epiphanes' attack on the temple and the collaboration by those who "forsake/violate the covenant" (11:30–32). The description fits neatly with the sequence in First Maccabees where the nonviolent martyrs are spoken of in the immediate context of the profanation of the temple (1 Macc 2:6–12) and, before that, the persecution throughout Judea at the orders of the king, and of the "many . . . from Israel (who) gladly adopted his religion" (1 Macc 1:41–61). Daniel then informs us that "the people who are loyal to their God shall stand firm and take action. The wise among the people shall give understanding to many; for some days, however, they shall fall by sword and flame, and suffer captivity and plunder" (Dan 11:32–33). The Hebrew here for "the wise" is *maskilim* (also translated as "those with insight" or "with skill in interpretation"), and with this name we are given a group classification that rises to sudden, key prominence. The collective name is repeated three more times (11:35, 12:3, 12:10), and, as we shall see, with world-shaking significance. At 1:4 and 1:17, it was already used to describe Daniel, and thus the group indicated at 11:33 is associated intimately with the hero of the book. As John Collins says,

> There is no doubt that the visionary [primary author of the Book of Daniel] identifies with the *maskilim*. If the "people of the saints of the Most High" are to share in the victory of Michael and receive a kingdom, this "people" is not co-extensive with the state of Judah but is confined to the wise teachers and the section of the populace which responds to them . . . It is highly important to note how this elect group is defined. It is not by race, geography or nationality, but by wisdom and understanding . . . Further, the maskilim do not guide the people simply by exhorting them to loyalty, but by *making them understand*.[12]

This is a critical point. A group that suffers, and yet depends not on race or nationalism, must have a transcendent teaching. What is it? Generally, according to Collins, the teaching comes via the interpretation of dreams and visions. But what is the content of the interpretation? A vital clue is given in the explanation of what happens to the *maskilim* experientially. We have just heard of the violence they have endured: sword, flame, captivity, plunder. Then, "Some of the wise (*maskilim*) shall fall,

---

12. Collins, *Apocalyptic Vision*, 168.

so that they may be refined, purified, and cleansed, until the time of the end . . ." (Dan 11:35). There is a distinct purpose to the suffering, to the dying—and it belongs to a process toward a definitive change in time itself. The descriptives of "refinement" may be associated with temple offerings and their required purity, and this could easily be associated with the desert refugees from a corrupt Jerusalem temple. It might, at first blush, then be argued that it is the *sacrificial* death of the holy ones that makes them holy, transferring to them the holiness of the altar out in the desert. But sacrifice provides a closure within and for the present order—a temple anthropology; whereas the suffering spoken of here belongs to the opening up of a temporal sequence—"until the time of the end." This is a radically different dynamic, looking to a definitive transformation of the created human space.

We have to ask, then, what is the human sensation or phenomenology that placed the *maskilim* in this consciously transformed condition. It is not acceptance of violence as generative before God because that would, again, simply restore the present order. It must be, therefore, the breakthrough of a new transcendence, a *sui generis* awareness of God communicated in and through the vulnerability and nonviolence of these wise men and women. And, once more, this is itself the nature of "one like a son of man" brought on heavenly clouds into the presence of God, as it were, from before the world was made, the Ancient of Days.[13]

The dramatically new transcendence is connected organically to the abrupt and astonishing scenario that follows at the beginning of chapter 12:

> At that time Michael, the great prince, the protector of your people, shall arise. There shall be a time of anguish, such as never occurred since nations first came into existence. But at that time your people shall be delivered, everyone who is found written in the book. Many of those who sleep in the dust of the earth shall awake, some to everlasting life, and some to shame

---

13. Because the nonviolent transcendence is not spelled out explicitly—how could it be among men and women who are sensing its first glimmering on the horizon?—it has been much easier to assimilate it back to the old norms. The account of the martyrs at Second Maccabees 7 appears again to be a reassimilation of the wilderness martyrs' revelatory breakthrough to the all-powerful mechanics of violence. See 2 Macc 7:38, where the last of the brothers in the sequence seems to suggest their sufferings have an atoning function in "bring(ing) to an end the wrath of the Almighty . . ." In New Testament terms, this would perhaps be an example of violent humans "hijacking" the kingdom (Matt 11:12).

and everlasting contempt. Those who are wise (*maskilim*) shall shine like the brightness of the sky, and those who lead many to righteousness, like the stars forever and ever. (Dan 12:1–3)

The transcendence of nonviolence places the *maskilim,* and those taught by them, into assured connection with the end state of the universe intended and brought by a God of nonviolence. This new humanity will experience full realization in this final state, and those whose being is through violence (i.e., the kingdoms of history) cannot help but experience the awareness of never again being restored—i.e., irreversible shame. (The very fact that they awaken to this moral experience suggests not punishment but possibility of conversion.) Collins expresses the transformation clearly in terms of its basic conditions, arriving at the same necessary analysis as offered here. The only difference is the metaphysical shift to an alternate heavenly realm, rather than seeing it in terms of radically new human meaning:

> It is clear that this transformation cannot be brought about by militant action. Unlike the Maccabees, even the martyrs of 2 Maccabees 7, the *maskilim* envisage no goal which can be attained by violent revolution. For them, the kingdom is the heavenly angelic kingdom. The victory then must be completely the work of God and/or the heavenly host.[14]

But even with this conclusion, it should be evident that such nonviolent faith cannot be the result of any purely mythico-cosmic thinking. How would that be strong enough to hold out against the vivid and practical realism of the Maccabees? There had to be authentic (relational) spiritual content to the position of the *maskilim,* one that sustained through the Syrian crisis and all the way through until the time and experience of Jesus. Indeed, Collins himself traces the *earlier* lineage of a living spirituality. He references research that shows

> that the *maskilim* are described in terms of the suffering servant in Isaiah 53. Like the servant, the *maskilim* are said "to justify the many." Like the servant, they submit to death, but at the end they are exalted. Even the term *maskilim* itself corresponds to Isa 52:13: "Behold my servant *yaskil.*" The word *yaskil* is usually translated "will prosper" in this passage. However, it more usually means "will understand," or "will cause to understand, instruct" . . . The *maskilim* were precisely those who had

14. Collins, *Apocalyptic Vision,* 209.

understanding and sought to justify the many by instructing them. They were therefore acting out the role of the servant and could hope for a like reward of exaltation.[15]

With all these links, therefore, it becomes very difficult to draw a persuasive boundary between the *maskilim* and the nonviolent martyrs of First Maccabees. Their death had to be a catalyst in the emergence of the vision of Daniel 7, if not its direct spiritual-phenomenal source. In sum, the spiritual impact of a thousand nonresisting deaths cannot be separated out from the apocalyptic insights of the *maskilim*, and of their ideal visionary selves, the holy ones. It was the moment when the veil separating earth and heaven, gods and humans, was shattered in a new immediacy of sheer (nonviolent) divine relation. The effect of "cosmic" forces, of angels and spiritual "battles," flow from the generative power of this relation, not the other way round.

When the "wise . . . fall" the refinement and purification that happen is the removal of violence as a constitutive human theme and this goes on "until the time of the end" (11:35). The witness of the martyrs has the effect of disrupting the order of the world, which is the order of violence. In its place, the transformed condition of a nonviolent way of being draws near. This is, exactly as with the suffering servant, the equivalent of redemptive instruction. People affected by the *maskilim* learn a new way of being, one that brings righteousness with it.

As we have seen, the end result is complete transformation, including resurrection from the dead. By the time of the New Testament, resurrection of the dead was a core teaching not just for the Jesus movement, but also for the Pharisees (Acts 23:8), indicating the roots of both in the Daniel experience. We also see how the teaching had become a matter of controversy with other more conservative, non-apocalyptic groups in Judaism (Luke 20:27–40). We can imagine how the "idea" became the object of debate, or simply a matter of doctrine, knocked around and argued, separated from its existential roots. But in an account such as the present, the critical element of nonviolence to the teaching is regained and must not be set aside.

If the holy ones/one-like-a-son-of-man entered into the presence of God and there were given all authority on earth, it is because their nonviolence revealed something substantive to the acute sensibilities of

15. Collins, *Apocalyptic Vision*, 170. Note the "pedagogy of the servant" in chapter 4 above.

the author or authors of Daniel. The nonviolence of the wise/holy ones establishes an authentic companionship at the level of the divine, one that will endure through and out of death and into ages to come. The shining "like the brightness of the sky [*raquia*, 'the vault of heaven']" and "like the stars" means these individuals have achieved a level of existence proper to God and his heavenly host. This is not some Platonic idea worked up from the death of Socrates and the immortality of his intellectual soul. It is a much more daring yet consistent overturning of the entire order of the world, arising directly from the witness of the martyrs against the brutality of the Antiochene persecution. It was a sudden penetrating insight, like an arrow, into the true character of the divine, and therefore, necessarily, the ultimate shape of God's creation. The resurrection is simply a parallel way of saying that the holy ones/one-like-a son-of-man come into the presence of the Ancient One and inherit the future of an earth freed from all violence.

Proof of this phenomenology is that those opposed to the wise do not rise to everlasting fury of punishment, which would be the automatic response of standard anthropology, i.e., a reciprocity constructed out of violence. They rise to shame and contempt because their lives have been ordered by a meaning that is not the ultimate truth of creation. Shame comes from having been found so badly in the wrong. Contempt comes from universal knowledge of that wrong. These are judgments of meaning and truth, not judicial sentences to punishment. The same lack of punitive motifs is repeated in the New Testament, in the Gospel of John's account of the resurrection of the wicked bringing "judgment" (Greek *krisis*, John 5:29). Other places in the New Testament which seem to present a resurrection to violent punishment need at least to take account of the generative conditions of the doctrine in Daniel and their lack of reciprocal violence. "Punishment" in these New Testament instances may either be another expression of pedagogy, or simply a degrading of the original insight. In the latter case, research into the historical roots of the doctrine must be taken as a corrective. If the authentic roots of resurrection are a revelatory experience surrounding nonviolent witness and its divine relation, then what lies on the other side of resurrection must be fully consistent with that experience.

In any case, the claim is still a kind of anthropological gamble. It is the discovery of the DNA of God and God's creation but with only the tools of traumatic spiritual experience to verify it. To the challenge that this is simply self-comfort, the reply is that it is only in the extreme circumstances of the wounding of this world that another world breaks in. The atheist philosopher (or "materialist theologian") Slavoj Žižek understands the traumatic structure of the Christian mystery, arguing the death of God (through Christ) *signifies* the possibility of new human community—because the figure of authority has negated itself for the sake of love. He points out "[I]t is God himself who made a Pascalian wager. By dying on the cross, he made a risky gesture with no guaranteed final outcome . . . Far from providing the conclusive dot on the 'i,' the divine act rather stands for the openness of a New Beginning, and it falls to humanity to live up to it . . ."[16] He therefore recognizes the generative semiosis out of the death of Christ—and would certainly do so also out of the death of the sabbath martyrs/holy ones. He says, "Only a lacking, vulnerable being is capable of love," and this must be true of all those who communicate the semiosis of love.[17] But why should this generative anthropology of love not also encompass, or be encompassed by, an actual theology, a genuine revelation of God? Does not the semiotics of love draw us into the most transcendent of all human senses, bringing us into contact with something that exceeds all place and time? In effect, the loving nonviolence of the martyrs opened a relational aperture that enabled the visionary to see what before had been almost completely hidden, and remains almost so until today. When we get to our account of Jesus' own gamble in vulnerability, we will begin to recognize perhaps how this relational hiddenness can be reversed when we read it as an astonishing exercise in Daniel-style redemptive instruction.

16. Žižek, *God in Pain*, 85.

17. Žižek, *Puppet and the Dwarf*, 115.

7

Jonah

Parody as Prophecy

THE PROPHET JONAH ARRIVES in Nineveh, the heart of Assyria famed for its violence and cruelty. But he's there in the strength of something more powerful than violence, and the Ninevites are converted—from their violence!

This story of the reluctant prophet, and the last in our essays from the Old Testament, assumes its place as essential finale. Jonah claims pole position in the sequence of semiotic transformations because this book of the Bible most clearly makes our case. As pure story or fable, it most obviously acts as an instance of code transformation, and explicitly in relation to violence. More to the point even, Jesus used this story as a formal *signification* for what he was doing. He said, "No *sign* shall be given to you except the sign of Jonah" (Matt 16:4) It is essential, therefore, to reflect on this book as a parade example and conclusion to the systematic argument made here.

Jonah is a Jewish reflection which comes with no textual clues as to where and when it was written. The literary conceit of the book is that it's about an historical figure, the prophet mentioned in Second Kings. Jonah son of Amittai (Jonah 1:1) was active in the court of Jeroboam II of Israel, and, according to the brief description, a key prophetic encouragement for the king's successful military policy. "He [the king] restored the border of Israel from Lebohamath as far as the Sea of Arabah, according to the word of the Lord, the God of Israel, which he spoke by his servant Jonah son of Amittai, the prophet who was from Gath-hepher" (2 Kgs

14:25). Jeroboam II is counted a wicked king by the Deuteronomic author of Kings, but nevertheless the Lord granted him success for the sake of Israel (vv. 15–16). In the Book of Jonah, we hear right at the outset that the Lord orders the prophet to go to Nineveh and "cry out against it; for their wickedness has come up before me" (Jonah 1:2). Jonah in the book is not to deliver an oracle of doom on the enemy from within the echo-chamber of a king's court, but a denunciation of evil face-to-face in the hostile city itself. There is necessarily implied a possibility of repentance and conversion, just as would be the case if the prophecy was directed against Israel: thus, the historical dissonance between the militant northern prophet and the command of the Lord in the prophetic book is immediately and startlingly clear.

The name Jonah actually means "dove," and his father's name, Amittai, means "true" or "faithful," and these are further parts of the firework display of irony running through the Jonah text. It seems the author picked on the content of the single verse in Kings—a prophet with a peaceful name and warlike message—as the ironic hinge on which to swing his whole turning-things-on-their-head story. Reading it like this means the book could be written at almost any point from the exile onward. As we have seen, again and again, the exile is the core semiotic event in the Bible whereby everything becomes ironic for the Jewish people. They are punished nearly to the point of annihilation, but God still cares, and this is actually a way of strengthening their relationship. They are punished but the punishment turns to compassion, and the compassion of the Servant becomes a transformative pathway to bring many to righteousness. They are punished according to a logic of retribution, but an inspired writer demonstrates that retribution masks the logic of the scapegoat. The religious project of Judea is driven into the wilderness and yet its nonviolent martyrs open up a dramatic new possibility of divine life. The story of Jonah fits entirely and thematically into a structural semiotics of irony. The eighth-century prophet sent to Nineveh is a deeply ironic fable and, as such, is an integral part of a core communicative strategy of the Old Testament. For that reason, as I say, it can take place culturally anywhere within the post-exilic period. At the same time, however, I would set it in the Persian period when a calmer attitude to the nations was more the norm.

In literary terms, we should say the real prophet of Nineveh is Nahum. The seventh-century prophet worked somewhere close to Nineveh's downfall at the hands of the Babylonians and Medes, and Nahum hated

Nineveh, "[T]he city of blood, full of lies, full of plunder, never without victims!" (Nah 3:1 NIV). His hatred was entirely shared by his fellow Israelites. The great reforming king, Josiah, lost his life in an ill-advised attempt to block the Pharaoh Neco from coming to the aid of the Assyrians when they were under attack by the Babylonians. Josiah could have stayed well out of the fight (cf. 2 Chr 35:21–22), but desire to see the end of the Assyrian empire was irresistible. Afterward, the horrible shock of the righteous king's military disaster on the plane of Megiddo prompted the name for the place as a location of the final cataclysmic battle with evil, "Armageddon."

The first line of Nahum is this: "An oracle concerning Nineveh: the book of the vision of Nahum of Elkosh. A jealous and avenging God is the Lord, the Lord is avenging and wrathful; the Lord takes vengeance on his adversaries and rages against his enemies. The Lord is slow to anger but great in power, and the Lord will by no means clear the guilty" (Nah 1:1–3). It is more than possible that the Book of Jonah is written as a direct riposte to Nahum, countering its lead oracle of God's unmitigated wrath. "Slow to anger" in Nahum's lines is a clear echo of the theophany to Moses at Exod 34:6–7, referencing it while reinforcing an entirely different sense of God. In my calculation, where the Exodus passage has seven expressions of God's mercy, Nahum has the same multiple given to God's vengeance. In the Jonah story, toward the end, the recalcitrant prophet explicitly quotes Exod 34:6 and its benign understanding, saying how he *knew* this was the way God was and for *that* reason he had run away from him (Jonah 4:2). It is difficult to negate the impression that the writer of Jonah has deliberately constructed Jonah as a parody of Nahum, both a representation of his bitter spirit and a hilarious turning-it-on-its-head.

To achieve this and still get a hearing, the author must do two things. First, the writer must sufficiently embed the story within biblical language to convince readers this is an authentic account of Israelite prophecy. Then, even more crucially, a plot and a text must be produced which make an inversion of the popular viewpoint possible without lapsing into mere preachiness. A code transformation must be carried through with the reader hardly knowing it and left thinking entirely new possibilities at the end of the book.

The first requirement is achieved with great intertextual skill. Apart from the obvious hinge device of Jonah, son of Ammitai, there are at least twenty direct allusions to other prophetic texts found in Jonah's brief forty-eight verses.[1] The story is so skillfully interwoven with textual prophetic motifs that it lives and breathes the world of biblical prophecy. For example, Jonah is closely modeled on the prophet Elijah, especially at 1 Kgs 19:4, where the despondent opponent of Ahab and Jezebel flees into the wilderness, sits down under a tree, and asks to die. Jonah basically does the same at Jonah 4:3–5. This is just one of many textual echoes of canonical prophecy. But if creative intertexuality is what makes the "prophecy" of Jonah work as prophecy, then it is the writer themself who has produced it, in solitude on a desk and a roll of papyrus. It makes a theory of semiotic transformation that much more urgent and persuasive, telling us that this work of prophecy is first of all the mimicking of a code, aiming at giving itself an identity. It is a deliberate manipulation of familiar biblical DNA to produce a remarkably new mutation.

To understand the "writing" of the book in this way—as the pivotal feature of the work—displaces the dogmatic genre of "prophecy," even though the author did everything possible to get prophecy's imprimatur. It brings the work into parallel with other biblical writing like Job, Ruth, or even Genesis. Such creative writing is a mode of reflection and production which belongs to the overall biblical pathway and at key points is able to generate definitive works of code creation. "Wisdom literature" may be the broad category encompassing this activity,[2] but it needs to be emphasized that this "wisdom" is not at all conventional. It is about as radical as you can get, more akin to postmodern deconstruction than books of maxims like Proverbs and Sirach. Indeed, it is this radical wisdom which paradoxically warrants us considering Jonah correctly as prophecy: it is the speaking forth of a message challenging Nineveh, and the rest of us, to our roots.

A Marvelous Plotline

It follows necessarily that the other thing that is required is a massively creative effect in the writing. A plot and text are needed capable of bringing a crucial shift from the conventional to the new. In Jonah, the choice of the ship, the storm, and the great fish are inspired settings and motifs which by their very daring, and yet symbolic integrity and power, bring the reader to something wonderfully fresh and different. The enduring

1. Dell, "Reinventing the Wheel," 89–91.
2. Dell, "Reinventing the Wheel," 91.

popularity of the story witnesses to the success of Jonah on this score. The story starts with Jonah getting on board a ship going in the opposite direction from Nineveh. The ship's destination is Tarshish, a place known in the Bible as a source of precious metals and identified with a variety of Western Mediterranean locations from Carthage to Sardinia. The point is this is a ship's destination as remote and "other" as the biblical writers know (akin to any impossibly outposted mining colony in the Star Wars sagas!). It is the very place Jonah wants to go to, to get away from any merciful possibilities of the biblical God.[3]

But the Lord is not done with Jonah. He "hurled a great wind [*gadowlah ruah*] upon the sea" (1:4), and a mighty storm comes up threatening to smash the boat to bits.[4] The scene is reminiscent of creation itself where "a wind from God swept over the face of the waters" (Gen 1:2). We are in the realm of primordial divine action and in the biblical repertoire of signs the violence of the storm must echo Genesis, including the episode of the flood. The sailors (who are pagans; cf. 1:5) cast lots to find out "on whose account this calamity has come upon us" (1:7). The author abruptly introduces the theme of cosmic blame, the thought structure telling human beings that natural disaster comes on account of human wrongdoing with reactive divine vengeance. The author does not feel the need to explain this: it is given, and there is another rich Jonah irony here in the sense of Deuteronomic guilt (which Jonah does not feel!) now substituted by a common human—anthropological—theme of seeking-out-the-one-to-blame for any given disaster. There are obvious thematic connections to Job here, but the author takes the Bible revelation of the scapegoat in a further and deeper direction. The narrative does not pause on the topic, because something even more profoundly revelatory is at stake.

The sailors use a word to describe the storm—*ha ra'ah*, translated as "calamity" (1:7)—which is used five more times in the book and in ways that constantly overlap human evil and the evil of the storm (1:8, 3:8, 3:10 twice, 4:2). As everyone know, the sailors end up throwing Jonah in the sea and straight away the sea "cease[s] from its raging" (1:15). Jonah

---

3. Georges Landes explains that the geography of Tarshish suggests a space where the cultic presence of the Lord has never been known, thus somewhere Jonah won't have to encounter the commands of his God and their benign outcomes (Landes, "Kerygma of the Book of Jonah," 19–20).

4. For Hebrew text, see Limburgh, *Jonah*; also, Phyllis Trible's evocative *Rhetorical Criticism, Context, Method and the Book of Jonah.*

is definitely a scapegoat for the sailors, but in this case, there is also an open merging of Jonah's personal condition of spiritual alienation and the terrifying alienation of the deeps. In a literary and mythical sense, Jonah has joined the abyssal monsters of violence that the Book of Daniel so signally presented as forces of actual historical violence. In Daniel and Jonah, the feature of anthropological violence is given the same formal symbolism—that of the violent deep. But Jonah goes beyond even Daniel. The sea quietens down not because a necessary victim has been offered to the god, but because Jonah's anger has disappeared into its own primordial space. The Book of Jonah reveals the primordial violence sealed inside the scapegoat by making Jonah as protagonist take willing-but-resentful responsibility for cosmic violence. Jonah is a highly unusual biblical scapegoat because he embraces that condition in an astonishingly modern adoption of victim status. And even as he does so, he reveals the continuity of human and cosmic violence. "Pick me up," he says to the sailors, "and throw me into the sea; then the sea will quiet down for you; for I know it is because of me that this great storm has come upon you" (1:12)[5].

We can come to this conclusion—that "cosmic" violence has its source in the human heart—because this is the direction the overall text is moving. On one level, we can still think that God sent the violent storm because God, after all, can behave as God wants, including violently. But very soon we discover that God, marvelously, uses a creature of the deep to deliver Jonah—in order to continue to pursue his intention. In terms of the prophecy, this involves centrally the overcoming of violence, both that of the Ninevites and Jonah. We will return to Jonah's deliverance in the deep shortly, but first we underline how further elements of the story continue to shade together human and cosmic violence.

At 3:6–9, where Jonah has at last conformed—grudgingly—to God's initial command to cry out against Nineveh, the king of the wicked city responds wholeheartedly. He proclaims a fast for humans and animals, including from water, and commands that "all shall turn from their evil ways [ha ra'ah] and from the violence [he hamas] that is in their hands."

---

5. We have to note here that "cosmic" is a signifier for an essentially human experience of the physical universe, one tied to mimetic meaning. It is extremely difficult, if not impossible, for humans to have a purely neutral sense of the universe: it is "either for us or against us." The anger or forgiveness of the human psyche one way or another recruits the universe to its side. Jonah is noteworthy because it is as victim that he embraces a violent universe.

The evil that was the violence of the storm is now directly parallel with human-on-human violence. An evident semiotic slippage is set up between the two planes or codes of meaning. A little later, when God has "changed his mind" about bringing the "calamity" (*ha ra'ah*) on Nineveh, we hear how this is deeply offensive to Jonah (4:1). The Hebrew then uses the same term as an intensive attached to an expression of Jonah's displeasure, and it is deployed in parallel with a further expression of anger. Thus Jonah "was greatly displeased [*ra'ah . . . way-yera*] and became very angry [*way-yihar gedowlah*]." The words have obvious strong assonance in Hebrew, the sentence sounding something like "Jonah was in an exceedingly evil, evil-mood, and incandescently angry." The repeated emphatic vowel sounds make for a continually redoubled sense of murderous wrath. Finally, to underline the point, the verb for being displeased is the same verb used to express Cain's state of mind before he murders his brother (Gen 4:5)!

In sum, Jonah fulfills textually and emotionally the very same character as the violent storm and the evil it brings about. The text has doubled back on itself, returning Jonah to the same murderous state he embraced when he was thrown in the raging sea—and beyond that to the very first murder of history, thus once more knitting together the themes of human and cosmic violence. Meanwhile, the king and the Ninevites renounce the selfsame evil and violence, and, following on, God does too.

The episode in the middle, between the two instances of Jonah's terrible anger, and preceding the people's repentance, is that of the great fish. It represents the way in which the author (literally) navigates between Jonah's anger and something wonderfully new. "But the Lord provided a large [*gadowl*] fish to swallow up Jonah; and Jonah was in the belly of the fish three days and three nights" (1:17).

The fish matches the size both of the storm and Jonah's evil mood and so acts as a semiotic foil to their violence. The great fish is technically a monster of the deep, intimate to its primordial chaos, a cultural parallel to Daniel's beasts from the depths. But, paradoxically, by God's power the fish provides the original "safe space" for Jonah, a place where he is rescued and can come face to face with a God of redemption. The psalm Jonah then utters (2:1–9) is a fairly conventional piece of Old Testament piety, a fugue of motifs that can be found scattered throughout other psalms. What makes it different is its fabulous setting, the belly of the fish which of course strains all credulity but still succeeds because of its wonderful metaphorical tenor. As an image of proximity to death, of Sheol

(2:2), it is unrivalled: the slippery, dark, amorphous belly of a fish, itself surrounded by unfathomable deeps, carries us at once to the obscure but real feelings humans project for the experience of death. At the same time, it is a bold, disruptive thought for biblical culture, a mountain-and-desert imagination which saw the sea as alien and hostile.[6] Following from this, and in a turn of brilliant daring, the author changes this foul hostile space to one of safety. In one trope a deadly, oppositional theme becomes one of nonviolence and salvation. This is how we should understand Jonah's "whale," explaining its enduring popularity as a stunning metaphor of redemption.

Transformational Code

But by what right did the author do this? How could he take an enduring mythic image of violence and death and transform it to one of hope and deliverance. It could only be by the deepest instinct of Hebrew faith, including an eruptive insight of nonviolence, parallel in its way to the insight gained from the nonviolent martyrs of Maccabees. Where, in particular, did it come from? We cannot know. We only have Jonah's fishy tale to go on. And yet the insight stood, gained traction, and established its rightful space among the prophets; and, strikingly so, with Jesus. It is an example of pure code invention, and perhaps the very purest example of this in the Old Testament. In the depths of Sheol and the turmoil of the sea, the God of creation establishes a space of enduring life. One moreover that is intended for external historical awareness and impact. Because, "the Lord spoke to the fish, and it spewed Jonah out upon the dry land" (3:10).

The deep nonviolence of the Lord's will in creation ejects Jonah into history. The force of the "spewing" onto land suggests that Jonah has no choice but to witness to the abyssal nonviolence propelling him onto the land. Indeed, the disappearance of violence at the end of chapter 1 depends for its secure meaning on this later statement. Jonah identifies with the abyss in his anger and this quietens the sea, but his drowning could very easily lapse into scapegoating—i.e., not a revelation of anthropological violence but a normal mythology that Jonah was the indeed the guilty source of the god's anger. Only the creation of a nonviolent space at the

---

6. See especially Isa 51:9–11, where the Lord defeats Rahab the sea-monster in the miracle of the Exodus; cf. Job 26:12, 41.1; Pss. 74:14, 89:10; also Isa 27:1.

heart of the ocean, one that could also deliver Jonah to the land in the power of nonviolence, could ensure that Jonah's presence in the abyss would truly calm the waves. The passive aggression of Jonah's "throw me in . . . for I know it is because of me . . ." will not bring peace unless there is a larger nonviolence which can form a healing capsule around the militant prophet. The calming of the waters thus depends on the further narrative of the great fish; it is a diptych where the second panel fully displays the meaning of the first. The revelation of the continuum of human and primordial violence could not be definitive unless the continuity was profoundly subverted from within.

This is the central sign of the semiotic concerto that is Jonah. The abyssal overcoming of violence. And the people of Nineveh immediately "get it." It is not Jonah's minimalist, still-hostile proclamation that convinces them: "Forty days more, and Nineveh shall be overthrown!" (3:4). It is the phenomenon of Jonah's deliverance that truly changes things: this is why the king at once focuses on the issue of violence (3:8). It is not stated in the narrative but thematically the two events are inseparable, and it is the reason why the king and the people's conversion is credible. Their sudden transformation is all one with the revelatory nonviolence of the great fish.

And then, in the great literary coup of the whole story, God too changes vis-à-vis the Ninevites. Explicitly. "When God saw what they did, how they turned from their evil [ha ra'ah] ways, God changed his mind about the calamity [ha ra'ah] that he had said he would bring upon them; and he did not do it" (3:10). Once again, we see how tightly woven are the term's various inflections for evil. Not only are human and cosmic violence implicated, but now human and divine "evil" are put in direct, astonishing, proximity. In the Hebrew text, the two uses of the term are even closer together, reading like this: when God "saw they turned from *the evil* relented God of *the evil.*" The proximity is much closer than simple legal consequence in a Deuteronomic sense, i.e., if they repent, then God decides not to punish. There is a semiotic and thematic identity of the instances of evil. The evil contemplated by "God" forms a direct, even ontological, continuation of the evil in the hands of humankind. We cannot avoid the impression, therefore, that the meaning and identity of God are changed, from violence to nonviolence, by the equivalent change in humans. Even if the plot mechanism tells us God had pre-constructed the "safe place" at the heart of the tempest, it depends, in a full hermeneutic circle, on the Ninevites' renunciation of violence to achieve its full value as meaning. There is a semio-ontological shift in the identity of God and the cosmos dependent on the change of human relationship from violence to nonviolence.

This then becomes the crowning effect of the Book of Jonah: the provocative sense that God is changed substantively by human change, and precisely by the in-breaking of nonviolence. The Prophet Jonah wishes to hang on to a violent God despite the dramatic revelation of nonviolence derived by his deliverance from the belly of the fish. He also knows that many of the great biblical confessions about God are against him. As already mentioned, he quotes from one of the greatest. In perhaps the single most ironic verse of the whole Bible, he prays, "O Lord! Is not this what I said while I was still in my own country? That is why I fled to Tarshish at the beginning; for I knew that you are a gracious God and merciful, slow to anger, and abounding in steadfast love, and ready to relent from punishing" (4:2). As noted, the description of God is from Exod 34:6, but it stops short of verse 7 and its codicil of "by no means excus(ing) the guilty." In place of the latter, the author of Jonah adds another, further, and deeper commitment to mercy, one, moreover, tied yet again to the previous language. "Ready to relent from punishing" is actually "ready to repent concerning the evil [ha ra'ah]. The verb "repent" is the same as the verb used earlier about the Ninevites when they repented their violence (3:10, nacham). So it is that God mimics the action of the nonviolent Ninevites, repenting of his own violence in identity with the new Ninevite way of being.

Sadly, however, Jonah is entirely in the old way. This is the great paradox: a prophet of Israel out of synch with the transformative being of his God, fighting bitterly to retain his theological semiotics of violence, despite all persuasions to the contrary. Yet God does not give up. He continues to try to give Jonah the new optic of nonviolence. The continuation of the Jonah story is a coda to the story of the Ninevites, but clearly it is the point of the whole book. The Lord intercedes with Jonah, asking, "Is it right for you to be angry?" (4:4). The question echoes God's question to Cain back in Genesis, "Why are you angry?" (Gen 4:6). But this time, God is much more proactive, as befits a God who is progressively discovered to be nonviolent in and through the whole of subsequent Genesis. The Lord provides a parable and continues to intercede. Jonah has set up camp outside of the city, malevolently waiting to see what would happen. He builds a "booth" for himself—reminiscent of the temporary structures built for the in-gathering Feast of Booths (the same word, sukkah). But the Lord upstages such religious practice by providing his own back-to-nature bush to shade Jonah from the sun (4:6). Then, in quick succession, he provides a worm to destroy the bush and a sultry east wind to wear Jonah out. The embittered prophet repeats his default solution, the same as the one on the ship when he told the sailors to throw him in, but now made definitive: "It is better for me to die than to live" (4:8). The successful prophetic preaching is fully inverted: if he has to suffer and Nineveh not, then he would rather experience annihilation.

Yet the Lord continues to seek an empathic response, once again asking if it is right for the prophet to be angry. He compares the bush to the great city and questions whether Jonah should be concerned about the bush and he (God) not care about the city: "[T]hat great city, in which there are more than a hundred and twenty thousand persons who do not know their right hand from their left, and also many animals" (4:11).

The dialogue evokes the one between Abraham and the Lord when the former was interceding for Sodom. But in that case, Abraham tried to bargain on the basis of the small number of the "righteous" who might be found in the city, bargaining against Sodom's imminent destruction by God. Here the tables are turned, and it is the Lord who is bargaining for the city. Moreover, he bargains on the basis of the absolute number of his creatures, human beings *and* animals! Nothing to do with the righteous! So much has changed since those early stories! So much so that the author of Jonah has turned everything on its head. Yes, of course it's true, the people of Sodom had not repented, while the people of Nineveh had. But did God provide a prophet to preach to the people of Sodom, let alone such an amazing backstory for that prophet? Much more to the point, we remember that all this is just a story! There is absolutely no historical record of a mass conversion by the Ninevites. Nahum's verdict on the "city of blood . . . never without victims" is the historical one. On the other hand, it is the very compassion of Abraham working itself out in the history of Israel that eventuates in a writer able to construct such an outrageously tall tale. It is the writing of the Book of Genesis itself bearing fruit. The Book of Jonah could not exist unless the author had seen that Abraham was compassionate, because a compassionate God had first blessed him to be so! Unless it were not the deep destiny of Israel to bless all the tribes of the earth with divine compassion!

But it had taken centuries of reflection to get to this point, to get to the moment when the subversive coding present in the Abraham story could finally fully express itself in the sign of the nonviolent God of

Jonah. The primitive coding of a violent god/gods is so fundamental to our human existence that it cannot be revoked overnight. Such a change of code depends first on human transformation out of violence, and this is what Abraham and the story of Sodom represents. But working this up into a nonviolent theology depended on prolonged meditation against the background of exile and national loss. If God still loved and cared for his people when they had lost their land, if he had given up the direct use of war-fighting and encouraged the people to seek the welfare of the city among whom they were in exile (Jer 27:9), it meant this God could be, and might very well prove to be, essentially nonviolent. The prophecy of Jonah creates a coding where the "could be" becomes a reality. There is a dynamic sign of nonviolence—the great fish from the deep spewing a prophet on the shore—which changed a people, and, in turn, this change in the people changed the meaning of God, completing the semiotic circle. In the story of Jonah itself, the story starts with a certain ambivalence—God hurls the wind and the storm at Jonah and, collaterally, at the sailors. But by the end of the story, we recognize that all these things are just signifiers on the way to the massive reversal from the deeps. This is the semiotic miracle of writing—the radical and progressive coding producing a dramatic change in the meaning both of being human and being God.

It is this plenary sense that Jesus intends by the "sign of Jonah," as in "no other sign will be given" apart from it (Matt 12:39). We can be assured that Jesus meditated often and deeply on this text, and that is why he invoked it as a sign. The "sign" includes both the method and the content of code transformation represented by the whole text, and it was on this that he staked his life. Jesus chose to go to the abyss of violence and death on the strength of a Jonah-style insight telling him that the God of nonviolence would rescue him and so change the semiotics of that event itself. It is fitting, therefore, that we now turn to the story of this extraordinary man.

8

Jesus

Global Icon

PUTTING "JESUS" AT THE head of the page in a sequence like this might seem foolhardy. There are so many questions, issues, and metaphysics surrounding the figure at the heart of Christianity, it would seem preposterous to fit him into a semiotic framework.

Jesus comes to us as a theological entity in one of the most over-determined senses known to human culture: the sole-begotten Son of the eternal God, made flesh! To place this once-and-only status in continuity with codes and textual signifiers seems a category error at best, blasphemy a possibility! Like someone trying to push a balloon under water—it must continually rebound back to its natural, rarified medium.

At the same time, there can be no doubt that "Jesus" does perform the function of code, and massively so. As the legendary footballer Pele remarked, "Wherever you go, there are three icons that everyone knows: Jesus Christ, Pele, and Coca Cola." Allowing for the football genius' only slightly exaggerated self-importance, it is clear that the fixed point of iconic comparison is Jesus. It is impossible to think of another claimant to supreme *sign-value* that would rank equally across the globe next to him. There is no question, therefore, that "Jesus" is an extremely dynamic piece of semiosis. He *means* a great deal.

But if we do try to analyze this status, to dig into it, we come upon some serious problems. It's as if examining the foundations of this colossus brings us to nothing but loose shale and the imminent danger of the whole edifice crashing down.

The problem does not lie with theological doctrine, as such. The metaphysical definitions of Jesus as the second person of the Trinity, eternally begotten by the Father, were worked out in the early centuries of Christianity. They are contained in tight formulae surrounded by highly technical and specific discussions. The definitions have stood the test of time, taking on a sacred patina, a kind of self-contained inevitability. No, the problem lies with the strange, paradoxical connection of this eternal status to historical fact: Jesus lived in first-century Palestine, ate, spoke, and taught there, and died a hard death under the Roman prefect, Pontius Pilate. What has the iconic, Elvis-status "Jesus" to do with these brute facts?

We get the simple concrete details from the Gospels. But there are a lot of things also in Matthew, Mark, Luke, and John which seem fanciful or contradictory, or both. Once the Gospel accounts are thought about in a systematic, scientific way, you set in motion an industrial-scale inquiry as to what, if anything, we can know for certain about this person. So, suddenly, from the factual-historical side, the sign-value of Jesus seems ready to evaporate. The evocatively named "Quest for the Historical Jesus" first began in the nineteenth century. Its eponymous account by Albert Schweizer was published in 1906, and gave us a description of historical hypotheses about Jesus created by mostly German scholarship over the course of the previous century. The quest did not end there, but was renewed in what is currently known as "the second" and "third" quests in the middle and end of the twentieth century, respectively. With this sporadic but sustained inquiry over two hundred years, it is pretty obvious there was, and is, little scientific consensus about the historical Jesus. And as we continue to dig, we see how complex the questions get. Crucial bits of understanding all seem to be connected to each other in a kind of tangled mass of reinforcement which seems to rest on nothing but itself, each bit holding up the other. Is it possible to find a grounding that is both historical and semiotically fertile, so that we can find some basis for the massive iconic value known as Jesus? This is the question that will guide us and, even though we have not approached a theme quite in this way before, it is not entirely unique. As we have seen, some of the critical semiotic shifts we have described from the Old Testament are grounded in particular history. Especially the themes of the servant and "one like a son of man" belong to decisive historical events. The methodology we are adopting here has in fact already been sketched in the earlier essays. It is just being made crucial and systematic in relation to the pivotal semiotic value that is "Jesus."

An Unexplained Death

Dale Allison is a scholar of the Third Quest who wrote *The Historical Christ and the Theological Jesus*, a somewhat elegiac account of where he personally ended up in the wake of these inquiries. He first formulates the questions he sees as central to the Jesus quest. "Why did Jesus go up to Jerusalem? Did he anticipate his own death, or even deliberately provoke others to engineer it? If he did sense where things were tending, with what categories did he interpret his imagined future?"[1]

As we shall see shortly, these are vital questions for the historical Jesus. But the very fact that there could be doubt about the answers seems again to question the iconic status of this man. If we don't know what he really did or intended, then is his fame justified? Here then lies the semiotic conundrum. Could it be that his semiotic value is essentially all fictitious, secondary, dependent on an imaginary or mythical value attributed to him? Or is it in any way the other way round, i.e., the semiotics (and, somewhere in parallel, the metaphysics) are rooted in fact?

In the eighteenth century, a scholar named G. E. Lessing gave a memorable rebuke to Christian theology. He was considering the first disciples' testimony as an historical event, but the idea that this should then determine the understanding of God was a step too far. His ringing dictum was: "[The] accidental truths of history can never become the proof of necessary truths of reason." Historical truths cannot be demonstrated, only rational ones can. Lessing accepted the disciples' *report* of the resurrection as historical, but that could tell us nothing about eternal truths—there are any number of reasons why a report can be mistaken. The distance between history and eternal truth was, as he said, "the ugly, broad ditch which I cannot get across."[2] But if the claim of resurrection cannot give us anything transcendent, how much less the ordinary details of Jesus' life?

I remember when I first heard Lessing's axiom in a course on the New Testament. It was used by our professor as a way of marking his

1. Allison, *Historical Christ*, 9.
2. Lessing, *Theological Writings*, 51–55.

credentials as a representative of Christian orthodoxy and yet teaching a fairly skeptical assessment of the historical gospel tradition. In other words, the doctrine about Jesus works at its own level, the history is something else. It struck me then that this was unsatisfactory and somehow a wrong way to present the problem, although I could not give any kind of good argument. Before, however, we get to the possible terms of an answer, we should return to the work of the "quests." What, if anything, have they been able to contribute to a solid and meaningful history about Jesus?

As already underlined in the quotation from Allison, central to everything must be his death. Another Jesus scholar, Scot McKnight, wrote his own historical Jesus summation book, one where the title makes the concern patent: *Jesus and His Death: Historiography, the Historical Jesus and Atonement Theory.* The book has a feeling of marking the end of the late-twenieth century inquiry, and this time a further layer is added to the questioning, the issue of what is known as "atonement." This term is a theological "weasel word," one that implies various meanings on an important theme, and yet always carrying with it a certain toxic freight. (Did Jesus have to "pay" his brutal suffering to his Father to put us in the clear from punishment?) This is not the concern here, and McKnight does not go into the theory in any detail. His problem is simply the connection of the historical Jesus to the pivotal Christian concept of his death as beneficial to others, however conceived. Here is how he puts it:

> [D]oes Jesus' death have ontological or narratological but not historical value? Did his death set into motion a sort of reflection on his death, a reflection that had little to do with the intention of the one who died? Apart from faith—Christian faith at that—one cannot state that Jesus' death outside of Jerusalem in (say) 30 CE was an act of God in history. But, apart from faith, one *can* try to determine if Jesus thought his death was atoning. And, if one were to conclude that Jesus did not think in such categories, well, then I believe the history of Christianity ought to be given a reappraisal. If the religion of Christianity has given to Jesus' death both a central significance and an importance never given it by Jesus, then *the religion itself becomes completely separated from Jesus himself.*[3]

In short, the human individual who started all this may have very little to do with what he started. And this gets down to his salvific death: if he

3. McKnight, *Jesus and His Death*, 49; my italics.

didn't think about it, or intend it in any reflective way, then the whole edifice of atonement (and, with it, salvation) appears on very shaky ground. For any kind of evangelical Christianity, this is an absolutely central question, and the problem seems a very contemporary one. Up to now, everything has been built on Jesus' body, in a very literal and automatic sense, while what was in his mind and heart appeared secondary, even neutral, to the vast monument constructed on top of him. This is in fact a formally *sacrificial* understanding of the work of Jesus—in the end, the thoughts of the victim have nothing to do with the value of his death. It is, I believe, a major reason why we can still talk in this manner about "the faith" of Christianity apart from the historical mind and heart at its source. Jesus has been understood over the Christian centuries as an object-sacrifice to God, and that is all that matters to make salvation work. But we now live in a time when the sacrificial worldview is more and more breaking down. McKnight's anxiety is very much a product of a sacrificial theology at the point of its progressive collapse. Because, meanwhile, history raises its head from the deeps. The phenomenal violence of our era—in every sense—has made the forensic use of violence, to "satisfy" God, deeply problematic.

Standing behind Allison and Mcknight's reflections there is a small army of scholars who have been working on questions of the historical Jesus, as I say, for two hundred years and more. It is an astonishing phenomenon—the depth and range of scholarship devoted to an issue remaining still somehow inconclusive. To review it would be significantly beyond the scope of the present work, but I can indicate some main lines that describe the spectrum of attitudes. They fall essentially between a degree of realism in the life of Jesus, as an apocalyptic prophet or agent, and a dismissal of the core of the Gospels as essentially early Christian construction or myth.

Albert Schweizer penned probably the most influential historical Jesus book ever, one which we have already had cause to mention and which still sets the bar for the drama of its account. His *Quest of the Historical Jesus* argues that Jesus died to set the final tribulation underway in his own person, and thus bring in the reign of God. A number of scholars follow this road of historical Jesus-realism, but with less of Schweizer's anguished first-century apocalypticism. We can mention a few of the influential authors in the English-speaking world and their major books: W. Manson, *Jesus the Messiah* (1944), Morna Hooker, *Jesus and the Servant* (1959), C. K. Barrett, *Jesus and the Gospel Tradition* (1967), C.H. Dodd,

The Founder of Christianity (1970), Joachim Jeremias, *New Testament Theology* (1971), B. F. Meyer, *The Aims of Jesus* (1979), Martin Hengel, *The Atonement* (1981), Ben Witherington III, *Jesus the Sage* (1994), N. T. Wright, *Jesus: The Victory of God* (1996). For all these authors, one way or another Jesus can be rooted intelligibly and integrally in both the Old Testament and his first-century Jewish context. In particular, the motifs of "servant" from Second Isaiah and "like a son of man" from Daniel, and the symbol and role of "Israel" itself, to one degree or another provide coherent motivation for Jesus' historical actions.

N. T. Wright represents perhaps the most vigorous attempt at a dramatic narrative of Jesus since Schweizer. His *Jesus: The Victory of God* looks to multiple Old Testament sources, including both the servant and son of man. He concludes Jesus took on the identity of Israel in order to bring about a new exodus, the end of exile, the eschatological redemption which is the defeat of the power of Satan in the world.

Against all of the above, however, has to be balanced the epochal impact of Rudolf Bultmann. His *History of the Synoptic Tradition* (1921) continues to resonate as a hyper-skeptical analysis, producing a Jesus largely without a story. The critical method he used, known as "form criticism," saw the Gospel texts composed of numerous standard forms worked up by the early church for its own purposes and then presented as authentic Jesus teaching and history: forms such as preaching, pronouncements, controversy, miracles, etc. Bultmann's approach is itself influenced by the nineteenth-century critical thought of German New Testament scholars like David Strauss (1808–1874) and William Wrede (1859–1906) who saw New Testament writers as purveyors of religious myth and little more. This optic on the Gospels, passed on through Bultmann, is felt all the way through to the famous, if partisan, Jesus Seminar. A group assembled by Robert Funk, chair of the religion department at Vanderbilt University, the Seminar assessed the authenticity of the Gospel texts by voting. Their overall result was that only 18 percent of Gospel words attributed to Jesus are historical.[4] As for Jesus' story, this is largely evaporated, producing a "laconic sage" with no end-times vision. For the Seminar, Jesus intended nothing by his death and the empty tomb is a fiction of the early church.[5]

4. Funk et al., *Five Gospels*, 5: "Eighty-two percent of the words ascribed to Jesus in the gospels were not actually spoken by him, according to the Jesus Seminar."

5. The agenda of Funk is summarized by Dale Allison: "It is time, insisted Funk, to grow up . . . to recognize that Christians have been captive to a false religion, from

Turning the Temple Key

Standing somewhere off to the side of our list of Old Testament Messiah/Servant/Son of Man themed portraits, and far removed from the Bultmann-style ones where the historical Jesus is glimpsed within an absent landscape, there is the work of E. P. Sanders. His *Jesus and Judaism* published in 1985 represented an historiographical breakthrough.[6] It defined a method where contextual background, actions, and intentions-deduced-from-actions (rather than sayings) enable a continuous account. Sanders' book places Jesus squarely and credibly in his time and space. Because of this, and despite his rather minimal conclusions, the one that he does offer moves Jesus forward as a semiotic agent and thus provides a vital starting point for answers to our question.

According to Sanders, a good hypothesis about Jesus should situate him believably in Judaism, and yet be capable of explaining why the movement begun by him triggered persecution from the Jewish authorities and ultimately broke from Judaism itself.[7] He identifies Jesus' action in the Temple as the realistic core of such a hypothesis. He points to a coherent stream of thought in late-Second Temple Judaism anticipating a restored Temple. Jesus took up this theme and acted upon it, both preaching the existing Temple's destruction prior to something new, and doing something powerfully to signify it, thus bringing about his death.[8] It is inconceivable for Sanders that Jesus did not realize that interrupting the physical business of the Temple affronted not only the priestly authorities, but also Moses and the God who commanded Moses.[9] "A blow against the Temple, even if a physically minor one, was a blow against the basic religio-political entity, Israel."[10] In other words, this was an incredibly serious thing to do. Sanders stresses this also to argue for a coherence in Jesus' action and his teaching. According to Sanders,

---

which knowledge of Jesus of Nazareth as he really was will set us free" (Allison, *Historical Christ*, 7). There can be little doubt that Funk and many of those with him wished to be free of a Jesus story brokered by any ecclesial system, whether Evangelical or Catholic. But it's the very thing that is so easily dismissed as myth that has to be explained. The opening up by the Bible of an entirely new human meaning and history—one of radical nonviolence—demands a process rooted in human history.

6. McKnight, *Jesus and His Death*, 73.

7. Sanders, *Jesus and Judaism*, 5, 18.

8. Sanders, *Jesus and Judaism*, 305.

9. Sanders, *Jesus and Judaism*, 57.

10. Sanders, *Jesus and Judaism*, 296.

for Jesus just to wander into town and decide to sabotage the Temple is entirely implausible. If he did not have a coherent, intelligible teaching prior to the event, one actually forecasting the Temple's destruction, it would mean he literally did not know what he was doing.[11] Jesus must, therefore, have intended his action in Jerusalem as part of a connected, thought-out purpose and meaning.

Sander's thesis necessarily includes Jesus stopping the sacrifices, and it's worth underlining the point. He takes issue with the traditional viewpoint that Jesus' action was "cleansing the Temple," that he was engaged in a reformist expulsion of traders and money-changers who had introduced an over-mercenary, materialist aspect into spiritual matters.[12] He says, "In the view of Jesus and his contemporaries, the requirement to sacrifice must always have involved the supply of sacrificial animals, their inspection, and the changing of money . . . Just what would be left of the service if the supposedly corrupting externalism of sacrifices, and the trade necessary to them, were purged?"[13] The accent on the money and marketplace are in fact a result of the Gospels' *embarrassment* at the radicalism of the action, a smoke-screen for what is in fact a fearful cultural scandal.[14] Sanders restores Jesus' radicalism front and center, and very much implied in the scandal of this radicalism is that nobody would have made it up!

He points out that stopping the sacrifices had an implicit political dimension. Quoting Josephus, he shows how withholding sacrifice for the Roman nation and its emperor was the signal for the Judeo-Roman war in 66 CE: "This action laid the foundation of the war with the Romans."[15] Thus Jesus' action in the Temple was simultaneously a profound religious offense and a stark political risk. Sanders also underlines the symbolic character of Jesus' action. A continuous blocking of the sacrifices would have "required an army,"[16] but Jesus' action *signified* the same thing. It

---

11. Sanders, *Jesus and Judaism*, 58.

12. J. D. Crossan (with Funk a co-chair of the Jesus Seminar) maintains a version of this: Jesus carried through a symbolic destruction of the temple because it represented, in a single space, everything his egalitarian message in Galilee had fought against. But the action undoubtedly brought about his death. See Crossan, *Historical Jesus*, 357, and *Who Killed Jesus?*, 64–65.

13. Sanders, *Jesus and Judaism*, 63.

14. Sanders, *Jesus and Judaism*, 75.

15. Josephus, *Bellum Judaicum* II:408, quoted in Sanders, *Jesus and Judaism*, 64.

16. Hengel, *Was Jesus a Revolutionist?*, 16, quoted in Sanders, *Jesus and Judaism*, 70.

was sufficiently dramatic to brand itself in the memory of the tradition, despite embarrassment (cf. Mark 11, Matthew 21, John 2, and Acts 7, where Luke has transferred the drama), and it explains the decision by the high priests to kill Jesus with the co-operation of the Romans.[17] Sanders points out that his interpretation has the added advantage of explaining the early Jerusalem community's continued acceptance of Temple worship: they did not consider the Temple impure, only that an end had been set for it.[18] At the same time, it neatly provides a reason for the early persecution by the chief priests of the infant Christian movement (Acts 4–5). The priests had a sense that the embryonic movement, like its founder, threatened the Temple—tying together the primitive community and Jesus' symbolic destruction.[19]

Given such a clear concept of such a dramatic act on Jesus' part, it is curious that Sanders refuses any holistic or deeper understanding of Jesus' motivations. Yes, Jesus' action in the Temple was preparatory of a new age and a new Temple to be established from heaven.[20] But this appears in nearly a formal sense, without any clear continuum for Jesus with the main fabric of his Scriptures, nor, in parallel, with many of the traditions about Jesus in the Gospels. Neither is there a clear recognition of the fearfully violent repercussions the scenario carried. Stopping Temple sacrifice had truly apocalyptic consequence and if it was impossible that Jesus lacked a coherent teaching about his action, it seems equally implausible he had no sense of the cosmic powers he would unleash.

As already mentioned, even the New Testament is embarrassed about the Temple action. All the Gospels seem to highlight the commercial transactions, and Luke reduces the event to one verse, informing us emphatically it is about those "selling things there" (Luke 19:45). Sanders himself seems to suffer from this traditional malaise, albeit in a more subtle form. Even though he identifies the bedrock historical value of the Temple action, he fails to take in the enormity of his discovery. The shutting down of the sacrifices is a semiotic clue of rosetta-stone value, opening up the whole story of Jesus to a chain of meanings that tell us a

17. Sanders, *Jesus and Judaism*, 302–5.

18. Sanders, *Jesus and Judaism*, 76. It's also probable that many early Jerusalem Christians did not fully grasp the meaning of Jesus' action; it was the movement around Stephen which resonated most consciously with its significance and aftermath. See Hengel, *Between Jesus and Paul*, ch. 1.

19. Sanders, *Jesus and Judaism*, 285–86.

20. Sanders, *Jesus and Judaism*, 73.

vast amount about his program and the character of his work. The symbolic destruction of the Temple is not simply a goal-directed function,
preparatory—in Jesus' mind—to some alternative heaven-sent architecture. Rather, it provides for us a scientifically grounded *sign* around
which the meaning-value of Jesus can be seen forcefully to coalesce and
be disclosed. Divorced from this sign value—as in Sanders' treatment—it
remains interesting but finally inconsequential. Jesus can even appear as
a kind of Temple fetishist, when, in reality, the meaning of his act is to
transform the human condition as such. We can say this because to attack
the Temple and not have a *wider* spiritual, indeed apocalyptic strategy, is
unintelligible, and unintelligible within the context of Judaism.

Militant or Nonviolent?

The evidence of the sectarian community which produced the Dead Sea
Scrolls emphatically illustrates the point. These writings belong to Jesus'
cultural timeframe, straddling the last two centuries BCE and the first
century CE.[21] Among them is something called "The War Scroll" and its
link to the Temple is highly instructive. Following the unfolding drama
of the work we can see the intense violence associated with any kind of
Temple restoration. The scroll gives a description of the final military
struggle between the sons of light and the sons of darkness allied with the
army of Belial, the angel of darkness. There is a seven-stage battle involving men and angels, on both sides, and concluded by "the mighty hand of
God" striking down Belial and his host.[22] Directly after the victory there
is the establishment of a purified Temple and its worship. In sum, the goal
of the apocalyptic conflict is restoration of the Temple, and the latter does
not happen without the former.

The thing that Jesus does is to reverse the order, but the significant
connection would not have been lost on the Temple scribes and authorities. If in the religious imagination of an established sectarian group of

---

21. VanderKam and Flint, *Meaning of the Dead Sea Scrolls*, 20–32. The ruins at the
site known as Qumran, on the shores of the Dead Sea, are considered by most scholars
to be related to the community which produced the scrolls. The community is often
associated with the Essenes, a sect within Judaism well known in the ancient world for
their communal lifestyle, rejection of money, celibacy among some members, daily
immersions, and piety. The Roman historian, Pliny the elder, gave as their location a
place north of Ein Gedi on the Dead Sea (Pliny, *Natural History,* V:73).

22. Vermes, *Complete Dead Sea Scrolls,* 163–65.

Jesus' contemporaries, a truly reconstituted, purified Temple can only happen after a cosmic war, then any interruption of the Temple, if only symbolic, must at least invoke the cultural tremor of that war. In Girardian terms, any measures against the Temple would have to reckon with a generative crisis of violence to go with them. This was in fact the real-world conclusion that the chief priests and Pharisees in John's Gospel took from Jesus' general activity: "If we let him go on like this, everyone will believe in him, and the Romans will come and destroy both our holy place and our nation" (John 11:48). The Temple system constituted the bulwark against chaos, as important to the Romans as it is to the priests, and once it is undermined, the Romans must necessarily come to impose their own imperial, supremely violent version of sacrificial security.

This is an anthropological and semiotic analysis, but it is both coherent in itself and very hard to contradict in the actual history of first-century Judaism. As we know, within two generations after Jesus' death, a cataclysmic war broke out, bringing the actual destruction of the Temple and signaling, instead of a vindicated Israel, the glorious triumph of Rome.[23] There is a simmering crisis of violence building in the neural pathways of Judea at that time, and the Temple was at the center of it all.[24] The Temple story was one of an accumulating "sacrificial crisis," in the full Girardian sense. Any disruption of the present fragile order of the Temple would have signaled, however remotely, an avalanche of force, a signal no educated and politically sensitive Jewish observer would have missed or ignored.

In sum, if Jesus reversed the War Scroll sequence, that would do nothing to negate the crisis implied in the scene. The iron dust of the legions would have been just over the horizon. Matthew's Gospel has Jesus himself say in response to Peter's fiery sword-strike: "Are you not

23. Josephus calculates that 1.1 million people died in the siege of Jerusalem and 67,000 were carried off into slavery (Josephus, *Jewish War* VI:420). The *Arch of Titus*, still standing in Rome, graphically celebrates the Roman general's triumph with Temple treasures and captives.

24. The period from the death of Herod the Great in 4 BCE through until the first Roman-Jewish war (66–70 CE) was marked by roiling disturbance, what N. T. Wright calls "widespread disaffection and readiness to revolt in this period," including incidents of violent rebellion and corresponding Roman suppression (Wright, *New Testament and the People of God*, 171, 172–76). The Temple was the indispensable core and symbol of this national struggle. See, for example Philo's *Embassy to Gaius*, describing the intense reaction of the Jews—including mass civil disobedience—to the plan of the emperor Gaius to install a statue of himself as Jupiter in the Temple in Jerusalem (40 CE) (Philo, *Embassy to Gaius*, XXXII.225–42).

aware that I can call on my Father, and he will at once put at my disposal more than twelve legions of angels?" (Matt 26:53). This sort of expectation would have been part of the apocalyptic *zeitgeist* shared by John the Baptist, the Dead Sea sectarians, and others. "Twelve legions" is roughly double the size of the Roman force used to quell the Jewish revolt 66–70 CE, and Jesus' remark reflects the amount of force needed, on the Judean side, if in fact the issue were to be resolved by violence.

Of course, Jesus did not look at a violent outcome: he was working toward something very different, as we shall see. But the comment illustrates the amount of violence at stake as a result of his action. Just because Jesus did not bring an army with him does not mean that he did not know, no less than the sectarians, that in prophetically enacting the Temple's destruction, he was detonating an anthropological timebomb. If the sacrifices were suspended, that meant the war had already begun.

However, in addition to this we must at once point out a counter feature. If Jesus acted in any way in a spirit of militant defiance of the Temple, if his action contained any mimetic opposition toward it, then he would be caught in the same anthropological equation as the writers of the scroll. He would need those heavenly armies on his side to protect and vindicate him. Short of this, any ordinary human being, let alone someone of Jesus' prescience, would have instinctively feared to oppose the sacrifices in the Jerusalem Temple. The whole of archaic humanity, and one thousand years of intense Jewish religious history culminating in the present crisis of Roman occupation, would have risen up against him. They would say, "We are all that stands between you and horribly undifferentiated violence, and it will come down on you first!" Thus, if he were anything like the Essenes of Qumran he would have retired to the Mount of Olives and watched the sky quietly but eagerly for the armed hosts arriving on his side. *Instead* Jesus meekly submits to his arrest and death, and finds meaning in this course of events, not in any kind of apocalyptic showdown. This, in itself, necessarily suggests a profoundly conceived attitude and program.

As regards the evangelists, the apparently effortless way in which the synoptic gospels slide the Temple event into the story of Jesus' final period in Jerusalem not only masks its intensely provocative nature, but also suggests that it carried no overtone of violent revolt, no sense that here was a militant rebellion against the Temple and its authorities. Rather, again, it has the feeling of a planned sequence of action within an overall program of nonviolent surrender. It is, thus, a *sign*, an enacted parable, not any kind of reciprocal attack. The Temple authorities understood the sign within *their* overall generative anthropology and reacted accordingly. But the sign stands for itself and grows steadily in stature and power. It belongs to an entirely different *nonviolent* project going on in Jesus, one that makes it both possible and intelligible.

We know this, not just because it is what the gospels present, but because the movement resulting from him never hinted at armed insurrection. As many have pointed out, the Romans did not arrest any of the followers of Jesus, indicating they did not see them as a threat. And, as just indicated, the very act which prompted Jesus' execution, and about which the gospels are embarrassed, left no trace of anger with the Temple itself among the very first community in Jerusalem. We have, therefore, to conclude that Jesus' action—despite its apocalyptic profile and fatal consequences for himself—left no residue of violence among his immediate followers. The act was apocalyptic in meaning, but it did not view the Temple in a sectarian way as impure or hateful. Indeed, Jesus agrees with its role as "a house of prayer" (Mark 11:17). So, the act was apocalyptic in meaning, but non-sectarian and nonviolent in spirit. It is vital to get this distinction, otherwise Jesus' act does not truly displace the Temple, only creates another one on the basis of a new round of violence.

Semiotic Portal

Thus, the action in the Temple was carried through with a profound authority of *nonviolence*—a distinctive sensibility which incurred immense danger from the authorities, but did nothing to provoke or render militant either the crowds or his followers. Such an attitude is consistent and continuous with a willingness to suffer and not retaliate—i.e., the cross. If Jesus was not simply stupid about what he did, he knew the consequences that would come for him, and he already knew he would pay them. *And by that token the content of what he did already implied the cross*: it tells us that he *already embodied an alternative mode of humanity which subverted sacrifice and replaced it with nonviolent life, forgiveness, and love.* This can only be seen fully and clearly by tracing a line forward to the cross, and then back again. The anthropological disruption of the action in the Temple is only anthropologically intelligible through the cross.

This is an historical, anthropological, and semiotic argument and through it we reach a point where we can tie together two crucial aspects, the *historical* and the *transformative*. It is this that creates the very peculiar dynamic attached to Jesus where meaning seems in excess of what we can positively derive from history. Where Jesus as icon seems completely to outstrip historical possibility. It is because of this excess that a broad strand of German scholarship concluded that the gospels must be myth. But—turning the thing on its head—it is the very character of this dynamic which demands that the history be, in fact, something very close to what is described in the New Testament! The human transformation depends on it. This will continue to become clearer as we go ahead, but, at the moment, we underline again that the history of very early Christianity is a logically consistent spillover from the anthropology of Jesus' Temple action. Both the shock *and* the nonviolence of the event connect intimately with the cross, and the whole thing provides the historiographical bedrock of the primitive movement. First, as already underlined, the early Jerusalem community did not see the Temple as something to be opposed in a sectarian or separatist way; but then, subsequently, there was enough charismatic authority in Jesus' action to expose a profound fissure between the movement and the Temple, culminating in the events around Stephen (Acts 7). Effectively, Jesus had announced the end of the Temple but without detonating sectarian "apocalyptic" violence, rather bringing that violence down on himself. Jesus consumed the "cup of wrath" not as any kind of appeasement, but—as the image more radically suggests—to drain violence from human history.

I will claim, therefore, the "thorough-going nonviolence" of Jesus' Temple action, both in its inherent content and experienced manner. It makes sense of the evidence and establishes a crucial interpretive arc between Temple and cross. With this arch, I believe we have come to the solid historical portal for the semiotic explosion that is the gospel. There is also, of course, the resurrection to take into view, a third element creating a triad; but, consistently, this has to be seen as semiotically continuous with what went before, the shutting down of the Temple and then the cross. The resurrection accomplishes the transcendence of nonviolence and *per se* this is a world-making event, the kind which leaves the disciples in Mark terror-struck before the second genesis it offers. The tomb was genuinely empty of its corpse, and the sense of that was a qualitative novum which for the disciples did not collapse into a perverse sense of conspiracy. This is crucial: the initial mindset of the disciples had to be that of the normal intended impact of crucifixion—abjection and despair: otherwise, why would this brutal instrument be employed at all by the Romans?[25] For this condition to translate into an eruption of relationship, of forgiveness, and of nonviolence is historically unfathomable, short of a real physical event of overcoming death. And yet this is still semiotic: it is something that happened to the disciples, in the fabric of their minds and hearts. The subsequent appearances play this transformation out in recognizable language of physical encounters, but what really counts is the transformation of the root humanity of the witnesses, something that made them into a different kind of people, something which could in turn be passed on to others. Thus, the resurrection *means* the breakthrough of a nonviolent God into the human system, where the portal represented by the arch first made that possible. The arch provided the radical opening for the abyssal love of the Father/Mother to enter seamlessly into the human system.

It is important again to underline the twin aspect—of history and transformation—but now from a theological perspective. First, the historical basis for the semiotic explosion of the Gospels, and then the same space as the space of transformation where the nonviolent God breaks through into history. The first is an historical source for the extraordinary iconicity of Jesus. The second is grounds for development of metaphysical doctrine about Jesus. Ultimately, however, we are looking at the same semiotic root for the emergence of both possibilities. Understanding things this way, we have perhaps arrived at "the semiotic Jesus." In a way, he would be the same as Dale Allison's "theological Jesus." Allison argues that the Jesus of the Gospels is already a theological creation, but that does not mean that the actual Jesus of history did not have a hand in creating the theology! Only, that it is very hard to pull the two things apart. He comments that in the discourses of John—almost universally recognized as post-Jesus theological constructs—Jesus, nevertheless, "remains a real presence."[26] Even so, the semiotic Jesus produces a "real presence," but in a very much more urgent and dynamic manner, one that does not simply depend on an end-of-the-day opinion of a New Testament scholar, soon to be replaced later by another's. As I argued in *TBM*, a sign both subsists within and produces an *ontological relation*;[27] even so, the semiotic Jesus of the Gospels produces "a real relation," one that continues to resound through history. It is because of him especially that the victim has been

25. See Hengel, *Atonement*, for multiple references to the horror which crucifixion inspired.

26. Allison, *Historical Christ*, 29.

27. Bartlett, *TBM*, 109–11, 116–17, 132–33.

revealed and behind the victim a nonviolent transcendence, and these are the crux of his semiotic identity. We can reach out and touch him, and that is because the semiotic portal of the Temple and the cross infuses a dramatic new truth into our world. *It produces (leads forth) its own reality.*

There follows here some further strategic account of Jesus from the gospels fitting this semiotic understanding, and continuing to fill in a picture consistent with the through-going nonviolence of the Temple action.

John the Baptist

Mentor and Master

A man appears, in the wilderness! That's a good enough beginning to any story.

But famously, it is the beginning of the gospel, the good news.

Where this man got his inspiration from nobody knows. He could have spent time in the Essene community which was, as we have seen, likely located at the site known as Qumran. This is only eight or nine miles off the Jericho road, and appearing "in the wilderness" close to the river Jordan puts him conceivably no more than a day's hike from this location.

But the Baptist had none of the sectarianism of this group. None of the apparent obsessive need to separate itself from what is wicked and impure. This man had another solution, no less radical, but one of startling originality and creativity. Instead of separating himself *in* the land, in a far-off, inhospitable corner, he made use of the land itself, grabbing hold of it and using it as a symbol of itself and everything it stood for. He used the land as a duplicate—a representation and icon—of its own biblical history, starting at and in the river Jordan.

John the Baptist was the first semiotic revolutionary, a worthy forerunner of Gandhi's salt march protest. He changed the character of his environment by calling attention to it directly and dramatically. He subverted the meaning of things dictated by the powerful, by the elite who claimed to speak for everyone else. He is the mentor and teacher of the semiotic Jesus, and it is no accident that the story of Jesus begins with him.

John "baptizes" at the river Jordan, practicing a "baptism of repentance" (Acts 19:4). The Temple in Jerusalem had institutional requirement of washings needed for priestly Temple purity. Archeology tells us that there were numerous ritual baths (*miqvaot*) in Jerusalem during the Herodian period.[28] The Pharisees according to Mark (7:2ff) practiced extra washings, aiming, it seems, at a priestly level of purity in daily life. Sanders attributes this to the *haberim*—a group known from the Mishna which practiced regular eating together with strict rules. There was overlap between these and the Pharisees.[29] The community at Qumran appear to have evolved a sophisticated method of water collection essential for survival at this desolate site, but thought also by many to supply ritual baths for community practice of purity.[30] All this is a way of saying that purification was a prevalent concern in the time of the Baptist, and John's "water bath" in the Jordan clearly held that connotation. But the Jordan is much more than a convenient supply of running water.

If we associate John's practice with the words describing him in all four Gospels ("a voice in the wilderness . . . prepare the way of the Lord," Isa 40:3), we see that his ministry is connected to the return of God to Zion bringing the exiles with him. The theme is considered by N. T. Wright to be a major feature of Jesus' program: the sixth-century prophecy is not yet effective—there is need for a full and final realization of God and the exiles' return.[31] To my mind, John seems to anticipate some version of this perspective by his geographical choice. Returning from exile in Mesopotamia would involve (at least mentally) crossing the line of the Jordan at some point. For John to bring people out to a desolate spot by the river could not help but evoke the original entry to land across Israel's national river, and, after that, the more recent return from Babylon. John's "baptism of repentance" worked at multiple levels. The water was cleansing, but this water also meant the land, its gift by God to the people, and subsequently a fraught history in which God took the land away because of sin and gave it back again in an experience of renewed relationship. To be baptized in the Jordan was to be immersed in that whole story of Israel and to emerge in a dramatically new realization of its truth and meaning. No wonder "all Judea" went out to John, and no wonder the Temple authorities viewed him with suspicion and rejection (Matt 21:23–27). To a large degree, he rendered them irrelevant, if not roundly condemned.

28. Sanders, *Jesus and Judaism*, 184.

29. Sanders, *Jesus and Judaism*, 187.

30. Galor, "Plastered Pools," 291–320, especially 317.

31. Wright, *Jesus and the Victory of God*, multiple index entries, especially 613–31.

Jesus' relationship with John was profound and irreplaceable. As everyone knows, he was baptized by John—or, rather, he entered John's semiotic revolution—in the waters of the Jordan. What is less recognized is that Jesus was initially a disciple of John and John was his mentor.[32] The Gospel of John shows this clearly, with Jesus practicing a ministry of baptism alongside John (John 3:22–23). What then happened? There was obviously some kind of break, and it seems more and more evidently to be over the issue of divine violence. The fact that his has not been generally acknowledged is witness to the generative power of violence itself, controlling human discourse against all-comers. In this standard perspective, Jesus is the "Son of God" and so of course he had to have his own privileged ministry. Any real disagreement as to the nature of God in respect to violence is completely occluded. But the evidence is substantial.

Galilean Semiotics, Different from John's

Jesus leaves the Jordan and sets up his headquarters next to the Sea of Galilee. More water! The Sea of Galilee is remarkable for being so prominent in the Gospels and playing virtually no part in the Old Testament. This corresponds to the nature of the Hebrews/Israelites as a smallholder people, for whom land was paramount. Jesus abandons the Jordan and with that he abandons the national land reference of Israel. Why were his first disciples fishermen? It has to be because they made their living on the waters in complete difference from the ideal Israelite who lives "beneath his vine and fig tree" (Mic 4:4). Simon, Andrew, James, and John were economically insecure, disinherited Israelites whose occupation as fishermen obliged them to set sail on the alien deep where storms and malign forces threatened. In Jesus' choice of the deeps of Galilee as his base, we cannot avoid the sign-value that had been built up to in the Hebrew Scriptures regarding the sea. Not only was there Canaanite mythology about primeval battles of gods and sea-monsters represented in Scripture (Isa 27:1, 51:9–10; Job 26:12; Ps 74:14), by the time of Jesus there is also the powerful imagery of the books of Jonah and Daniel. The sea is that place where primordial violence is kept at bay, but able to break out in fearful dreams and visions, which are again representative

32. The most extensive treatment is Meier, *Marginal Jew*, vol. II: *Mentor, Message, and Miracles.*

of actual historical (imperial) violence. Ultimately, however, the sea and its monsters will submit to God's sovereign nonviolence. Jesus, with his invocation of the "sign of Jonah," was clearly cognizant of the sea's semiotic value (more on this below). By moving the center of his ministry to the shore of the sea of Galilee, Jesus announced in easily decipherable code that he was not simply about calling Israel to repentance: he was announcing his engagement with both "natural" and deep anthropogenic violence.

Jesus' actual verbal commentary on John confirms this is the reason he broke with his mentor. In a sustained discourse, represented in both Luke and Matthew, Jesus is seen reflecting on what John means to him (Luke 7:24–3; Matt 11:7–19). This is the only instance in the Gospels where Jesus speaks at length about a contemporary, let alone in such laudatory terms. It is clear that Jesus' relationship with John is pivotal. The immediate context is the arrival of messengers sent from John to inquire, "Are you the one who is to come, or are we to wait for another?" (Luke 7:19). John is in prison and the question is fraught with both apocalyptic and personal anxiety. It suggests that John had placed his faith in Jesus in respect of some expected scenario but is now seriously doubting that Jesus was the figure he thought he was. Part of Jesus' response, "Blessed is anyone who takes no offense at me" (Luke 7:23), strongly implies that John was indeed offended at Jesus.

The phrase "the one who is to come" is often understood in a default Christian manner as "the expected Messiah/Christ." But it's important to know that an "expected Messiah" was just one of the scenarios of how God could intervene in the current crisis of Jerusalem and Judea, and not a terribly plausible one, as it normally implied an actual Davidic military king who would be able to lead a successful attack against the Romans. Much more attractive was the scene, presented in the prophecy of Malachi, of "the day [of the Lord] . . . burning like an oven, when all the arrogant and all evildoers will be stubble; the day that comes shall burn them up . . ." (Mal 4:1). It is the unleashing of direct divine power, against which even the might of Rome must quail. A core part of Malachi's prophecy was the coming of a "messenger" ("indeed he is coming," 3:1), to prepare the way, a figure who is subsequently identified with Elijah. "Lo, I will send you the prophet Elijah before the great and terrible day of the Lord" (Mal 4:5). It is this prophecy which much more likely lies behind John's unhappy question. The crucial role of the Elijah figure is underlined in Jesus' conversation with his disciples at Matt 17:10–13, where the "coming" Elijah is plainly identified by Jesus to be John the Baptist himself! It seems pretty clear that John's thought was the converse, where he saw Jesus as Elijah, and was then severely disappointed that Jesus did not show Elijah-like characteristics.

Elijah did not suffer opposition meekly. He is famous for ordering the slaughter of the prophets of Baal, after summoning heavenly fire on his holocausts. Also, gratuitously calling down fire on two companies of soldiers sent to be his escort to the king (2 Kgs 1:9–12). Fire is his weapon of choice and seems reason enough for his association with a day of the Lord as intense conflagration. John references the same kind of fiery future in his own prophecy (Matt 3:7–12). Thus, the coming Elijah scenario is by far the most plausible understanding of John's words, and it is one that Jesus rebuts with his very different version of the way of the Lord in the world. "Go and tell John what you have seen and heard: the blind receive their sight, the lame walk, the lepers are cleansed, the deaf hear, the dead are raised, the poor have good news brought to them" (Luke 7:22). It would be hard to imagine a more contrasting to-do-list to the threatened one of burning. All of Jesus' list is drawn from biblical prophecy, especially Isaiah (26:19, 42:7, 61:1), and it amounts to a diametrically alternative biblical code to John's tropes of fiery divine intervention. In which case, we must understand Jesus as having made a profoundly different judgment as to the nature of God's return to Zion. If John was preparing for a day of conflagration of enemies, Jesus was to bear their assaults with forgiveness.

In the Matthew version of Jesus' discourse on John he directly addresses the issue of violence. These words have never been highlighted in general pastoral preaching, but they are central to understanding how Jesus saw his own ministry and its meaning in regard to this decisive issue. Jesus says, "Truly I tell you, among those born of women no one has arisen greater than John the Baptist; yet the least in the kingdom of heaven is greater than he. From the days of John the Baptist until now the kingdom of heaven has suffered violence, and the violent take it by force. For all the prophets and law prophesied until John came; and if you are willing to accept it, he is Elijah who is to come" (Matt 11:11–14).

There is the straightforward identification of John with Elijah, setting up the remarks in Matt 17:10–13 already mentioned. This could itself be part of Jesus' strategy which emerges clearly as one drawing a line-in-the-sand between himself and John. The distinction between the "greatest" of those born of women and "the least in the kingdom" is startling, and in its doubly paradoxical character (born of women/of the kingdom, greatest/least) seems to reflect Jesus' distinctive style of discourse, his *ipsissima verba*. In short, John represents something of incredible stature in the world before the announcement of the kingdom made by Jesus. But once that announcement is made, all previous world evaluations are null and void. A qualitatively new way of being human had entered history and commenced its revolutionary effect. What was it?

The only explanatory remark is verses 12 through to 14. Verse 12 sets out a timeframe: "from the days of John the Baptist until now . . ." and "violence" is the crucial feature which governs everything in this frame. Thus, from the days of John the kingdom of heaven has been subjected to violence, or, has "been violated." There is a possible alternative translation from the Greek—"has come or worked violently"—but it does not matter because it still has violence as the pivotal agency which governs the days of John. The following phrase—"and the violent take it by force"—can go with both translations, but either way it makes plain that "those who are violent" are taking over or hijacking God's kingdom and its meaning. This is the key. Violence as a theme and activity violates the kingdom. It possesses the kingdom in a way that is alien to the kingdom itself. The rest of the passage goes on pointedly to underline the continuity of meaning between John and the law and the prophets, also naming John as the "Elijah who is to come." Jesus has drawn a seismic distinction between his preaching and John, and much too of the tradition before him. In the substantive context of the Baptist—his preaching, his identification with Elijah, his doubts about Jesus, and his distinction from the kingdom—there can be little doubt Jesus is here indicating violence as the core phenomenon which separates him from the Baptist. As far as Jesus is concerned, John hijacked the kingdom with his violent apocalyptic!

This is an immense critical point. The Gospels cannot help but accord great respect to John, something which must initially stem from Jesus. They recognize and repeat this respect and yet there is a jarring note in it. The baptism narratives in Mark, Matthew, and Luke are testimony to John's irreplaceable role in the Jesus story and at the same time, they mark a qualitative distinction, via the descent of the Holy Spirit. The effort to mark a distinction continues—even more insistently—in John's Gospel. The Baptist is not shown physically to baptize Jesus, but to witness to him as "lamb of God" and "Son of God" (1:26–34), and later as Israel's bridegroom and "the one who comes from heaven" (3:29–31). John says, "He must increase but I must decrease" (3:30). There is evident need to continue pointing out and naming where Jesus differed from and transcended the program of the Baptist. If Jesus was, at one time, a disciple of John's, how could it turn out that he was different and, indeed, greater? It seems to me that this would have been a serious objection on the part of those remaining within the Judean/Palestinian context and who awaited the coming of Elijah and its associated hope for purification and deliverance. They would not have understood how Jesus improved on John. Even if Jesus was personally raised from the dead, this did not right the wrongs of the world—the Romans were still very much in charge!

Thus, the problem about accepting Jesus is the radically changed code he offered—forgiveness and nonviolence, and each entirely coincident with the other. This changed coding had to be experienced either through a personal loyalty to him, as with his personally recruited disciples, or through the dramatic reorientation and new affect experienced and named as "Holy Spirit." Anyone still within the mind-frame of a vengeful Elijah apocalyptic could not have "gotten" Jesus. In many ways, therefore, militant hold-out disciples of the Baptist after his death seem much more honest than a broad continuum of Christians who think they believe in Jesus and yet do not recognize the profoundly changed human coding he offered in respect of violence. This is a problem of inherited religio-institutional Christianity. The advantage we have today, however, is that we are able to name *semiotically* what in New Testament times could only be marked "spiritually." I underline at once that I am by no means denying the truth of the Holy Spirit, either in Christian experience or doctrine. I am stating that both experience and doctrine have a human substrate (a semiosis) which is encoded by Jesus' definitive witness of nonviolence. All that is necessary is to understand that the Baptist represents a true crossroads for Jesus, one that Jesus navigated in an irreversible way. We are able today to name that crossroads accurately because the long permeation of humanity by the revolutionary coding of the Gospels has finally thrown up *violence* as its most radical question. We are therefore able systematically to name Jesus' break from John perhaps for the first time.

The figure of John the Baptist stands in the Gospels both as the "forerunner" of Jesus and his disappointed mentor. As the one who opened the way for him semiotically, and yet became in the end scandalized by the signs Jesus gave. Jesus began as his disciple, without doubt, but ultimately journeyed far beyond his teacher, plunging into depths much deeper and wider than the Jordan. As deep and wide in fact as the figure of humanity itself. This leads us directly to another key Jesus motif, enabling us to trace his transforming semiosis.

The Jonah Journey

Meaning of the Jonah Saying

We can never know for sure what provoked Jesus' fateful decision to go to Jerusalem. Was it planned right from the beginning? Was it something that arose slowly in his thoughts? Or was there something in particular that happened, something which forced his hand? The parables of growth and metamorphosis that he seems to preach early in his ministry give a sense of joyful inevitability (see, for example, Mark 4). There is no hint of a need to suffer. Why, if the harvest is bound to come, would Jesus decide that he had to go to the Temple and shut down the sacrifices—if only symbolically—and thus incur the certain fate of arrest and capital charges? Is this not a very different scenario from the wondrous work of yeast effortlessly transforming the dough (Matt 13:33)? The questions seem irresolvable, unless perhaps there is another sign or parable (Hebrew *mashal*) governing Jesus' perceptions and actions, one that would work somehow in parallel to the tropes of seed, leaven, and growth.

As explained earlier, Jesus' initial choice of setting for his ministry—the sea of Galilee—is undoubtedly deliberate and is its own kind of *mashal*, in a life littered with parables spoken and enacted. In Mark, Jesus' goings back and forth over the lake continue to be referenced and end up gripping the reader's attention. Up to chapter 8 and the shift away from Galilee, there are seventeen references to "sea" with geographical meaning, plus frequent independent instances of "getting into the boat" for a journey, together with several parallel mentions of crossing over "to the other side." The sensation of constant crisscrossing the lake works in tandem with traditions of Jesus' strange affinity for the waters and his uncanny power over them (miracles of fish, calming the waves etc.). If Mark is the first written of the synoptics, providing their narrative template, we have to ask what was it about this role of water that so powerfully frames his narrative movement? The evangelist gives no explanation but appears on the surface simply to include the lake as a semi-theatrical device bringing staging and unity to the story. But the framing of the lake is at once so central and thematically urgent it cannot help but demonstrate a dramatic intention, either in Mark's sources or going back to Jesus himself. It seems to me that the easiest and most coherent explanation is the one suggested: Jesus deliberately chose the lake as a *mashal* in his overall ministry, signifying that he was bringing peace and nonviolence to the violent depths of human existence. This would then work as a parallel theme to the one of natural growth, a minor chord, so to speak, but ultimately rising as the *leitmotif* of the whole story. It also seems plain that Jesus got much of his scriptural warrant from the Book of Jonah. If we track the references to Jonah in the Gospels, we can see how this deeper theme was always present, and one day it would bring Jesus to direct confrontation with violent anthropology—in the figures of the Temple and the Roman occupation.

The name "Jonah" does not appear in Mark's Gospel. But there are vivid textual echoes of the Old Testament book, and specifically in relation to a wild tempest at sea. At the end of chapter 4, after the segment on parables of growth, Jesus says "Let us go across to the other side" (4:35). Then "A great windstorm arose, and the waves beat into the boat, so that the boat was already being swamped" (4:37). This follows the selfsame pattern of the *mise en scène* of Jonah: "The Lord hurled a great wind on the sea and there was a great storm on the sea, so that the ship was about to break up" (Jonah 1:4 NASB). There follows a direct superimposition of images of Jonah and Jesus: Jonah is asleep in the hold of the ship (1:5)— Jesus is asleep in the stern (Mark 4:38); the captain upbraids Jonah, demanding that he "call upon (his) God . . . so that we may not perish" (Jonah 1:6)—the disciples show the same reaction, down to using the very same verb: "Teacher, do you not care that we are perishing?" (Mark 4:38, Greek *apollumetha*, "we perish"; in LXX, *apolōmetha*). Finally, calm returns, in the one case because Jonah is thrown into the deep, in the other because Jesus commands peace to the waves. The sailors and disciples both experience a transcendent awe, in near identical language— they fear with a great fear (Jonah 1:16 LXX, *ephobēthēsan phobō megalō*; Mark 4:41, *ephobēthēsan phobon megan*).

How did Jonah get superimposed on Jesus? Is it one of those instances of "taking the prophecy and making a history"? If it is, it is a very strange one. What benefit is there in comparing Jesus with Jonah, a disreputable figure who was running away from his God? If it is a deeper matter of seeing Jesus as a Jonah-style undoing of cosmic violence, then it is a totally remarkable insight, one that seems nowhere else explicitly recognized or represented in the New Testament. (If Matthew and Luke used Mark in the composition of their Gospels, then they played the whole parallel down: their accounts are substantially shorter, omitting tell-tale details.) Maybe the author of Mark constructed the teaching but only gave it allusively. But it is very difficult to understand the value of such a shadowy, indirect outline. Much easier, I think, to see the episode as going back to the very first levels of the Jesus tradition, meaning that Jesus directly associated himself with Jonah and did so as an interpretative key. And eventually this got "reported" in the story of the calming of the sea.[33] In which case, it may in fact be seen as part of the deeper core of Jesus' ministry, one that dramatically counters worldly violence, including implied reference to imperial Roman violence. Considerably strengthening the overall possibility is Jesus' saying of "the sign of Jonah."

The saying is not present in Mark, but in Matthew and Luke (Matt 12:38–42; Luke 11:29–32). Jesus' words come in response to the request for "a sign," a direct request by the scribes and Pharisees in Matthew, and in Luke reflected by Jesus as a general demand of the present "evil generation." A "sign" in this context would mean something along the lines of Elijah's violent miracle of lighting his sacrifices with fire from heaven after having soaked the wood in water. The contagious consequence is the slaughter of the prophets of Baal after their inability to replicate the show of firepower. The return of Elijah discussed in the segment on John the Baptist would have put this kind of sign very much in the air around a commanding figure like Jesus. However, on the contrary, Jesus insists "no sign will be given except the sign of Jonah." But the different ways that Matthew and Luke parse the sign tell us that that there was no clear understanding of what that reference meant. Matthew gives us a literal read-out, obviously coming from the post-Easter Jesus community. "For just as Jonah was three days and three nights in the belly of the sea monster, so for three days and three nights the Son of Man will be in the heart of the earth" (Matt 12:40). Luke is more vague, and perhaps nearer the

33. Properly to understand this passage in Mark we have to add its direct sequel, the bringing of peace to the Gerasene demoniac (5:1–21). There is an emotional, literary, and hermeneutic continuity between the two episodes. The Gerasene demoniac is effectively the city of Nineveh liberated from its violence. His name is "Legion," glossed as "many," to avoid an obvious anti-Rome connotation, but unmistakably in the context of the time it means the mob-like-but-organized supreme military tool of Roman empire. Mark reveals himself as fully deliberate about the emotional, interpretive connection because of the way the episodes are framed and sutured by the continual presence of the sea (the storm, crossing the sea, getting out of the boat, the swine entering the sea, Jesus getting into the boat and crossing back again). The demoniac and his terrifying internalized violence act as an anthropological abyss and substitute for the systemic violence of the Roman empire in first-century Levant.

truth, telling us that Jonah's sign-value to the Ninevites is a cipher for the Son of Man's sign-value to the present generation (Luke 11:30).

The question is further muddied by the saying of the sign being attached to a separate logion about the "something greater" than Solomon or Jonah. The alternative linking verses in Matthew and Luke ("three days and three nights in the belly of the sea monster" and "Jonah/Nineveh—the Son of Man/this generation") are an obvious suture to the following independent saying whose verbal subjects are not Jonah, but "the queen of the south" and "the people of Nineveh." Nonetheless, the fact that Jonah is evoked so powerfully, in parallel to Solomon, as a model of Jesus' identity tells us quite a bit about the "sign." Solomon is a paragon of Wisdom and to be "greater" must surely invoke the identity of Wisdom herself. What then is Jonah a paragon of, and what does he tell us in a parabolic way about the identity of Jesus? Once we put aside Jonah's curmudgeonly attitude, we see that he is a prophet who comes from afar to confront the depths of anthropo-cosmic violence, who is delivered by God from those depths, and in the power of that deliverance proceeds (scandalously) to turn the very worst, imperial offenders from their violence. But if Jesus is saying that he will be a sign like Jonah to "*this* generation," he is telling his audience that he will in fact represent the meaning "Jonah" to his Jewish brothers and sisters, not just to some hostile foreign power!

The sign of Jonah is mentioned one other time in Matthew's Gospel. At 16:1, we have a passage that repeats Mark 8:11. The episode takes place following the feeding of the four thousand, but Matthew has stripped away mention of the boat and "the other side." Mark's Gospel does not mention the sign of Jonah. It is thought by scholars that Mark removed it because of his concern to maintain the sense of a "messianic secret" of Jesus in the face of the world.[34] But I think Mark in fact has his own version of the sign, in the enigmatic way his gospel is written. Jesus is asked for a sign "to test him" (Mark 8:11), where testing means to put someone under stress in order to break their equanimity, to make them retaliate in mimetic terms. Indeed, part of the meaning of the "secret" is, I believe, Mark's conscious desire to prevent the gospel falling prey to this mimetic interference, to point rather to a "hidden" gospel zone of peace and transformation which is the experience of God's kingdom. It is Jesus, of course, who makes this possible. In Mark's version, Jesus does not cite Jonah, but "he sighed deeply in his spirit," saying "no sign will be given

34. See Witherington, *Christology of Jesus*, 168.

to this generation" (8:12). He then got into the boat again, and "went across to the other side" (8:13). Without mentioning Jonah, we see Jesus entering the abyss of the human situation "in his spirit," and then once more embarking in the boat as a *mashal* of the Jonah journey to the heart of the human tempest.

Thus, the Gospel of Mark demonstrates its acute awareness of what Jesus is doing to transform the human situation. At the same time, it recognizes how dangerous and conflictual the attempt is, first in terms of interpersonal mimesis, and ultimately as a threat to the messenger's own personal safety and very life.

The Way to the Temple

For if Jesus is embarking on the Jonah journey in a deliberate fashion, he must at some point head toward Jerusalem and its institutions of violent power. He must open up the Jonah abyss under the very rock of human security on which the nation is based in contradiction to the will of his Father. He will do so as Wisdom-in-person (as the Solomon comparison implied), which means assuming her role in the Temple: "In the holy tent [where in the beginning] I ministered before him, and . . . was established in Zion" (Sir 24:10). This is where the showdown will be, the climactic confrontation which will both establish Jesus' Wisdom authority and bring his precipitate death. In the same way, and by the same token, he will go to the same place as Jonah: Sheol, the scene of destruction and death. He will enter it in a terrifying, palpable way, but from there God will rescue him.

Jonah's psalm or prayer from the belly of the fish stands in tension to the ironic narrative around it, but it contains vital information. The psalm seems to break the storyline, for it tells of a repentant and pious Jonah crying out to God for help. Despite the dissonance, the prayer serves to hinge everything, leading directly to God's startling act of deliverance, getting the fish to vomit Jonah out on the land (Jonah 2:10):

> Out of the belly of Sheol I cried, and you heard my voice. You cast me into the deep, into the heart of the seas, and the flood surrounded me . . . Then I said, 'I am driven away from your sight; how shall I look again upon your holy Temple? . . . The waters closed in over me; the deep surrounded me . . . As my life was ebbing away, I remembered the Lord, and my prayer came to you, into your holy Temple. (Jonah 2:2-7)

The destination of Jonah's prayer is the Jerusalem Temple, and so the arc of salvation appears between Sheol and the Temple. But what kind of Temple is it? If there is one point of self-recognition and repentance in the psalm it comes at 2:8. The verse is often translated along the lines of "Those who worship vain idols forsake their true loyalty," which suggests Jonah is preserving his hostility toward the foreigners with their idols. But it can also be rendered: "Those who hold on to lying vanities forsake their true loyalty." (See the JPS Tanakh 1917: "They that regard lying vanities forsake their own mercy.") This could favor a reading where Jonah comes to see his nationalist violence as empty and meaningless and counter to divine faithfulness/mercy. Jonah's subsequent words then break open a dramatically different sense of Temple: "But I with the voice of thanksgiving will sacrifice to you, what I have vowed I will pay: Deliverance belongs to the Lord!"

"With the voice of thanksgiving" is instrumental—meaning that this is how he will sacrifice, not with animals' blood. He will pay what he has vowed, and the implication of the direct exclamation or testimony bursting through is that *this* in fact is how he will pay—by heartfelt proclamation of Yahweh's salvation.

We are drawing close once more to Jesus' action in the Temple. Jonah's story points Jesus toward the Temple, and it does so, if only allusively, in non-sacrificial terms. We will come again to the deep radicalism of Jesus' action in the next segment, but before we do, we need to look back once more to the theme of Sheol. At Luke 10:13–15 (parallel to Matt 11:20–24), Jesus denounces the Galilean lake towns Chorazin, Bethsaida, and Capernaum, for lack of belief. He says in respect of Capernaum, "Will you be exalted to heaven? No, you will be brought down to Hades [Sheol]" (Luke 10:15). Why should Jesus pick on these lakeshore towns when he is reported as ministering throughout Galilee (Mark 1:39)? What he says of Capernaum in particular, reminds us of Jonah cast into the deep, into the belly of Sheol. It appears again, therefore, that the setting of the lake is for Jesus a mirror of the Jonah story, and when he is forecasting judgment on these places, he is forecasting for them a Jonah-style reckoning.

Later, and most strikingly, this seems also to be the fate forecast for Zion and the Temple Mount. In Mark's Gospel, Jesus' makes his way to the Temple, coming from Bethany. On the way, he seeks fruit from a fig tree. Finding none, he says, "May no one ever eat fruit from you again" (Mark 11:14). He then proceeds to the Temple to stop the sacrifices and later that night, leaves the city. On the following day, he and the disciples return to Jerusalem once more, looking toward the Temple Mount as they go. They find the fig tree withered. Peter remarks on what has happened, and Jesus replies, "Have faith in God. Truly I tell you, if you say to this mountain, 'Be taken up and thrown into the sea,' and if you do not doubt in your heart, but believe that what you say will come to pass, it will be done for you" (Mark 11:22–23). These words have often been taken as a challenge to faith as a quasi-magical faculty, literally able "to move mountains." Even the evangelist seems to take it this way. But why would Jesus say something so outlandish and apparently irrelevant to the pivotal drama that has just taken place in the Temple the day before? It is much more intelligible to hear him referring exactly to this event, using the withering of the fig tree as a parable of what will now happen to the Temple and its sacrificial order. We should see him gesturing toward the Temple Mount as he says these words, describing its being cast in the Jonah abyss, the same terminus predicted for the lakeshore towns which had refused his message. The faith required is not some type of religious straining of the mind until we are able to transfer any old outcrop of rock and dirt into the ocean. Rather, it is staying faithful to a God of infinite nonviolence while the human institutions which rely on violence for their being are rendered transparent, and thus—like Jonah—opened to an entirely new and transforming way.

Jesus' "No sign will be given to you except the sign of Jonah" has to be read, therefore, as a comprehensive reference to the whole of the book. "Jonah" is to be understood as a spiritual-cosmic road map both to Jesus' own destiny and that of the world. Jesus would go first, but the world will follow, or, rather, be brought there with him. The end goal was always God's deliverance, the shout of salvation for everyone and everything. The sign, or we could say the code's final, holistic meaning is the plunging of all humanity into the depths of its own existence, where it may recognize its congenital violence and turn at the very last to be healed.

Jerusalem and the Temple: Final Choreography

After the previous segments, it is now relatively easy to follow the events at the Temple and Jesus' subsequent death. We start back with Jesus' entry into Jerusalem. The instructions to the disciples to find a "colt that has never been ridden" (Mark 11:2) is expanded in Matthew to a donkey with her foal (Matt 21:2) on which the disciples spread their cloaks. And Jesus "sat on them" (Matt 21:6). Matthew glosses the unlikely picture by quoting the prophecy from Zechariah. "Tell the daughter of Zion, look, your king is coming to you, humble and mounted on a donkey, and on a colt, the foal of a donkey" (21:5). The specification of a young animal by Jesus is in both Mark and Matthew, and the literal elements of the request in Matthew signal very deliberate reference to Zechariah's prophecy of the coming king. It explains the ensuing enthusiasm of the crowd, waving branches and shouting "Hosanna!" Which in turn tells us how Jesus was able to assemble a large enough crowd around him in the Temple that he could block the sacrifices.

The actual prophecy in Zechariah reads, "Rejoice greatly, O daughter Zion! Shout aloud, O daughter Jerusalem! Lo, your king comes to you: triumphant and victorious is he, humble and riding on a donkey, on a colt, the foal of a donkey" (Zech 9:9). The Hebrew word translated "victorious" is from the same root as the word given as "deliverance" in Jonah (2:9). The word for "humble" is *ani,* which also translates as "poor," "oppressed," or "afflicted." Elsewhere in the Bible, the *ani* is the victim of murder (Job 24:14), or the poor man who is obliged to give his single cloak as security for a loan (Deut 24:12–13). In contemporary terms, we could easily say this king is unarmed, powerless, and so must bring deliverance without violence. And this is the unarguable connotation of the following verse, Zech 9:10: "He will cut off the chariot from Ephraim and the war-horse from Jerusalem; and the battle bow shall be cut off and he shall command peace to the nations; his dominion shall be from sea to sea, and from the River to the ends of the earth." With this contrast, the meaning of "the foal of a donkey" is unmistakable. The foal is no match for the war-horse or chariot; thus, the victory of this king has to come by other, nonviolent means. In Matthew's Greek version of the prophecy, the word rendering *ani* is *praus,* often translated as "gentle" or "meek." It is the word for the third group or category in the Beatitudes: "Blessed are the meek" (Matt 5:5). In both instances it refers to those who cannot avail of forms and instruments of violence to defend themselves, either through condition or choice. It means Jesus is unarmed.

It is nothing less than astonishing that this meaning has rarely if ever been drawn from the figure of Jesus on the colt. The very first people not to get the cue was the yelling crowd! Reading the whole prophecy, and knowing the deliberate choice of the colt, it is impossible to miss the *mashal.* But a notorious prophet and healer who always walked, now riding a donkey, is ambiguous enough to set off an excitable, power-hungry crowd. Here comes the king!

It seems certain, therefore, that Jesus brought a finely controlled choreography to the situation, delicately balanced between transformative dynamic and the popular messianism that would propel him to brief, mesmerizing power. Even the evangelists seem to stress the kingly role—not making reference to Zechariah's verse 10 and its explicit nonviolence.

In doing so, they stopped short of the full text and its meaning and essentially got the story at most half right. Much more coherent in the whole scheme of the enacted gospel (and of the Old Testament before it) is to understand that the depth of meaning Jesus brought was truly revolutionary, and so at best was poorly understood or represented even by the gospel tradition. If a new light comes into the world, it cannot at once transform the eye which has been constructed by the old. Things at first will be blurry and without depth. But enough is definitely caught to slowly bring the new outline to focus, step by step with the deep reconstruction of the eye itself. The argument here is always that the semiotic shift performed by the whole Bible is too radical to be produced by human intelligences internal to violent culture. It has to be molded by something beyond itself. In the case of Jesus, he is simply of an intelligence that is already fully molded by the radical meaning of his Jewish tradition. As such, what he does must always be interpreted as a living *mashal* of that meaning. We may understand, therefore, that Jesus privately arranged for the colt in order to evoke the prophecy of Zechariah, at the same time as consciously setting up the next stage of his overall communication, which is his taking control of the Temple.

In Mark, after the triumphal entry to Jerusalem, Jesus goes straight to the Temple, and after "he had looked around at everything" (11:11), he leaves for Bethany. The sequence has the hint of planning, of scouting the situation to know where he will position himself. The following day he returns, and it is on his way in that he "curses" the fig tree. In N. T. Wright's words, Jesus' action toward the fig tree is a "visual aid"[35] of the fate henceforth of the Temple. Jesus says to the fig tree, "May no one eat fruit of you again" (Mark 11:14). If the saying is transferred to the Temple, Jesus is saying, "May no one derive religious/sacrificial benefit from you again." By following through this enacted parable with his action in the Temple, Jesus denudes Jerusalem—at the symbolic level—of

---

35. Wright, *Jesus and the Victory of God*, 334.

sacrificial protections: precisely the thing that the priests knew they were providing, and for the sake of which they decided instinctively they had to get rid of Jesus. Jesus is not a milquetoast messiah. He is intervening proactively in the human situation, offering it complete transformation, even as he neutralizes and draws a line under the failsafe protections that have been with humanity from the very beginning. We might say, "Please leave us alone, Jesus," as did the people of the country of the Gerasenes (Mark 5:17). But it is already too late. Jesus has acted as the climactic example of the prophetic tradition: denouncing and disabling the false truth of the human situation, announcing the possibility of a new earth given by a God of (nonviolent) deliverance.

After his words to the fig tree, Jesus goes to the Temple and proceeds to drive out those who were selling and buying there, overturning the tables of the money-lenders and the seats of those who sold doves (Mark 11:15). The initial accent on buying and selling sends everyone off on a false trail—the idea that Jesus was upset at the gross commercialization of the Temple activities. But as we saw above, E. P. Sanders effectively argued that money was a perennial and necessary part of the provision of animals for sacrifice. No one would have been shocked at these transactions. On the other hand, depriving the Temple of the flow of sacrificial offerings provided to and by the customers, this was an immensely provocative and dangerous act. It is equivalent to shutting down the Temple itself.

Another sentence added by Mark is so often ignored because its translation renders it trivial. "And he would not allow anyone to carry anything through the Temple" (11:16). This again seems like Jesus piously fussing over trivia—people carrying their packages through the Temple courts! But the word rendered "anything" is Greek *skeuos*, which has a technical meaning in the context of Temple sacrifices. All we have to do is look at Heb 9:21, where the word is used in connection with the sprinkling of blood on "all the vessels [plural, *skeuē*] used in worship." In short, there is a whole paraphernalia necessary for the conduct of sacrifice—shovels, barrels, buckets, bowls, pans, trays, censers, etc. These would have been used to ferry wood, ashes, oil and grain offerings, grain cakes, and the animal body parts remaining in sin offerings, peace offerings/thanksgiving sacrifices (cf. Leviticus 2–7). If from the distance of two thousand years and non-blood-sacrifice religion, we can re-create in our minds the conditions of the Jerusalem Temple—sole locus of physical sacrifice for Israel—then without a doubt there has to be a huge bustling and continuous service maintaining the business of slaughter and burning. It was this that Jesus was blocking. He was able to do so because of the crowd's ongoing fascination for his person and his words, and the triumphant outcome they still envisaged (see Luke 19:47–8).

Jesus' words in Mark underline the violent nature of what he is opposing. "Is it not written, 'My house shall be called a house of prayer for all the nations'? But you have made it a den of robbers" (Mark 11:17). The first part is taken from Third Isaiah, a prophecy of universal inclusivity which, at least in the segment quoted, emphasizes prayer, not sacrifice (Isa 56:7). The latter part is from Jeremiah (7:11) and the context is Jeremiah's denunciation of the offenses of the worshippers—oppression of the alien, the orphan, the widow, and the "shed(ding) of innocent blood in this place" (7:5). Again, in the Gospel it is a matter of English translation: the word rendered "robber" is Greek *lēstēs*, which typically means a bandit who employs violence. Jesus is echoing classic prophetic critique of the Temple which sees the institution of the Temple as a shelter for murder and violent cultural mores.

John's Gospel seems to underline the standard optic of Jesus being concerned with the buying and selling—especially in the words, "Take these things out of here! Stop making my Father's house a marketplace!" (John 2:16). But John also contains the astonishing image of the whip of cords and the driving out of the sheep and the cattle (John 2:15). Despite the explanatory words, the driving out of the animals changes the focus emphatically to the sacrificial victims. This reading is reinforced in chapter 10 of John where the figure of the sheepfold can stand as the enclosure for sheep for sacrifice. This is made possible by the words at 10:8–10: "All who come before me are thieves and bandits [pl. *lēstēs*] . . . the thief comes only to steal and kill and destroy." The word given as "kill" is Greek *thuō*, frequently also translated "sacrifice" (see Mark 14:12). The words at verse four are "When he has brought out all his own, he goes ahead of them. . .," but the word "brought" is actually from *ekballo,* which is the same verb used at 2:15 for Jesus' action of *driving* out the sheep. There seems then an obvious layering of the gathering of Jesus' flock with the driving out from the Temple of the sacrificial animals and their deliverance from sacrificial violence. The creation of a new human community freed from violence is the selfsame event as the prevention of sacrifice by the expulsion of the animals. Therefore, at some level the Johannine tradition is clearly aware that Jesus' action in the Temple was consciously putting an end to Temple sacrifice.

The interplay of the shutting down of the Temple and the creation of a new humanity brings us now a final element in the sequence. If Jesus has negated the traditional mechanism of ritual bringing unity to human beings, what is to go in its place? At this point, Jesus seems to have left an aching void at the heart of humanity, but he does not disappoint. He moves directly to fill it, creating a final single code for what he is doing in contrast to all that went before. He produces a definitive *mashal* of the new, one that will go on translating human identity throughout history. It is entirely appropriate that this parable comes in the middle of the arc between Temple and cross. It is effectively the keystone of what I have called the semiotic portal which Jesus forms between these two.

Eucharist

Beginning with Mark, the Synoptics present Jesus' last meal emphatically as a Passover meal (Mark 14:12–16; Matt 26:17–19; Luke 22:7–13). The problem is that John's account equally emphatically tells us the meal occurred *before* the Passover, and therefore could not be such. (See John 19.14: Jesus' trial and execution takes place on "the day of Preparation for the Passover." The Passover lambs are sacrificed on that day, in readiness for the meal which takes place after sundown—only *then* Passover and its meal begin.) But the exact chronology of the meal does not matter. From the New Testament evidence, it is indisputable that Jesus celebrated a meal with his disciples shortly before his death, one that immediately garnered a high-value significance for the infant movement.[36] It is noteworthy that the repetition of this meal could take place daily (Acts 2:42; cf. Luke 24:35): something which counts against it being a Passover celebration which obviously happened just once a year. This strongly suggests Jesus was acting with creative freedom in re-ordering the basic symbols of Israel—he said and did enough to point to Passover, but what he was doing went far beyond:

> [T]here is no reason to suppose that Jesus might not have celebrated what we might call a *quasi*-Passover meal a day ahead of the real thing . . . Granted that Jesus had, throughout his work, reorganized the symbolic world of his contemporaries around his own life and mission . . . it certainly does not strain credulity

36. Jeremias, *Eucharistic Words of Jesus*, 105, 189.

to think that he might organize a special quasi-Passover meal a day early.[37]

What counts is the performative sign-value of the meal, the meanings it concentrated into itself, and in order to establish this we have to see the meal in conjunction with the action in the Temple. The Jewish scholar, Jacob Neusner, ties the meal to Jesus' overturning of the tables which—agreeing with Sanders—he sees as directed precisely against the sacrifices. He believes that Jesus saw the daily "whole offering" (Exod 30:16) in the Temple as useless for providing "atonement" for sins of Jewish people; consequently, Jesus acted to put a stop to it. But at the very same time, he moved to institute an alternative act of atonement, one enacted in his last meal before the passion, and continually performed thereafter—the celebration known as Eucharist.

> [T]he counterpart of Jesus' negative action in overturning one table must be his affirmative action in establishing or setting up another table . . . The negative is that the atonement for sin achieved by the daily whole offering is null, and the positive, that atonement for sin is achieved by the Eucharist: one table overturned, another table set up in place, and both for the same purpose of atonement and expiation of sin.[38]

Neusner is giving a very traditional understanding of Jesus' last meal, regarding it as opposed to the Temple but still doing the same thing, "atonement and expiation." This is no different from the broad Christian tradition which erected a Temple over Jesus' new semiosis, making it conform to the very thing he was subverting. Nevertheless, Neusner is structurally correct, even if the significance he draws is mistaken. Neusner gives Jesus the credit of shaping his own world of meaning after having acted to remove a fundamental prop of institutional Israelite meaning. But Jesus' actions go well beyond Neusner's concept, which would appear simply idiosyncratic on Jesus' part. After all, Neusner obviously does not think that Jesus out-atoned the Temple, so from a Jewish perspective there can be nothing special about his death. But if Jesus was neutralizing age-old sacrificial protections which had always provided "atonement" for humankind, including Israel, then there was so much more at stake. Jesus was denuding the landscape of temples, so he had to give something

---

37. Wright, *Jesus and the Victory of God*, 556.
38. Neusner, "Money Changers in the Temple," 290.

absolutely transformative in their place, for the sake of human existence and its peace. And this is precisely what he did in his amazing final meal.

There are three accounts of this meal in the New Testament: Matthew/Mark, Luke, and Paul. Here is not the place for a comparative analysis of these texts,[39] but what immediately impresses itself in the overall picture is the way Jesus is giving spoken meaning to elements of a meal: bread and wine. This parallels Passover practice as we know it from the Jewish *Haggadah*, giving spoken meaning to the unleavened bread, bitter herbs, etc. The dating of this Jewish material is uncertain (perhaps from after the fall of Jerusalem, 70 CE), but it is anyway certain that the Passover meal always had symbolic reference. It was a code with generative meaning in Jewish life (see, for example, Exod 13:3–10, where the unleavened bread "shall serve for you as a sign . . ."). Jesus manipulated for his own purposes this cultural topos, giving it his own meaning. What then comes clearly into focus is the elements he chooses and how he makes them into a sememe of self-giving life.

As others have also argued, the elements of bread and wine, along with thanksgiving, could go perfectly well with other "ordinary" Jewish meals in the ritual traditions developing in the timeframe of the first century.[40] In which case, rather than looking strictly at Passover, Jesus first best source for the meal could be the figure of Wisdom calling out, "Come, eat of my bread, and drink of the wine I have mixed" (Prov 9:2–5). He has simply chosen the context of Passover, with his imminently approaching death, to construct the most profound sense of his Wisdom meal. The signification of the elements, of "body" and "blood," have always represented to interpreters the supposed "sacrificial" meaning of what Jesus was doing. If Neusner is one of the latest, we can perhaps take Paul as one of the earliest: the "Passover Lamb (which) has been sacrificed" (1 Cor 5:7).[41] But this sacrificial reading has, as far as I can tell, prevented one very salient—and counter-indicative—factor from coming to the surface. In the biblical tradition of sacrifice, it was imperative that the blood be

---

39. The classic work is Jeremias, *Eucharistic Words of Jesus*.

40. Bouyer, *Eucharist*, 99.

41. For example, Jeremias' insistence on the sacrificial meaning of the twin elements, body/blood (*Eucharistic Words*, 221–22). Paul's expression has to be read semiotically within the overall transformative meaning he gives to Christ's death. Anthropologically speaking, if blood rituals have been at the core of meaning for human beings, then a code which transforms that actual framework will feasibly use the same signifiers while giving them revolutionary significance.

separated from the body and spilt on the ground or at the altar (Gen 9:4; Lev 17:10–14). It was impossible that the blood be consumed, for the "life was in the blood" and the life belonged to God alone. Even among the early Christian community, the horror of consuming blood remained (Acts 15:29). By telling his disciples to drink (a symbol of) his blood, Jesus was transgressing the central vector of sacrifice as it had been formulated in Jewish practice, and he was going against formal sacrificial practice generally. Indeed, he was turning sacrifice into something other than sacrifice! He was producing an anti-sacrifice that could superficially be mistaken for actual sacrifice because its active agent was blood, but the blood had been given an entirely different, new semiosis.

The blood contained absolutely no violence—on the contrary, it contained *non*violence, which is positive forgiveness, peace, love. Only in that way would it be possible to drink and not feel the Temple universe crashing down on you in outrage. Thus, the ritual meaning of blood—its elemental sign value—had been turned from the place where the violence of the group is poured away, removed as "sacred," to become an inner agent that contains no violence and works proactively to transform the group into nonviolence and love. This is what it means to eat and drink the Eucharist. It is about as nonsacrificial as you can get.[42]

The images of wine and blood easily evoke a "pouring out" (Mark 14:24; Matt 26:28; Luke 22:20). This connects with the suffering servant and the words used of him at Isa 53:12. The Hebrew is "he poured out his soul unto death," with the verb *arah*, which can also carries a meaning of "lay bare" or "strip." There is a wide literature on the topic of the servant and its connection to Jesus,[43] but it seems to me inevitable that if Jesus was engaged in a thoroughgoing rereading of his Scriptures, capable of changing our violent way of being to one of nonviolence, then the figure of the servant provided a ready-made template for him. And there is also a natural segue from Jonah to the servant, and vice versa. In his prayer from the belly of the fish, Jonah says, "When my soul fainted within me, I remembered the Lord" (JPS Tanakh 1917). The Hebrew refers to "soul" (*nephesh*) as in the Isa 53:12 passage. The verb and its action ("faint," "grow feeble" or "be overwhelmed") picture Jonah's situation of drowning

---

42. René Girard's first instinct was this, to draw a definitive line between the term "sacrifice" and the meaning of Christ's death: "[I]f you absolutely must have the word 'sacrifice', then you must do without it in the case of all forms of sacrifice except the Passion, which is clearly impossible." (*Things Hidden*, 453, n. 66).

43. See Bellinger and Farmer, *Jesus and the Suffering Servant*.

in the deep, remembering that *nephesh* can equally be translated "life." "Fainting" is different from "pouring out," but what the servant does is take Jonah's passive situation and turn it into something proactive; he embraces Jonah's unwilling "drowning" and makes it his own, hence he "pours out his soul." By reading these Scriptures together, we could say Jesus "servantises" Jonah, just as in all the other connections we have seen Jesus embrace and translate the prophet of the deep. He is going indeed to the same place as he has cast the towns of Galilee and the Temple Mount, and he is going there as Servant-Jonah, in order to transform the absyssal space of human violence into the space of love. Only in this final zone of encounter can these towns and this Temple be saved—from themselves.

The *mashal* of the Eucharist communicates a new mode of being to humankind. It does so over long ages because the sun must prompt the evolution of the eye which over time is able to see what it reveals. The command, "Do this in remembrance of me" (Luke 22:19; 1 Cor 11:24) refers to this process. The Greek has *poiete eis tēn emēn anamnēsin*. Anamnesis/memorial has been shown by scholars as having a technical reference. According to Louis Bouyer, it is "a pledge [of memory] given by God to his faithful, precisely so that they will re-present it *to him*."[44] The key New Testament example is Acts 10:4 where Cornelius' prayers and alms are said to "have ascended as a memorial before God" (*eis mnēmosynon*). Jeremias highlights this, plus other examples from first-century Jewish usage, to claim the "in remembrance" of the Eucharist is directed to God that *he* may remember Jesus and bring his work to completion.[45] Apart from reversing—at the crucial moment of his life—Jesus' standard practice of using signs both spoken and enacted to communicate his meaning *to people*, this suggests that nothing definitive had been accomplished, that the gospel has not in fact been preached. The Christian Jews were in the same condition as regular Jews who prayed to God every Passover for God's "remembrance of the Messiah," i.e., that God would bring about the Messiah's kingdom.[46] Much more likely, it seems to me, that Jesus took the established formula and turned it around, so it did indeed apply to human beings, calling them to remember him in the breaking of the bread and the pouring out of the wine. He took God's act of fidelity—the full story of the Messiah—and held it out in remembrance, not in some

---

44. Bouyer, *Eucharist*, 85; my italics.

45. Jeremias, *Eucharistic Words*, 244–54.

46. Jeremias, *Eucharistic Words*, 252.

heavenly space, but on a human table at the center of human concerns. The anamnesis is then a work of semiosis, a day-by-day performance of divine meaning for the sake of human transformation. At the end of the walk to Emmaus and a dense catechesis showing the necessity of the Messiah's suffering and non-retaliation, something happened; the living reality of this nonviolent Lord found its breakthrough point in the breaking of the bread (Luke 24:35).

Death and Resurrection

Intentional Actions

The four Gospels end with the resurrection of Jesus, and the story of the road to Emmaus is one of the more memorable vignettes of encounter with the risen Christ. But as we have just seen, this account presents itself as a semiotic conversion—a developing series of spoken and enacted signs bringing a radical shift of meaning. It therefore informs us that the resurrection is a semiotic event. Or, rather, a climactic part of a broad semiotic pathway encompassing the whole story of the gospel and, behind that, the Old Testament. Nevertheless, in terms of claimed event, the resurrection must be counted a semiotic explosion in its own right. Coming after Jesus' crucifixion and death, it represents an unparalleled reversal and transformation of meaning, one that is at the core of the Christian movement and the explanation of its historical vitality. The Emmaus story shows us human meaning for the disciples shifting progressively until there is an instantaneous, wondrous vision of Christ, followed at once by his disappearance. The appearance-disappearance affirms this is both a real "physical" event and yet it functions, and persists afterward, as a semiotic event, something that remains imprinted on the retina and brain and then is "told" to others. The question always is what is more important, the human progression of meaning or the actual physical vision of the Christ? And immediately there is a second question: Can you have one without the other? Or, put yet another way, if more mysteriously, do they perhaps amount to the same thing?

These are questions we will come to, but before we do, we must follow again the intensifying drumbeat of Jesus' last days before his execution and death. There is no minimizing the terror of the storm gathering around the protagonist of the gospel, but at the same time, we continue to infer the shape and meaning he continually gave to his situation. We've previously used the work of Tom Wright in describing the historical possibilities and probabilities of the life of Jesus, and Wright's particular methodology has special closeness to a semiotic reading. Wright lays out a pattern of praxis, story, and symbol in seeking to understand Jesus and the material about him given in the Gospels.[47] It is a way of doing history, recognizing that history is governed by structures of meaning which are repeatable and, at the same time, negotiable and transformable. It is also therefore a semiotic approach, a kind of semiotic history, recognizing that signs and meaning are not just spoken or written, but designed, built, performed, choreographed, lived. Wright's method brings results gauged by probability, not certainty, but by the same token it puts you in touch with real history—for that is the way (via signs) we always understand our world. Jesus becomes an axial figure, negotiating both a continuation and a revolutionary change in the meaning structures of his time and place. What is particular in the present study is the insistence on an inner coherence among signs based in nonviolence, something which brings you to a certain historical bedrock in relation to Jesus.

As already argued, Jesus' action in the Temple could not have been performed without an intrinsic nonviolence, if he was to avoid any expectation of mass violence to vindicate his action. Jesus upset the sacrificial order, and this can only result in a crisis of violence which would inevitably devolve on him. Unless he possessed an already-formed, profound ethic of nonviolence, the only intelligent response would be to invoke the protection of an army, either human or angelic. It is the traditional understanding of Jesus' death as a necessary sacrifice to God which has masked this requirement—effectively creating a new sacred (violent) order at a higher metaphysical level. But Jesus' nonretaliatory, nonviolent death contradicts every element of violence, including metaphysical. His saying to the women of Jerusalem—"Do not weep not for me, but for yourselves and your children" (Luke 23:28)—is prophetic warning of the consequences of Jerusalem's ongoing commitment to violence as human meaning, not a threat of vengeance. Most conclusively, at the level of the

47. Wright, *Jesus and the Victory of God*, 138–42; part 1, chapters 5–9, use these headings, and there are multiple examples elsewhere: e.g., 472–73, "His activities made sense, and were intended to make sense, within a Jewish worldview. His stories evoked, extended and in part redrew some standard Jewish storylines. The symbols of his own work challenged the permanence of the standard symbols of his Jewish contemporaries . . . Thus his praxis, his stories, and his symbols all pointed to his belief and claim that Israel's god was fulfilling his promises and purposes in and through what he himself was doing."

first century (long before the contortions of medieval atonement theory), it would be impossible to derive an exponential gospel of forgiveness from Jesus' death if there were any note of divine retaliation.

The Temple authorities acted to bring about Jesus' arrest and execution after his symbolic abolition of their sacrificial system. Dominic Crossan agrees that what Jesus did was "an attack on the Temple's very existence."[48] As a result, "Jesus was executed by some conjunction of Jewish and Roman authority."[49] What Crossan denies is that Jesus acted with any intention beyond a suicidal protest against the non-egalitarian social system he had contested in Galilee, one which had its effective headquarters in the Jerusalem Temple.[50] The problem with this is (at least) twofold: it makes of Jesus an entirely implausible figure on which to base a doctrine of divine forgiveness, redemption, and resurrection; in parallel it makes of the Gospel writers (primarily Mark and John) transcendent geniuses of theological illusion. Crossan's understanding displaces the semiotic novum of the man from Nazareth onto the evangelists, at the same time as not explaining any of the momentum of the first decades of the Christian movement, nor less the possible motive force for the evangelists' amazing fiction writing. Ockham's useful razor requires the simpler explanation: namely, that Jesus was an intelligent author of his own fate, including his death, for which he had a good reason and gave a good account.

He said to the High Priest, "You will see the Son of Man seated at the right hand of the Power, and coming with the clouds of heaven" (Mark 14:62). At which point, the High Priest tears his clothes and declares Jesus has spoken blasphemy. Just before, Jesus has answered a question as to his identity, declaring explicitly that he is the Messiah: "I am." He then offers this gloss on the Messiah's meaning, referring to Daniel 7:9 and 13. The former verse speaks of "thrones" set up for a judgment scene, one of them evidently for God: the accompanying implication is that the "one like a son of man" to whom all authority is given will occupy another. Wright points to a wide stream of speculation inspired by Daniel 7 in the orbit of the first century regarding such throne-sharing.[51] Jesus makes it his own, putting the two verses together. The High Priest clearly catches

48. Crossan, *Who Killed Jesus?*, 64.

49. Crossan, *Who Killed Jesus?*, 147.

50. Crossan, *Who Killed Jesus?*, 65.

51. Wright, *Jesus and the Victory of God*, 624–29.

the sense, immediately condemning Jesus' words as egregious blasphemy. The indirect way Jesus cites the passage in relation to himself (circumlocution) is taken by Wright as evidence of historicity.[52] Jesus keeps the listener off balance, challenging them to enter a new frame of meaning. And from everything we argued in the essay on Daniel, this meaning is one of revelatory nonviolence. Jesus is asserting that the very situation of powerlessness and nonretaliation he now occupies is somehow reflective of the divine nature, and in the immediate future he will sit beside God, judging humanity in and through nonviolence. By stating it the way he did, Jesus is saying, "You will see the new world of divine nonviolence established on earth through what is happening right now!" Of course, the High Priest only heard a claim to divine status in terms of a god of rivalry and violence!

The figure of "son of man," therefore, begins to make complete sense of Jesus' readiness to face death. For into this figure must also be sutured the experience and meaning of the "servant." Wright judges that the picture of the suffering righteous servant in Isaiah 40–55 was a core influence on Daniel. "Daniel 11–12, in particular, should be regarded as one of the earliest extant interpreters of the servant-figure in Isaiah: it looks as though he saw the martyrs of his own day as at least partial fulfilment of Isaiah 53."[53] We recall then our own conclusion that the death of the wise in Dan 11:33 cannot be separated from the nonviolent sabbath martyrs of First Maccabees. In this perspective, therefore, Isaiah's servant is part of a revelatory legacy sustained from Isaiah through the text of Daniel in the distinctive key of nonviolence. An intrinsic element of this legacy is God's vindication of the suffering one, which in Daniel becomes resurrection, and we shall arrive shortly at that crucial nexus.

If the writers of Second Isaiah and Daniel could see radically new meaning in the midst of suffering, why not Jesus? And why, therefore, should Jesus not assume the circumlocutory title of "the son of man" as synthetic code and sign for this new meaning? A sign is not a rationalistic idea framing an abstract reality; in contrast, it can suddenly put us in touch with what we have not clearly seen or known before. Picasso's Guernica, or a poem by Rilke, can give us sudden new, interruptive meaning; so why not, in an altogether more profound and life-determining sense, codes related to the liberating God of the Exodus? Thus, it seems to me

52. Wright, *Jesus and the Victory of God*, 644.
53. Wright, *Jesus and the Victory of God*, 589.

hidebound not to allow Jesus—a master of semiotic intelligence—to understand himself in terms of Daniel, specifically chapter 7. Wright recaps the figure of the "son of man" in relation to Jesus as follows: "Jesus as part of his prophetic work of announcing the kingdom, aligned himself with the 'people of the saints of the most high', that is, with the 'one like a son of man'. In other words, he regarded himself as the one who summed up Israel's vocation and destiny in himself."[54]

It then becomes entirely intelligible how Jesus could have had the inspiration, insight, and courage to construct the semiotic portal that he did. And then to produce a performative sign (the Eucharist) to continually hand on his vision, to enact his portal and invite people through it. Wright does not declare a method of semiotics, nor specifically a semiotics of nonviolence, to argue his thesis, but his final position converges closely:

> My proposal is that Jesus took his own story seriously . . . He would turn the other cheek; he would go the second mile; he would take up the cross. He would be the means of the kingdom's coming, both in that he would embody in himself the renewed Israel and in that he would defeat evil once and for all. But the way in which he would defeat evil would be the way consistent with the deeply subversive nature of his own kingdom-announcement. He would defeat evil by letting it do its worst to him . . .[55]

There is no substitutionary atonement here, no satisfying God's offended honor: there is only the display of an acute physical nonviolence in fulfillment of a distinct Old Testament storyline, something which in itself changes human meaning, beginning with the meaning of God. We have to grasp the magnitude of what is at stake, the catastrophic transformation intended by Jesus. Intrinsic to this there is the terror of confronting the old world-order with only faith in a nonviolent God able to redeem and reverse the annihilation intended by that order. On the reading given here, we now come to the point where resurrection becomes indispensable to the gospel. Resurrection is the piece of the gospel code that makes the whole thing work, that completes the radical re-coding of the human condition. Traditional atonement does not really need the resurrection. But a story, a praxis, a series of gestures that culminate in the crucifixion,

---

54. Wright, *Jesus and the Victory of God*, 517.

55. Wright, *Jesus and the Victory of God*, 564–65.

this can only succeed as nonviolent *meaning* if the Jesus of the cross truly is vindicated.

Materialist Semiosis

"Early on the first day of the week . . . Mary Magdalene came to the tomb" (John 20:1) and found it empty. In all the canonical Gospels, the accounts of resurrection begin with the empty tomb. That in itself proves nothing: just as Mary first thought, someone could have taken the body. What then follows is a series of encounters which apparently do not exclude doubt, nor descriptions of a prolonged moment/experience of perceptual shifting which bring a final recognition (Luke 24:13–35; Matt 28:16–17; John 20:11–18, 20:24–29). This is not Hollywood, not the age-old human preference for manifest visual evidence, something declarative, patent, overwhelming. The Gospels inherently leave space for the organic process which is essential if we are talking about a root change of human meaning. Even the account of Paul's conversion in Acts—the one which, with its blinding light, comes closest to a violent epiphany (Acts 9:1–4)— includes the transformative words presenting the revelatory victim of violence: "Saul, Saul, why do you persecute me?" Saul then needs three days before he is baptized (and years after that plumbing the meaning of what had happened). Resurrection is an unresolvable mix of physical event and semiotic transformation. Without the empty tomb, the triumph of Jesus over the violent condition of humanity would at once be negated. The corpse of Jesus would prove irrefutably Rome had won, no matter the tattered dreams of life that clung to it. More positively, it is very hard to see how a generative gospel of forgiveness could get its start from a bloodied cadaver abandoned in a shallow grave. The reversal of Jesus' defeat by means other than violent seems the only credible explanation. And yet the resurrection remains itself a sign—if we take "sign" (any sign) as ontological relation which links us to something real, but unknown "in itself." If this is true of any sign, how much more for a sign that claims to transform the meaning and substance of human existence? In which case, the gospel asks us to "believe," not as an intellectual acceptance of a metaphysical state of affairs, but as a joining in with the relationship proposed by the multiple signs of the gospel. They climax in the death and resurrection of Jesus, signs which in themselves relate us to a new nonviolent way of being willed by God while, at the same time, (re) defining the very meaning of God.

The disciples' grief-sourced projection of a fantasy Jesus could not have brought about this revolution in meaning. It is semiotically impossible. We have to remember that the dominant form of "truth" at the time was either legalistic or metaphysical, either subject to the law, or belonging to another "perfect" world. To intrude a claim that a dead person was no longer subject to the world-construct ordered by violence, but was generated anew in a nonviolent order still somehow of this world, could not happen simply by shifting chains of signifiers. There had to be an eruption of some sort in the density of "the real" for this to be apprehended.

The only way we can think otherwise (i.e., that the gospel of Jesus' resurrection could arise out of already constituted human meaning) is because *our* symbolic realm has been *de facto* changed by the Easter proclamation. And so we think that it must have always been this way: that the abyssal revolution in meaning was always somehow a potential of the symbolic order, a pure potential of its web of signs. But to believe this, we have to comfortably separate out in our thought the ontic force of violence in human affairs. We have to separate out the way violence violently composes the real, and think instead that human beings can compose the real of forgiveness and nonviolence simply by a speculative convulsion of emotion in reaction to murder and betrayal.

Death is the denial of giving, and in fact the dead person is a claim on the subject, not a giving *to* her. For death to be turned around and made a moment of giving requires an intervention in death itself. It is no longer a constitutive drain on life, the core generator of a violent symbolic order where peace is only discovered in the blameworthy victim. Rather, it is the inverse, a deconstruction of that order's power—so that now the believer is capable of giving without reserve, of going the extra mile, turning the other cheek, suffering without resentment, draining life's dregs without hatred. The witness of resurrection is an actual moment in history with consequences of universal historical significance. And once again, the only reason why we do not see this is because the symbolic order has been changed and we think, therefore, that there always was the possibility of "imagining" a bodily, forgiving, nonviolent resurrection. But, historically speaking, there was an actual moment when this happened.

At the same time—and again—we recognize that the very transformation of the symbolic order (by resurrection) is part of its essential mode of operation in the world. We accept the "normality" of a thought of resurrection because our semiotic system has been infiltrated by this "word." An apostle is a witness of the resurrection, but apostles are a quite limited category. After them there come all those who believe in their word, but are not witnesses. John's Gospel says explicitly: "Blessed are those who have not seen yet have believed." Why? Why—if there is a material reality behind it—not visit an indefinite number of people with the vision of the risen Christ, rather than a restricted few? Would that not constitute the triumph of the gospel? The reason is the obvious one: any clamorous publicity or evidentiality of a risen Christ would simply amount to more of the same of a violent world: the eyes which received this evidence would receive it in the present system of meaning and so appropriate it simply as a new form of imperialism. (Certainly, this is what much of historical Christianity has effectively and anyway produced in many cultural situations.) So it is that the gospel must quickly become proclamation, semiosis, and communication. In that way, the individual can be invited into the new meaning and can appropriate it precisely as meaning, not force.

Thus, Mary's word on Easter Sunday morning is the crucial birth of new nonviolent human reality. Jesus says to her "Go tell my brothers . . ." Already a human word is addressed to the apostles despite the fact that they too are to become actual witnesses of the resurrection. Already the real of resurrection is introduced by semiosis, even though the recipients are to experience it also "at first hand." Is there, in fact, any way of completely separating out the "word" and "first hand," the semiotic and the materialist? Mary already heard her name spoken before she "turned" (John 20:16), and how much of this receptive word was an echo of the abyssal love she had experienced in contact with the flesh-and-blood Jesus in the numerous times she had heard her name spoken by him? Except this time, it is in the extraordinary circumstances of his unarguable prior death at the hands of authorities. In other words, the apostles also remain semiotic beings, and the new meaning of resurrection has to be communicated individually to their personal semiotic process, even as it serves absolutely to reverse the prior empire of death. What are the words that Mary is to say? She says that Jesus has announced, "I am ascending to my Father and your Father, to my God and your God" (John 20:17). The words carry a meaning, a relation to Jesus' Father, Jesus' God, and *this* is what is now real and the reason why it is impossible fully to separate the word and the experience. The relation of a sign is real, the real is relation. Here is the materialism of the resurrection, a transformative relation genuinely carried by the sign.

What is marvelous about the sign of Jesus is that it creates a relationship with a radically new way of being—where life flows spontaneously by love, not force—even if and as we remain in an old one. When creation is liberated from violence, then the physics of the resurrection may well be both possible and provable. Until then, the death and resurrection of Jesus remain a vibrant semiosis communicating a real relationship with an impossible but real universe. And by exactly the same measure, the God of this universe is the impossible but real God of nonviolence.

9

Paul

Quick through the Portal

IF JESUS OFFERS A semiotic portal, then Paul plunges through it without a backward glance. However, because of the very radicalism of his leap, together with the dispersed, occasional character of his writing, he is often notoriously difficult to get a handle on. Pauline scholarship is itself a dense undergrowth, going back to Luther, and before that through the Middle Ages to Augustine. Since the nineteenth century, critical analyses of Paul have multiplied, in many ways parallel to the multiplying studies of the historical Jesus. In a work like the present, there can be no question of a comprehensive study. So, what is possible and needed here is to show that Paul's gospel is genuinely one of divine nonviolence and to identify the authentic grounds for the claim. What follows then is a species of highlight marker illuminating the critical areas that release this understanding. Paul of course has his own story in the Book of Acts. But that is very much a constructed version with a particular vision of the early church guiding the approach. To get back to Paul himself, from within his letters and teaching, requires a particular attention and critical effort. But if we can supply this, the rewards are well worth it.

Someone who has done a great deal of the labor and produced results that are as meticulous as they are compelling is the Paul scholar, Douglas Campbell. Campbell has managed to change the center of gravity in Paul's letters—at least as largely perceived since the Reformation—replacing "justification by faith" by something much more humanly life-giving and transformative. In much that follows, I will be dependent upon Campbell while drawing on other sources. The cumulative effect is to discover Paul as the announcement of an entirely new human reality which is simultaneously the discovery of an entirely new language of divine reality. In sum, Paul through the course of his letters came conclusively to demonstrate divine nonviolence. It is implied in the core of his teaching, one summed up in his constant heartfelt salutation, "grace and peace!"

Campbell develops an essential framing of Paul's writing.[1] Framing means the sequence of his letters, the intervals between them and the occasion and reference that prompted each of them. The establishment of this frame, from the letters themselves, yields a strong sense of contingency in Paul's writings. Paul is not writing in a university library, working systematically, but responding with personal letters as circumstances and needs dictate. A particular situation draws out of him what he considers essential to the occasion. This approach prevents a dogmatic, formulaic approach, at the same time yielding a sense of what is most dynamic in Paul's heart in various moments of his astonishing ministry. Campbell delivers a persuasive account of Paul's biography in the letters, creating a firsthand account from Paul's own sources, and, with that, a sense of a living, developing theology.

One exceptional result is the placing of the letter to the Ephesians in the early heart of Paul's work.[2] Campbell argues convincingly for an early date by demonstrating (together with other considerations) how Ephesians can, with some elegance, be identified as Paul's "lost" letter to the Laodiceans mentioned in Colossians (Col 4:16).[3] For some the closeness of style, language, and themes between Ephesians and Colossians have led to suspicions of Ephesians as a confident forgery on the part of a later writer, based on the text of Colossians. (While Colossians is itself dismissed as non-Pauline by some, for separate but related reasons.) Campbell explains the closeness by the immediate proximity of the composition of the two letters and the overshadowing themes of Paul's

1. Campbell, *Framing Paul.*

2. Campbell, *Framing Paul,* 254–338. Ephesians and, connected to it, Colossians, are often regarded as pseudonymous, from an author other than Paul but influenced by him. See, for example, Ehrman, *New Testament,* 329.

3. How the name got changed to "Paul to Ephesians" is its own story, which Campbell relates along with second-century evidence that this is indeed what happened. See *Framing Paul,* 310–12, 387–91.

thinking at the time. Paul is in prison, somewhere on the road westward through modern day Turkey; he has time to reflect and he writes simultaneously to Colossae and its neighboring town of Laodicea. In the latter case, he is in fact "cold-calling," introducing himself to a community, none of whom he has met before, and he is writing in order to recruit them to the full vision and practice of the gospel as he understands it. In which case, the letter is actually going to give us a particularly clear exposition of that gospel, freed of any local circumstances that might stress it in one direction or another. In short, the generality of the letter is a product of its special conditions of composition, and these allow us to take it, along with Colossians, as Paul's most confident and central expression of the Christ-portal he had entered.

The exact year of composition is of great importance. Campbell places it in a relatively benign moment before a much more stressful year to come, and just *after* Paul's crucial meeting in Jerusalem with the apostle-leaders of the church, when the gospel he "proclaim[ed] among the Gentiles" was approved (Gal 2:2–9). The dating of this all-important Jerusalem "summit" meeting is deduced with a fair amount of certitude from the information and timespans Paul himself provides in his letters. In company with many other commentators, Campbell locates it to late 49 or early 50 CE,[4] which means that Paul was very likely then heading west across Asia Minor sometime in the year 50 CE, armed with the liberating power of his message which his meeting with the Jerusalem leaders had affirmed. This window of time, and its circumstances, provide the

---

4. 2 Cor 11:32–33 tells us that Paul escaped a hostile governor in Damascus, under the reign of a certain King Aretas of Nabataea. Using evidence from Josephus' *Jewish Antiquities*, Campbell narrows the precise year for this dramatic event to 36 CE (*Framing Paul*, 182–86). According to Galatians, the time of Paul's removal from Damascus was three years after his conversion, followed directly by a first visit to Jerusalem (Gal 1:18; cf. Acts 9:23–26). Reading on then from Gal 1:19 through to 2:1, we get a further "fourteen years" before the second and critical visit to Jerusalem, which brings us comfortably to the year 49 CE. It is worth underlining from this dating that Paul experienced his call/conversion in the period of 33 CE, i.e., within three or so years of the likely year of Jesus' death and resurrection. Paul is himself a responder to the very earliest phase of Christianity. Part of this response, as everyone knows, was an initial violent opposition, giving him every reason to identify fraud on the part of the first disciples. As it is, he simply has recourse to suppression, meaning that he encountered an apparently unified world of belief and testimony, at that first very early stage, requiring—as far as he was concerned—brute force to crush.

reader with an ideal optic in which to find Paul expressing what may be understood as the integral sweep of his gospel.[5]

In order to grasp how ideal the moment really is, it is necessary also to contrast it with the much more particular and conflictual concerns that are going to affect Paul directly after. Campbell calls 51 to 52 CE a "year of crisis" for Paul, when he is beset by numerous troubles arising in Corinth, and, even more painfully, by the hounding of "enemies" bearing another, law-bound version of the gospel. These will have to be responded to, all the way through to his pre-emptive letter to the infant Christian community in Rome.

Mention of Romans brings us up against this mighty flagship of Pauline thought, the epistolary dreadnought in whose wake every major interpretation of Paul will always need to make headway. A recent interpretive demarche by Campbell is enormously relevant. He has demonstrated that the text of Romans must itself be parsed according to a represented dialogue between Paul and an opponent dubbed "the Teacher."[6] This particular figure insists on the law as a necessary practice for Christian converts in order to avoid God's wrath against immorality. The key is recognizing a set of rhetorical devices—especially speech-in-person (*prosopopoeia*)—by which Paul in fact continues to represent the Teacher's thought while countering and overcoming it.[7] Unfortunately, in the past, the text has been generally misunderstood as all Paul's own (rather confused) presentation, creating essentially two "gospels." For example, when the text seems to launch out at 1:18, "For the wrath of God is revealed from heaven against all ungodliness and wickedness," it comes as pure shock against the background of almost all of Paul's other writings. And yet because of a literalist uptake of Scripture, it has

---

5. To the correspondence with churches in these two cities, we have to add the letter to Philemon which manifests very persuasive connections to Colossians, and therefore forms part of a nexus of circumstance supplying presence in this area and a basic context needed to produce the reflection of Ephesians and Colossians. "[T]he tight connections between these two letters [Colossians and Philemon] now allow these sets of data to be confidently combined, suggesting that Paul was somewhere in the Lycus valley when he wrote those letters, or nearby. That is, we now know with some confidence that he was not far from his recipients, and his recipients were Colossians . . . So, we can now confirm more confidently that the imprisonment in question was during 50 CE, apparently occurring while Paul was returning from Syrian Antioch and Jerusalem by way of Galatia" (*Framing Paul*, 274).

6. Campbell, *Deliverance of God*.

7. Campbell, *Deliverance of God*, 519–93.

sounded with just the same authority as everything else, as if Paul was suddenly relapsing into the most punitive legal mindset. However, if we read the verse immediately prior, the words ring with a completely different tone, while using exactly the same verb *apokaluptō* ("reveal"): ". . . in [the gospel] the righteousness of God is *revealed* through faith for faith." Righteousness revealed, *not* wrath, and from the (earthly) faith of Christ, not heaven! When we set these two verses in contrast in this way, we immediately recognize the two voices in the text, and we are set free from an apparently vindictive theology at the outset of Paul's major writing. We will return to further comment on these verses and Campbell below, but for the moment the contrast alerts us to a completely *different* apocalyptic in Paul, one that is decisively transformative and nonviolent.

Meaning of the Secret

A cursory reading of Ephesians will bring to attention the central function of "mystery" (*musterion*): "He has made known to us the mystery of his will . . . that he set forth in Christ, as a plan for the fulness of time, to gather up all things in him, things in heaven and things on earth" (1:9). Paul's introductory blessing celebrates the mystery or secret at the heart of the gospel. What is it? The language of secret goes back to the Book of Daniel and its revelation of the hidden meaning of history.[8] We have seen in the previous chapter how Jesus shared intimately in this worldview and always from the perspective of nonviolence. What we have in Ephesians is Paul's appropriation of the Daniel-Jesus "secret" and the devastating change to world reality it signified.

In the second chapter, Paul declares,

> [N]ow in Christ Jesus you who once were far off have been brought near by the blood of Christ. For he is our peace: in his flesh he has made both groups into one and has broken down the dividing wall, that is, the hostility between us. He has abolished the law with its commandments and ordinances, that he might create in himself one new humanity in place of the two, thus making peace, and might reconcile both groups to God in one body through the cross, thus putting to death that hostility through it. (Eph 2:13–16)

8. See Dan 2:47, where Aramaic *raz* (secret) is translated in the LXX as *musterion*; and see the practice of the *maskilim* above, with their skill in interpreting the hidden things of history. See pages 117–20 above.

What Paul is referring to is the abolition of the division between Jews and Gentiles stemming from the practice of the law, and by virtue of the revolutionary peace brought by Christ. On his way back from Jerusalem, flush with the approval of James, Cephas, and John, Paul writes the central tenet of his gospel to the Gentiles. It's not simply that the works or practices of the law are no longer valid; they are positively removed in the dramatic new relation of divine nonviolence made available in the cross, a relation which creates a new humanity of peace. It's impossible perhaps to say which came first—the sense of freedom from the law or the sense of making peace—but whatever it was, the two things are indivisible. This is the *musterion* to which Paul refers and, to my mind, it is the result of a sustained reflection throughout the forties of the first century. In this period, Paul came to the conclusion that the gospel to the Gentiles implied not simply an abrupt Second Coming "in time" (as in letters to the Thessalonians), but a progressive revolution "in space," changing the very basis and nature of human existence—as indeed the Parousia was intended to achieve.[9]

A little later on in Ephesians, Paul comments that "the mystery was made known to me by revelation" and that he had (already) stated it above "in a few words, a reading of which will enable you to perceive my understanding of the mystery of Christ" (Eph 3:3–4). He is referring, it seems obvious, to the most substantive thing written before, the verses just quoted, "Now in Christ Jesus . . ." He thus tells us explicitly that the *mystery* or secret is the breaking down of the dividing wall in the cross, primarily between Jews and Gentiles, rendering the latter "citizens with the saints" (Eph 2:19), i.e., with the "holy ones" of Daniel. Paul is of course vitally concerned with this on the controversial issue of whether Gentile Christians need to become law-observant Jews or not. But the implications of the discussion go well beyond even this explosive question. If Christ has broken down the dividing wall between Jew and Gentile in terms of a new humanity, then the same must apply to *every other* division in the human community. Paul points this out explicitly in the companion letter, Colossians, at 3:9–11: "[Y]ou have clothed yourselves with the new self [humanity, *anthrōpon*] . . . In that renewal there is no longer Greek and Jew, circumcised and uncircumcised, barbarian, Scythian, slave and free; but Christ is all in all!"[10] He even extends this

9. See Campbell, *Framing Paul*, 216–29, for dating of First and Second Thessalonians to the early forties.

10. The distinction between "barbarian" and "Scythian" is particularly ironic.

deconstruction of binaries to male and female in the subsequent letter to the Galatians (Gal 3:28): "There is no longer Jew or Greek, there is no longer slave or free, there is no longer male and female . . ." The new human derived from the cross is indeed gender liberated!

But what may be named as deconstruction is more originally the reverse, a positive truth. God's definitive intervention has taken place in the cross and amounts to the constructive breaking down of the human scheme of division, separation, and violence. There remains, however, an enormous discrepancy between the proclaimed gospel meaning of Christ and its factual, visible realization. The world does not admit the lordship of Christ! It is this discrepancy that demands that Pauline faith is indeed a semiotic shift, something that takes place in terms of personal meaning before it is reflected in actual reality. At the same time, the point is it is still a matter of real meaning, not fiction or fantasy. Something has happened in the inner structure of Paul's being such that the world *is* actually changed, even though it may not seem so on the outside. It is what I called an "ontological relation" in *TBM*,[11] a real relation brought into the world conceptually by the leaven of Christian thought, and existentially, or in fact, by the relation called faith. It becomes vital then to dig deeper into this pivotal concept in Paul.

The English word "faith" translates Greek *pistis*, and the range of meaning of the Greek includes "trust," "confidence," "faithfulness," "guarantee," even "proof" (viz. Acts 17:31). You can see how the sense moves from a personal subjective state to a warranty or persuasion communicated by and from another. The range in meaning is based in the verb root *peithō*, meaning in fact "to persuade." Faith, in this sense, is the state of persuasion by a testimony or guarantee put forward by another. At once we recognize how the act of "faith/faithfulness" may constitute both a source and resulting quality in another; i.e., there is an essential interpersonal arc in its meaning—of persuasion and being persuaded. Unfortunately, in Christian history the sense of *pistis* has morphed into intellectual acceptance of metaphysical truths, and/or a legal or contractual effect constituting entitlement to salvation. The dynamic arc of communication is lost. The semiotic relation of faith is lost.

Barbarians were the "other" of civilized Greeks, while "Scythian" was a category of captive slave to whom free barbarians considered themselves vastly superior (Campbell, *Framing Paul*, 272). The revolution of new humanity went well beyond social orders of just Greeks and Jews.

11. Bartlett, *TBM*, 109–11, 116–17, 132–33.

Recent scholarship, however, has shifted significantly the possibility of translation in respect to some of the New Testament instances of *pistis*.[12] The alternative of "faithfulness" has been highlighted, especially in relation to Christ: so, instances where the Greek has *pistis Christou*, and has most often been translated "faith *in* Christ," may much more aptly reflect the subjective genitive and be translated the "faithfulness *of* Christ/the Messiah." This at once lights up the page and creates the possibility of an arc of relation essential to semiotic transformation. N. T. Wright comments on Rom 3:21–26, identifying there a schematic outline of God's overall plan in which God's *own* faithfulness is shown working *through* the faithful Christ. It is this, most of all, which convinces him of the correct translation of *pistis*:

> Once we understand Christos as the Messiah, Israel's representative . . . the logic works out immaculately. (a) The covenant God promises to rescue and bless the world through Israel. (b) Israel as it stands is faithless to this commission. (c) The covenant God, however, is faithful, and will provide a faithful Israelite, *the* faithful Israelite, the Messiah. It is the tight coherence of this train of thought, rather than any verbal arguments . . . that persuaded me many years ago that Romans 3:22 speaks of the *Messiah's faithfulness*.[13]

Thus Rom 3:22, "the righteousness of God through faith in Jesus Christ for all who believe," should in fact be rendered "the righteousness of God through the faithfulness of Jesus Christ for all who have faith (in him)." In sum, the faithfulness of Jesus is something we have faith in, and that personal faith in turn *is* the faithfulness of Jesus. This is powerfully reinforced at verse 26 which is translated as "he justifies the one who has faith in Jesus," but should more properly be rendered "he justifies the one who has the faithfulness *of* Jesus." Which of course makes a great deal of sense: the righteousness/justice of God is communicated by means of the faithfulness of Jesus embraced integrally by the Christian. What this tells us is that faith is not something human beings *do* with their minds or wills, but it is the divine nonviolence of Christ which they *copy* with their whole neural mimetic selves. To paraphrase according to the overall thesis in the present book: the nonviolent faithfulness/righteousness of God

---

12. See Hays, *Faith of Jesus Christ.*
13. Wright, *Paul and the Faithfulness of God,* 839; last emphasis mine.

is communicated by the infinitely enduring nonviolence of Jesus which then becomes in turn the radical character of the believer.

The cross is, therefore, the core sign or semiosis by which God's own faithfulness is communicated, and this movement is represented within the whole passage Wright is commenting on. It is "the redemption that is in Christ Jesus, whom God put forward as a sacrifice of atonement by his blood, effective through faith."[14] The "sacrifice of atonement" is nothing like a faithful translation of the Greek *hilastērion*, which is most often represented as "cover" or "mercy seat" in translations of the LXX and Hebrew (e.g., Exod 25:17, Lev 16:15; see also Heb 9:5). Paul did not at all say "sacrifice"; instead, he referenced an item of Temple furniture, the place where the atoning event took place and thus a piece of coding *signifying* a phenomenology, a *meaning of what was happening*. Moreover, in the Romans passage, this is entirely not from the anthropological side of offered sacrifice; it is instead something "God put forward," which, of course, is intolerable as an anthropology of sacrifice. This was very deliberate on Paul's part. There were lots of other expressions he could have used more precisely if he wished to evoke "sacrifice." Instead, he chose, as I say, a "site" or "event" of mercy put forward by God, effecting the very thing that a Temple yearned toward but could never accomplish. In this way—because perhaps he is speaking to a group with exactly this style of Temple yearning—he uses a term that at once echoes and displaces sacrificial language. From the perspective of gospel semiotics as I have outlined them, the *hilastērion* is plainly another version of the semiotic portal which communicates God's infinite nonviolence to God's creation. As the text says, it is "effective through [divine] faith/faithfulness [*dia tēs pisteōs*]." The whole phrase might then be rendered: "The redemption that is in Christ Jesus whom God put forward as the portal of mercy (divine nonviolence) by his blood working through faithfulness." It is the simultaneous deconstruction of the Temple and the generative event of the cross. It is the *musterion*, the constructive event of the cross breaking down all barriers (cf. Rom 16:25).

The electric arc of transfer, by which God's own meaning is transmitted to humanity, is programmatically underlined right at the beginning of Romans, and we should refer there again to clarify further what was briefly glanced at above. Verses 16–17 say, "For I am not ashamed of the gospel . . . for in it the righteousness of God is revealed through faith for

14. Wright, *Paul and the Faithfulness of God*, 24–25.

faith." What could this possibly mean if we are talking simply about an individual effect connecting to God? What is the second instance of faith communicated from the first, if faith is only a private faculty? "My faith for the sake of my faith"?[15] Much rather, it has to mean God's righteousness is revealed through Christ's original faithfulness for the sake of the Christian's faith/faithfulness. Paul is very deliberately mining the range of meanings of *pistis* to construct the arc of communication which is the birth of Christian faithful nonviolence or nonviolent faithfulness—which itself is redemption.

Campbell describes Paul's language here in terms of punning, a deliberate employment of double meaning. He shows that the initial mention of *pistis*/faith in 1:17 must refer to Christ and his faithfulness because it looks to the quotation that the same verse offers from Hab 2:4, "the one who is righteous will live by faith." This quotation, in turn, is a fulfilment of the declaration at 1:2–3 that the gospel regarding the Son Jesus had been promised beforehand *through the prophets* (such as Habakkuk*).*[16] Campbell concludes, "So Paul is stating in 1:17a that God's *dikaiosunē* is being disclosed through the faithful Christ for those who trust/believe/ are faithful (literally, 'through fidelity for fidelity')."[17] "Faith," therefore, becomes a deliberately multivalent word, carrying within it the Christian's relationship in existence with the faithfulness of Christ, her own inner pledge of fidelity, and the organic imitation of divine being as nonviolence. Faith is the opening of the human self to an imitation or mimesis that is not historically available before the death and resurrection of Jesus. It is authentically, therefore, the engine of good news, of the gospel, because it brings to the world a way of being unavailable before, and yet capable, "in the now," of transforming the character of human life as such.

---

15. The same pleonasm (if faith is a private faculty) is present at Gal 3:22: "[T] he scripture has imprisoned all under the power of sin, so that what was promised through faith in Jesus Christ [genitive, *Iēsou Christou*] might be given to those who believe." It makes much more sense to read, "so that what was promised through the faithfulness *of* Jesus Christ might be given to those who believe."

16. Campbell, *Deliverance of God*, 615.

17. Campbell, *Deliverance of God*, 618. Campbell does not translate *dikaiosunē* ("justice," "righteousness"), ultimately giving it the sense of *deliverance*.

Romans

Campbell's scholarship, as I have already mentioned, is a massive intervention in the reading of Romans. Romans—or, at least, key passages
within it—is the core site for Luther's doctrine of justification by faith
alone. They provide what Campbell calls the "mighty fortress" textual
base for what he names "Justification Theory," something derived essentially from the German reformer although it now has a life well beyond
him.[18] We should turn once again to Campbell's work, to reinforce the
general shift that is being proposed here: from faith as contract to the
profound copying of a different (divine) humanity. Campbell presents
Justification Theory's formidable architecture as follows: humans are
rational actors who find the existence of God from the cosmos, and his
law from the workings of conscience; God's law is enforced retributively,
i.e., through punishment, above all the prospect of hell; all our efforts at
achieving righteousness in our own strength (works) are doomed to fail-
ure by innate sinfulness; the resulting despair is relieved by the death of
Christ, satisfying the demands of justice and imputing his righteousness
to sinners; these sinners lay hold of Christ's offer by the act of faith which
is the sole criterion of salvation. Christ provides the divine contract of
salvation, the Christian signs it—as simple as that.

Campbell lays out this theory in order to demolish it step by step,
demonstrating numerous internal and systematic difficulties.[19] By the
time he gets to the theory's textual stronghold in the first four chapters of
Romans, we sense how really shaky the edifice is. We are ready for a very
different take on what these pivotal chapters contain, and in the latter half
of the book, he provides a compelling account. Hand in hand we look
for a better version of the actual meaning of Paul's gospel, and Campbell

18. Campbell, *Deliverance of God*, 313ff. Campbell wants to distinguish between
the particular work of an historical figure like Luther and the contours of a theory as
such. For him "Justification Theory" has attained a kind of free-standing autonomy.

19. The most crucial difficulty seems to me to be the question of how can crippled
ethical capacity result in a correct estimate in respect of God or, indeed, any kind
of ethical response: "The darker the depraved non-Christian [pre-gospel] mind, the
more incoherent the divine expectation that important conclusions will be drawn ra-
tionally from the construction of the cosmos" (Campbell, *Deliverance of God*, 47). As
a matter of fact, it seems that the Christian gospel in this theory, rather than depending on a rational calculus, simply conforms to the depraved mind, threatening it with
terrible violence in order to extort from it the "submission of faith." A rationalist and
voluntarist version of faith cannot see the transforming good of the gospel, only the
violent threat of eternal torment.

does not disappoint here, either. He does not go into anything as great in length as in his work of demolition, but he certainly says enough to suggest a more coherent Pauline gospel. He outlines chapters *five to eight* of Romans as offering an authentic self-standing statement of Paul's proclamation of Christ, one that is as full of grace as it is free of penal threat.[20] There is no doubt that this Romans 5–8 gospel belongs fully to the in-breaking semiotic of a nonviolent God proposed in the present pages.

But what about the strategic chapters 1–4? What is actually contained there, given their attention-grabbing position at the beginning of the book? Campbell analyzes the actual writing style of 1:8–32 and shows that these verses almost certainly belong to a different voice from Paul's and represent in effect a strong thesis from *a different author*.[21] This understanding makes a whole lot of immediate sense, especially of the juxtaposition of verses 17 and 18 already highlighted. Commentators, including Campbell, question why the statement in verse 18 is in the present tense—*"for the wrath of God is revealed from heaven against all ungodliness and wickedness"*—when it is clear the wrath that is promised is coming in the future (cf. Rom 2:5)? The answer has to be that Paul is announcing *parallel, contrasting theses* (vv. 17–18). Paul is setting side by side, in deliberate dissonance, his own present-tense statement and that of an established Jewish-Christian teacher in Rome whose doctrine Paul is both rehearsing and demolishing at the outset of his letter. This, in a nutshell, is Campbell's whole interpretive argument, one which he goes on to lay out in detail. As mentioned above, he tells us that Paul is employing "speech in character" in chapters 1–4, both representing his opponent's argument and dismantling it. The Teacher, as Campbell capitalizes him, has a concept of the God of Jesus which demands obedience to the Jewish Law from Gentile converts—essentially for the sake of moral behavior. The generative force behind this teaching is the coming wrath and violence of God against the manifest wickedness of the age. In contrast, Paul is laboring to announce a gospel free of threat of violence, one whose generative force is entirely one of love, nonviolence, transformative faithfulness.[22]

20. Campbell, *Deliverance of God*, 62ff. See Campbell's later work, *Pauline Dogmatics*, for a positive presentation of Paul's gospel, especially pt. 2, chs. 11–15.

21. Campbell, *Deliverance of God*, 356–58, 543.

22. ". . . Paul seems to be stating in v.18 . . . that the initial and hence essential content of the Teacher's position is a vision of the future wrath of God—of God as retributively just. And Paul does not think that this is the essential nature of the God

The two present-tense statements in verses 17 and 18 headline the dramatically alternative *gospel(s)* at work. Such an exegesis then corresponds to Paul's further rhetorical parroting of his rival's thesis in order to discredit it. However, the reading of these two statements throughout the Christian era *as amounting to the same thing* also now presents as theologically disastrous. Because of a non-critical, sacral-textual reading of these verses in Romans, Christians have very often had a confused sense of the righteousness of God, as simultaneously nonviolent and violent, grace-filled and vengeful, transformative and archaic. The jarring dissonance of verses 18–32, with, for example, 5:1–5 or 8:31–39, has without doubt struck many, but it has either been put down to plain incoherence in Paul or been worked together into something as lovingly punitive and punitively loving as Justification Theory. We cannot forget that intrinsic to this theory is Anselmian atonement doctrine forged in the crusading Middle Ages,[23] so we are also talking about a long gestation from a textual fault line in Romans through a feudal culture of generative violence. It has taken both the acute new sensibilities and thinking resulting from the experience of modern global violence (and I include Girard here), and the steady elaboration of New Testament scholarship, to bring

---

of Jesus Christ. So he contrasts the Teacher's programmatic theological claim quite deliberately with the initial disclosure of his own position—his gospel—which speaks of the saving intervention of God and hence of the divine compassion (vv.16–17). Paul is stating here compactly that *fundamentally different conceptions of God are at stake* in these two gospels" (Campbell, *Deliverance of God*, 543). It is highly suggestive that after chapters 1–3—where he is echoing the mind of the Teacher, Paul in Romans does not predicate "wrath" (Greek *orgē*) as an attribute of God, i.e., he does not place the noun "God" in the genitive in relation to it. (For example, 4:15, 5:9, 12:19, even 9:22.) It becomes a neutral historical function, "*the* wrath," consistently mistranslated as "of God" in the various English versions. Wrath is in effect anthropological violence, in both its generative and chaotic phases. The celebrated case of Rom 13:4 where the civil sword "is the servant of God to execute wrath on the wrongdoer" simply passes on a general Old Testament understanding where human violence is a given contingency in the ordering of the world under God's rule. Habakkuk, for example, sees God as using violence to punish violence (2:8–17), and Genesis (chapter 4 especially, where Cain the murderer is given a protective mark) sees violence ambiguously under God's sovereignty. It is not surprising that Paul slips back into this "anthropological default" (cf. Col 3:6; Eph 5:6). When he is describing civil society and instructing Christians not to disrupt it, he is describing the inescapable condition of belonging to a new way of being human *while* living alongside the old way where it is still in force. The teaching is negative (*not* to rebel against it) rather than positive (becoming its agent). It is "authority" which bears the sword, not God (Rom 13:4); and at the same time, we know that Christ is "raised . . . far above all rule and authority" (Eph 1: 20–21).

23. See Bartlett, *Cross Purposes*; also, Campbell, *Deliverance of God*, 50–55.

us to the point where we can accurately distinguish the two voices in the first chapters of Romans.

Campbell's analysis shows that Paul is debating with the Teacher through chapter 4, although the latter's actual voice lessens a lot after chapter 2. Chapter 3 give us a synopsis of Paul's gospel in the midst of the argument, at 3:21–26, and we have already seen how N. T. Wright reads the "faith" here, in 3:22, as the Messiah's faithfulness. Campbell underlines this forcefully, and also does so while connecting the first instrumental use of *pistis* ("through faith/faithfulness") at 1:17 with the ones in 3:21–26, especially verse 22.[24] Seeing this axis makes conclusive the complete inadequacy, indeed distortion, of the usual reading. The first passage at 1:16–17, as we have said, contains the thesis statement, which is then given greater elaboration in the second passage. Campbell argues trenchantly that "faith" in the conventional reading of these passages is meaningless. It has to be something other than the believer contributing her feather-weight to the legal balance of salvation; i.e., it is rather the transformative faithfulness of Christ in and through the cross:

> [W]hat the conventional reading cannot explain is a "faith" that discloses or reveals the "righteousness of God" in instrumental terms . . . [Such] "Faith" simply does not function as the means by which something moves from a position of invisibility to one of visibility, from the unknown to the known, and to affirm that it does so is to make a basic semantic error—to assert something unmeaningful or ungrammatical.[25]

We can then complete the cycle of Campbell's thought by noting his complementary view that the faithfulness or fidelity of Christ—the true reference of *pistis* in these passages—is a code or metonym for the *whole* passion and it is this *entire* demonstration of the cross that reveals God's *dikaiosunē* ("righteousness"). "It is (Christ's) fidelity, interpreted metonymically with reference to the rest of the story of the passion, that reveals God's *dikaiosunē*."[26] We are thus very close to the semiotic portal which we described in respect of the historical Jesus, the one by which the nonviolent truth of God broke into the world. By misreading *pistis* in these passages as "faith in Christ" rather than the endlessly nonviolent

---

24. "[T]he righteousness of God through the faithfulness of Jesus Christ for all who have faith" (Campbell, *Deliverance of God*, 377–80).

25. Campbell, *Deliverance of God*, 379.

26. Campbell, *Deliverance of God*, 621.

"faithfulness of Christ," interpretation has dug a ditch between the story of the gospels and the gospel of Paul. In contrast, Paul's description of Christ as a *hilasterion* put forward by God ("through faithfulness in his blood," v. 25) tells us that the Temple is very probably in the back of Paul's mind (along with, possibly, Jesus' action there). What many commentators miss is the brutally public nature of this other mercy seat in Paul, as opposed to the original one hidden in the Holy of Holies and only visited by the High Priest once a year on the Day of Atonement.[27] Thus, the Temple meaning is ripped *as and by a revelation* from the sanctum to the place of execution; but this can only happen by means of the bottomless nonviolence of the Crucified, refusing any retaliatory gesture ("through faithfulness in his blood"). If not, we would need the Temple all over again to deal with the crisis of violence so exposed. Instead, the faithful nonviolence of the Christ displays the righteousness (nonviolence) of God for all to see—rather than the falsifying displacements and obscurity of sacrifice. Even as its apparatus is mentioned, the Temple is fundamentally subverted.

It is enormously important to grasp the radicalism of what Paul is attempting. Paul is asserting a gospel without moral and legal sanctions in the face of certainly the most moral of ancient religions—Judaism. Why is he doing this? He can only dare to do so because something unbelievably fresh and new has obtruded on the human scene: to wit, the righteousness of God as infinite nonviolence manifested in the semiotic supernova of the death and resurrection of Jesus. A gospel of God's wrath is in direct contradiction of this revelation: hence, Paul at once engages with and undermines its claim. It is a horrible principle on which to base a gospel, not simply because we can never be sure that anyone is good enough to escape its calculus—a basic part of Paul's argument against the Teacher in chapters 2–3—but because its very violence arouses in the human heart an imitative, conflictive violence, resulting in many of the very vices listed in chapter 1. Paul comes to understand this and reflect profoundly on its essential anthropological dysfunction in Romans 7. But here in argument with the Teacher, he sticks to the fact that Jewish people do sin, despite the Law, and so have no ultimate advantage over Gentiles. Paul refutes the Teacher by leading him into this rhetorical and logical

---

27. The verb at Rom 3:25, "put forward," is *proetheto*, which can easily bear the sense of "display publicly"; cf. Gal 3:1: "Christ was publicly exhibited [*prographō*] as crucified." Christ is "graphed out" on the cross—semiotically constructed and broadcast.

dead end, as Campbell demonstrates. In conclusion, if the Teacher retains wrath as a generative principle, his gospel is lost—it promises nothing as an advantage. Instead, Paul's gospel offers a new generative principle: Christ's faithfulness as manifestation of God's righteousness for the sake of human transformation.

Campbell does not insert the signifier of nonviolence into his descriptions of this gospel of Paul, but he comes close:

> Paul signals in 3:23–26 that the Christ event is the basis for the new and *much more effective* ethical reality that Christians now inhabit . . . Only this divinely provided solution can effect real ethical change in humanity. Moreover, that same Christ event signals unequivocally that Christians need not fear the wrath of God at the end of the age—indeed, far from it. A God who is prepared to offer up his son to suffer and die in order to effect atonement for sinful humanity—*free* atonement no less!—is clearly utterly benevolent [read nonviolent]. This is a God of love, not a God of punishment.[28]

Stoicheia and Other Dead-Ends

Having breached (with Campbell) the fortress of Justification Theory, we can travel back once more to what I have claimed as an Ephesians/ Colossians heartland. In these letters, Paul lets his soul and writer's hand range through the world with an expansiveness and confidence requiring no deployment for attacks from behind telling him his gospel is without merit. The palpable stress in Galatians and Romans (and for different reasons in the letters to the Corinthians) serves to distract from this broad vision, giving us instead a pressured Paul obliged to defend himself on several fronts. Let us look then at some of the content of these letters of the year 50, bringing into view the magnificent panorama of Christ's cosmic lordship which then filled Paul's mind.[29] One particular passage

28. Campbell, *Deliverance of God*, 608.

29. To place these letters later than Romans (late fifties, early sixties) would mean that Paul had somehow reversed his westward trajectory to Rome and Spain (engaging "behind him," and in close-grained local detail, especially as given in Philemon). Plus, if he is writing at this late date, he seems to have completely forgotten the opposition that had exploded around him in Galatians and Romans—while there is no reason to doubt this hostility continued to hound him. The only device left then is to make the letters pseudepigraphal. But this demands a tortuous forgery, especially in regard to Philemon and Colossians; and once we recognize the latter as genuine Ephesians

in Colossians leaps to mind for its sheer brilliance in pulling together multiple tropes in order to explain the work of Christ. "God made you alive together with him, when he forgave us all our trespasses, erasing the record that stood against us with its legal demands. He set this aside, nailing it to the cross. He disarmed the rulers and authorities and made a public example of them, triumphing over them in it" (Col 2:13–15). Here, instead of a breaking down of barriers (Eph 2:14), the cross volatilizes their legal form—undermining the potent mechanisms which would accuse, indict or penalize those whom God has set free. Paul expresses this transcendent act of liberation using a cloudburst of cultural, financial, military, and civic metaphors.

The "record" is literally *cheirographon* ("handwriting") suggesting that Paul is essentially aware of the semiotic quality of the unredeemed human condition. This is borne out by his reference a few verses earlier to "human tradition according to the elemental spirits of the universe" (something which takes people captive, 2:8). "Elemental spirits" is actually *stoicheia*, a term which can be applied to the letters of the alphabet, inasmuch as they belong to something which makes up a *stoichos*, a basic row or series of things. In this connection, therefore, Paul can be heard talking about something akin to primordial human order and difference. There is quite a bit to be remarked on this, but just at the moment we are concentrating on the writing/semiosis that stands against human beings and from which the cross sets us free. It is sometimes translated "record of debt," referring to a bill of debt held by a creditor. But the further elaboration is "handwriting in the decrees [*dogmasin*] against us." *Dogma* can refer to the rules or ordinances in the law of Moses *or* decrees issued by the emperor (Luke 2:1; Acts 17:7). The reference in the second sentence following, to "disarm(ing) the rulers and authorities," and the image of a military triumph, make it fairly unmistakable that Paul is referencing the whole system of world order and control. What the gospel does is nail the violent system of human meaning to the cross, bringing it to an end, in the inverse pattern of what the authorities intended for Jesus. Jesus was nailed to the cross in order to overpower and abolish him as a figure

---

becomes easy to accept. Essentially the claim of forgery cuts Ephesians thinking off from Paul in a tendentious way—i.e., the "genuine" Paul is a Paul with *only* a future eschatology (and basically one that is violent). In which case it becomes very difficult to understand all the notes of the present reign and human impact of Christ in what are considered the undisputed letters: e.g., Phil 2:9–10; 1 Cor 15:20–25; 2 Cor 5:14–19; Rom 8:37–39.

of historical worth and meaning. What actually happened is a complete reversal of this mechanism, an absolute shock to the imperial order of things. Instead of being crushed, Jesus overpowers the very system of crushing. Paul illustrates this reversal with the figure of a written document. Normally, the nailing of a piece of writing to something intends the power of that writing over the physical and social space to which it is nailed. But here the physical reality is the cross which, as a metonym for Jesus' death and resurrection, is itself a semiotic reality, communicating the divine nonviolence which reverses the flow of meaning. The cross overpowers whatever writing/meaning is directed in "dogmatic" condemnation of human beings in whatever situation they find themselves so condemned. It is a huge claim, but Paul does not hold back. He goes further. On the basis of the reversal there is a formal triumphant display (v. 15, *thriambeuo*): Christ is now the conqueror of human meaning, like a triumphant Roman general, but on the abyssal grounds of divine nonviolence. Paul is not arguing a philosophy, an intellectual understanding. He is talking about something that has happened on the most basic level of human constitution, such that all prior orders of human constitution and meaning are rendered obsolete. The thought of semiotic transformation seems to be the only adequate analysis of this change.

So, let us come back to *stoicheia*, a concept that has a master role here in Paul's thinking. As mentioned, the word comes from *stoichos*, meaning "rank," "line," or "sequence." *Stoicheia* are then the bits, items, or elements that together make up the continuum, and as such they both depend on the total system for their identity, and yet in turn make up that whole. The amazing thing now about Paul's usage is how he takes a term with essentially physical reference and gives it decisive cultural and social value. The most commonly known "elements" are the fundamental physics of the Greek world, "fire, water, earth, air."[30] Paul brings the word with these physical references together with cultural meaning in a seminal way. He makes a leap from the physical to the cultural, intuiting that the cultural construction of things also somehow encompasses the physical world, and vice versa. This is what I called the "semioverse" in *TBM*, the fundamental unity of cultural meaning and *things*. Paul declared this unity two millennia ago and its truth has been slowly making its way to headline status. As already quoted, Paul has warned the Colossians of the danger of "human tradition, according to the *stoicheia* of the world,"

30. This goes back at least to Plato (*Timaeus* 48B). See Leithart, *Delivered from the Elements of the World*, 31–32.

specifying this as being taken captive "through philosophy and empty deceit" (Col 2:8). What contrasts with this—throwing it into relief—is the fact of Christ and the Colossians' relation to him: "For in him the whole fullness of deity dwells bodily, and you have come to fullness in him, who is the head of every ruler and authority" (Col 2: 9–10). Christ represents an entirely new and alternative principle of reality, in "bodily" being, and this new way of being is above every other semiotic regime and its physical realization. Clearly this is a revolutionary position, but Paul is not interested in revolution, or at least not in *that* kind of revolution. What he is talking about is a radical new meaning based in the reality of the Risen Crucified, something to which each Christian becomes committed, and through which all meaning for them is transformed in the here and now. As regards Christ being head over "rulers and authorities," this can only possibly mean a radical subordination of the lifeworld of empire, with its inherent violence, to the new principle of meaning which is Christ.[31] This again is a huge claim but it flows naturally from a breakdown of all walls of separation. It is these walls that constitute empire, creating a simulacrum of unity between those within its walls, while continually excluding those outside through its practice of violence. Christ, as we have underlined, brings a totally new principle, one "raised up" by God and thus destined to overturn the rule of empire itself.

However, all religious expression has roots in sacrificial origins, and tendrils of difference and exclusion can re-emerge with great tenacity no matter how searing the vision of new reality possessed by Paul. So, the apostle to the Gentiles is obliged to challenge the Christians of Colossae, calling them to renewed awareness of their radical liberation from the *stoicheia*. "If with Christ you died to the elemental spirits of the universe, why do you live as if you still belonged to the world? Why do you submit to regulations? 'Do not handle. Do not taste. Do not touch'? All these regulations refer to things that perish with use; they are simply human commands and teachings" (Col 2:20–22). Here it is plain. Some of the basic constituents of culture and religion—prohibitions, taboos, purity markers—are at stake in Christian existence and at once roundly rejected by Paul as obsolete, as part of a world that has passed away. There can only be one fundamental reason for this. The purpose of prohibitions,

---

31. It is not by accident that Paul uses this kind of language as he is addressing places in the Roman province of Asia which includes the proximate cities of Pergamon, Smyrna, and Ephesus, all centers of imperial cult dedicated to Caesars Augustus and Tiberius. See Friesen, *Imperial Cults*, 25–41, 95–101.

according to Girard, is to prevent possible occasions of rivalry and inter-necine conflict. But in the same moment their basic purpose is fulfilled, they take on a role in and of themselves, giving shape and meaning to the universe: they *become* the universe. Peter Leithart in his book on "ele-ments of the world" makes this function explicit.

> Practices of purity imply a cosmos, a way of organizing and construing reality. Distinctions between clean and unclean map the social world into distinct regions. Purity regulations form an economy of signs, a symbolic universe, but the symbolic uni-verse is not self-enclosed. A symbolic map works with the world divvied up in specific ways. Purity regulations trace out a world that comes to seem natural to those who inhabit it.[32]

This is critical. The "divvying up" of the world, the creation of fundamen-tal difference, becomes and is part of the objective order of things, the ontological as such. How can we dispense with these *stoicheia* and not experience humanly the collapse of the universe itself? It has to be that the abolition of this difference in Christ is the product of an inbreak-ing divine nonviolence which creates not chaos but an entirely fresh and transformative source of reality. This is the reason why Paul uses such radical language, "If with Christ you have died . . ." The old world-order cannot become new meaning simply by intellectual judgment, or moral decision, continuous with the old world-scheme; it can only come with the death of its generative principle within the individual. It is a cataclys-mic shift to an entirely new human and earthly physics. The language of *stoicheia* is used by Paul, therefore, to signify a change of meaning that is at the same time a change of the universe as such, the cultural and the physical together. "Paul told everyone that the physics of religion and so-ciety had been transformed, and that the end of the old elemental system was the great moment of maturation, when the human race grew up from slaves to sons. A world beyond stoicheic order—that is a *saved* world, a world fulfilled as a new creation."[33]

The language of *stoicheia* is one of transformative semiosis, and, once again, this is never simply an internal, soulish, subjective change. The reality of things changes too, because this is the nature and condition of the Risen Christ and the consistent liberation from the elements he has brought. "If you have been raised with Christ, seek the things that

32. Leithart, *Delivered from the Elements of the World*, 40
33. Leithart, *Delivered from the Elements of the World*, 41.

are above [i.e., other than the worldly order], where Christ is, seated at the right hand of God" (Col 3:1). Or, as said in Ephesians: "He has put all things under his feet and has made him the head over all things for the church, which is his body, the fullness of him who fills all" (Eph 1:22–3). If the universe is submitted to the Risen Christ, and the church is the body of this Christ, it means that in principle—and at some level of phenomenological truth—all things are transformed for those who relate to this novum according to the relation he makes possible. This is the nature and consequence of liberation from the elements. Leithart's striking epigram makes this plain: "Nothing could express the root character of the change brought by the gospel more stunningly than the language of physics. Jesus did not merely rearrange the surface. The world works differently now, because it is no longer made up of the same stuff. It is as if Paul announced that *Jesus transformed the world right down to the quarks.*"[34]

The paraphrase for *stoicheia*, "elemental spirits of the universe," is, therefore, not correct, suggestive as it is of another order of "spiritual" reality that somehow interferes with this one: "fallen angels," etc. The Colossians apparently were themselves moving somewhere in this worldview, and Paul warned them against it (Col 2:18). In contrast, his language is grounded and concrete. *Stoicheia kosmou* is better rendered by "generative forces of this world," having in mind, of course, the Girardian account of original violence. "Divvying up" the world happens on the basis of the original murder, in the primary distinction of "sacred" and "everything else" beside it, made in and through and by the body of the original victim.[35] This primordial shape and structure carries on throughout history as the core architecture of functional human meaning, pervasive in all cultural forms. But when Christ dies and rises from death, this architecture is essentially fragmented and volatilized, displaced by a fount of nonviolent giving which continually renews itself. The primary distinctions erected from the sacred are no longer valid. Instead, all is made new, single, life-giving, and whole. The Christian bases her life continually in this revolutionary alternative wholeness, not in the old divisions, and so she makes known the transformed universe to all around.

---

34. Leithart, *Delivered from the Elements of the World*, 42; my italics.
35. Bartlett, *TBM*, 39–45.

Powers, Law, and Liberation

When Paul encountered a "return to the law" in the Galatian church, he reacted against this as precisely a return to *stoicheia*. The Mosaic law had no privilege,[36] except inasmuch as it looked toward fulfillment in Christ via promises to Abraham of universal blessing (Gal 3:15–18). Speaking to his fellow Jews, Paul equates being under the law to being a child under guardians, until the time when the child reaches majority (4:2). But these guardians too were *stoicheia*. "So with us, while we were minors we were enslaved to the *stoicheia* of the world" (Gal 4:3). It is indeed a matter of slavery, of the lack of human liberty and dignity under a regime of violence: "Now before faith came we were imprisoned and guarded under the law until faith would be revealed" (Gal 3:23). Only in the faithful divine nonviolence of Christ is full human freedom granted and attained. The sweep of Paul's thought becomes clear when he turns next to address Gentiles, switching from first to second person. "Formerly, when you did not know God, you were enslaved to beings that by nature are not gods. Now, however, that you have come to know God how can you turn back again to the weak and beggarly *stoicheia*? How can you want to be enslaved to them again? You are observing special days, and months, and seasons, and years" (Gal 4:8–10; see Col 2:16–17). The splitting of time on the basis of sacred days and seasons is a beggarly ("bent-over") *stoicheion*, which is necessarily an image of sacred violence, of slavery to beings that claim divinity but "by nature are not gods." Thus, any essential distinction between Jewish and Gentile religious practice is erased: everything that repeats the elements of an original generative sacred is *stoicheia*, regardless of whether it is Jewish or Gentile, whether it is purity requirements or calendric divisions of time.

Paul's vocabulary of "powers" is broader than *stoicheia* and can seem to suggest independent "personal" existences. For example, the graphic passage at Eph 6:12: "For our struggle is not against enemies of blood and flesh, but against the rulers, against the authorities, against the cosmic powers of this present darkness, against the spiritual forces of evil in the heavenly places [*pros ta pneumatika tēs ponērias en tois epouraniois*]." The work of Walter Wink has been pivotal in bringing these "powers" to focus in contemporary theology, understanding them in a demythologizing frame as human institutions or physical and structural forces which

36. Leithart, *Delivered from the Elements of the World*, 38: "Paul dramatically, radically flattens the difference between Jew and Gentile."

govern human life.[37] But by also identifying them with a claimed Jungian, "spiritual within" simultaneously connected to an external world, Wink risks simply changing the imaginal space of the "other world," effectively reaffirming a traditional dualism that has always dogged Christianity.

In contrast, the approach here tells us that the purported "spiritual" level of reality is the complex of mimetic relationships and signs which humans create together. This understanding does not belittle, let alone negate the world of powers. On the contrary, it accounts for its never-ending vitality, even as it explains consistently from where that power and vitality derive. As human beings are plunged together in a vast universe of objects and forces, they have created an even vaster sea of signs by which to interpret and control it. To begin with, violence was the generative power behind the miracle of organizing semiotics, but little by little human institutions, such as kingship, law, temple, and ritual, give permanent shape to the original fission and fusion of violence. It is these institutions that dispose of "power" in relation to human beings. Wink's analyses act as a kind of prolegomenon to this approach, charting the array of sign-forces at work in Paul's world and text—all of which Paul declares as subordinate to Christ.

There is a descriptive semiotic element directly present in Paul. Ephesians tells us God put his power "to work in Christ when he raised him from the dead and seated him at this right hand in the heavenly places, far above all rule and authority and power and dominion, and above every name that is named, not only in this age but also in the age to come" (Eph 1:20–21). Paul has recourse to "name" (*onoma*) alongside the

---

37. See Wink's trilogy, *Naming the Powers, Unmasking the Powers, Engaging the Powers.* The powers extend from obvious entities such as actual rulers, magistrates, police, army, through religious practices, ritual, temple, or the ceremonial Jewish law, to more sociological and economic structures such as class systems, nationalism, education, even philosophy, all the way to spiritual, demonic, or Satanic powers. Wink insists that all of these are demythologized because they are not projected on a cosmic level. "[T]he 'principalities and powers' are the inner and outer aspects of any given manifestation of power. As the inner aspect they are the spirituality of institutions, the 'within' of corporate structures and systems, the inner essence of outer organizations of power." However, because of this archetypal "within," his writing is often close to reaffirming the old dualism. "[The] sense of being held fast by some overwhelmingly powerful, higher being is common to all religions. Jung chose the term 'archetypes' as a more phenomenologically neutral way of speaking about what religions have called gods, spirits, angels and demons. The archetypes are the numinous, structural elements of the psyche that preform our experience in certain typical ways . . ." (*Unmasking the Powers,* 117–18).

vocabulary of rulers and dominions, telling us explicitly that language is the accompanying frame of powers present and future. It is an implied semiotics where words carry their own intrinsic weight in relation to materiality. The world of powers may then also morph and shift depending on our evolving language and signs, rendering what is newly meaningful and impactful in our world as the generations change. But in every case, the implication is the same: the name of Christ is raised above the other names, the other signs, involving a total reordering of all semiotic space. It is by virtue of this reordering of root meaning that believers themselves are then also raised above the powers: God "raised us up with him and seated us with him in the heavenly places in Christ Jesus" (Eph 2:6). Because believers are in the transformed semiotic space of the Crucified and Risen One, no other sign/power has power over them.

As with so much of Paul's writing, he is reaching for metaphors to explain a transformative event within a previous and now relativized master scriptural narrative, and nothing can entirely fit. It is very important to underline this: Paul is always working on a double register, sketching the breakthrough of the gospel prepared in and through the Jewish people, and yet proclaiming the breakthrough as absolute. He clearly says that before Christ, Israel (3:23), like the Gentiles, was enslaved to the *stoicheia of the world* (*tou kosmou*, Gal 4:3). The *stoicheia* are part of the generative forces of the human world prior to and other than the inbreaking nonviolence of Israel's God. The only thing that makes full sense of the double register is the anthropological constant of historical generative violence within which biblical revelation slowly develops its recoding—the apocalypse of divine nonviolence. All the code creations described in this present book look toward and prepare the breakthrough. Meanwhile, it is evident so much of the vehicle or medium in which they are carried forward belongs to the generative human order. Kingship and temple are obvious. And again, of course, is law. As we have seen, the law imposes itself in the figure of violence: as a guard, jailer, or discipline master (*paidagogos*, Gal 3:24). In Romans, Paul is even harsher: "For the law brings (*katergazetai*, "brings about") wrath, but where there is no law, neither is there violation" (Rom 4:15). The law not only imposes itself *through* violence, it actually works out *as* violence.

Paul says this in absolute terms—law issues in violence. The famous account of human incapacity in Rom 7:7–25 describes the terrible human condition in which the law itself provokes sin. The responsibility is—as Paul insists—that of "sin," but nevertheless the law itself becomes a mechanism, through "sin," of multiplied trespass. Paul, as always, is doubling round to validate what I have called a master scriptural narrative—thus the law is holy and good (Rom 7:12). Yet at the same time, if the law did not have some kind of affinity with sin, it could not possibly work to provide opportunities for it. The explanation then has to lie in mimetic desire. As Paul is very probably referencing, the account in Genesis is paradigmatic: unless God had given the prohibition against eating of the fruit of the tree there would have been nothing for the first parents to covet and so to transgress. Anthropologically speaking, prohibition is itself a product of the crisis of desire and its explosion. It comes out of desire and represents the negation of desire and yet it still works via desire, i.e., desire's high-point of violence which the crisis generates. Thus "sin" here is simply a metonym for mimetic desire and its function as both quelled, yet secretly preserved and enshrined, by law. Hence, sin is genetically linked to law, and vice versa. Even though in the short run, sin is held in check by law, its essence, germ, or mainspring is maintained in the very mechanism that so controls it. In this passage, Paul is talking at a profound anthropological level, not necessarily represented in his previous consciousness or action as a Jew; but—from the devastating perspective of the inbreaking of Christ—he comes to see that no matter its noble intentions, law still continues to operate in the same closed circle of violence and sin. Only the "clothing" in the radically new ontology of Christ (Gal 3:27) offers a way out.

The "flesh" is another of Paul's master tropes, pressed into service from ordinary language to describe something extraordinary. From a term rooted in the phenomenon of the body, its sexual generative power, and its inevitable mortality,[38] Paul extends the concept into apocalyptic meaning. "Flesh" cannot now be thought apart from the new thing in the world and its offer of life, and so it must now become itself an apocalyptic notion. Not only is flesh the human condition of bodily life and death, but now it becomes necessarily *a chosen way of death* when it deliberately refuses the nonviolent divine and its present resurrected life. Flesh becomes an assertive and recognizable semiosis of human life once the possibility of refusing the revelation comes together with the revelation. To use a modern parallel, it is not possible to refuse a vaccine until the vaccine arrives—but once it does, it is possible to refuse it on principle. Necessarily, therefore, the flesh becomes a way of life, one

38. Leithart, *Delivered from the Elements of the World*, 78–80.

rooted in generative violence. Leithart recognizes this in Paul's summary description with its decisive accent on conflict: "Fleshly society is exclusivist, divided and competitive. Flesh produces 'enmities, strife, jealousy, outbursts of anger, disputes, dissensions, factions, envying' (Gal 5:20–21 NASB)." He also makes the point with sharp contemporary relevance in terms of institutional violence. "If you want to see a concrete, structural expression of flesh, take a look at the budget for the US Department of Defense or the protective system of Homeland Security."[39]

The cross of Christ is a one-time-only event of extreme nonviolent suffering, carrying into an abyss of violence a countervailing forgiveness and love. The old core of human semiosis—the discharge of collective violence on the surrogate victim—is transformed into a meaning-bearing self-surrender and giving. Because the space of crucifixion is intended (by temple and empire) as the triumphant opacity of worldly violence, Jesus' endless visibility of nonviolence, brought to transcendent identity in the power of resurrection, becomes an apocalyptic breakthrough of new human meaning. The believer embraces this meaning by a relation called faith and so in turn follows Christ into the same bottomless space of death and new life: "Do you not know that all of us who have been baptized into Christ Jesus were baptized into his death? Therefore, we have been buried with him by baptism into death, so that, just as Christ was raised from the dead by the glory of the Father, so we too might walk in newness of life" (Rom 6:3–4).

The believer dies to the atavistic construct of violent human meaning, entirely. The cross becomes a window into a radically new existence, a portal to a different human meaning, renewed day after day, moment by moment. And here is the reason Paul opposed circumcision: it represented an ambivalence connected to the old order. Paul expresses this in terms of "boasting" (*kauchaomai*, Rom 2:23; Eph 2:9), a mimetic activity which goes on all the time—i.e., the constitutive "dialogue" with the other that says in the secret of our souls, "I am other and better than you." At Gal 6:13, he says that some of the circumcised "desire to have you circumcised so that they may boast in your flesh" (NASB). This is not a petty accusation about tribal score-keeping; it is about the construction of identity in opposition to the other, through the victory of rivalry and the rivalry of victory. The cross of Christ instead—as semiosis—disrupts this world from within. He "has broken down in his flesh the dividing

---

39. Leithart, *Delivered from the Elements of the World*, 84, 82.

wall of hostility by abolishing the law expressed in ordinances that he might create in himself one new humanity" (Eph 2:14). In Christ, the ontology of cutting-off and otherness has itself been dissolved, giving rise to an entirely new humanity. The ontology of difference is overwhelmed in the semiosis of love. Paul insisted on this meaning and this meaning only.

In the same vein, we also readily understand the freighted words "works of the law" employed in Ephesians, Galatians, and Romans. It has very little to do with any supposed proto-Roman Catholic religious practices ("works righteousness") in first-century Judaism.[40] In Ephesians, faith is opposed to works of the law where, in the latter, someone may boast (Eph 2:8–9). Already at this point—before the crises of Galatians and Romans—Paul understands that the basic issue with the external acts of the law is the dialectic of victory it creates with the other. As with "flesh," this would not be an issue unless Christ had broken into the bounded human sphere and created a new humanity without boundary walls. In which case, the acts of the law become themselves a counter-apocalyptic, a way of life that is blocked from the radical newness of the cross. "Grace" is the word that Paul uses here for the absolute nonviolence of God's act in Christ—a condition where there is no mimesis of exchange enacted, only the unstinted overflowing of love: "the immeasurable riches of his grace in kindness toward us in Christ Jesus. For by grace you have been saved through faith, and this is not your own doing; it is the gift of God—not the result of works, so that no one may boast" (Eph 2:7–9).

Grace is not some kind of arbitrary legal decision for the elect, still less a quantum of divine favor inexplicably doled out on selective occasions: it is a radically different principle of being, revealed to all in Christ and assimilated in the relation of faith. It is the impossible self-giving of God displayed in the mystery of the cross—Christ's remainderless self-outpouring to the final breath. It is the eruption on the scene of exchange of a life beyond exchange. When Paul engages in Galatians and Romans with agents who seek to preserve the law in Christian practice (Gal 5:1–4; Rom 2:17–29, 6:17, 16:17), he shows himself totally committed to this other, transformative vision. "I, Paul, am telling you that if you let yourself be circumcised, Christ will be of no benefit to you . . . You who want to be justified by the law have cut yourselves off from Christ, you have fallen away from grace" (Gal 5:2–4). "Justification" itself—another

40. See Sanders' protest in *Paul and Palestinian Judaism* against the concept that Jews had to earn salvation, on merit based assessment, rather than remain steadfastly within a divinely-given covenant (*Paul and Palestinian Judaism*, 57, 183).

historically fraught word in the Pauline lexicon—can be nothing other than the overcoming of wrath/violence in God through Christ, and the relational communication of that overcoming to human beings. If the Teacher of Romans starts his gospel with "the wrath of God has been revealed from heaven," and Paul, as we have seen, pre-empts him with "the gospel reveals the righteousness of God that comes by faith [of Christ] to faith" (Rom 1:17–18), it means that what produces justification or righteousness is what is *other* than wrath. Explicitly and essentially so—as the historical, earthly witness of nonviolence on the cross demonstrated. Meanwhile, the double register of a narrative of law and one of transformation must have its final explanation, in that the former provides the generative space in which the latter may emerge. Transformation has always been the secret soul, the lovechild, and final truth of the law, as the present book must show.

And so we come to the long-gestated heart of biblical and Pauline revelation, as Campbell states it at the end of his own long argument:

> *Dikaiosunē theou* speaks of God's liberating act in Christ, through which a captive and helpless humanity—and ultimately a screaming creation as well—are delivered. And because the content of this divine act is supplied by the Christ event, and because of its utterly saving character, Paul characterizes God consistently as a deliverer—a divine king who is acting with a right action and a "judgment" that does nothing other than save and save gratuitously. In short, for Paul, God as revealed by Christ, is benevolent [i.e., nonviolent] . . . There is no other character of God behind this acting God: this is God as he truly is—the God who delivers through Jesus Christ. Paul's root metaphor of God, then, is benevolent, or merciful. *There is no retributive character to the God revealed to Paul by Christ.*[41]

41. Campbell, *Deliverance of God*, 706. And it is worth continuing the quotation for the sake of the contrast with the doctrine of the Teacher, so germane to the argument here: "*And this is what lies at the heart of Paul's dispute with the Teacher.* The Teacher has not taken Christ's disclosure of God's benevolence with full seriousness; that disclosure has been subordinated and assimilated to some prior conception of God that is retributive. In this sense, then, the Teacher's conception of God is Christianized but not Christian; it is not revised by the Christ event at a fundamental level . . . [Paul's] gospel is rooted in a *dikaiosunē theou*. The Teacher's gospel is rooted, however, in an *orgē theou*—an 'anger' that responds to all actions retributively, and to sinful actions punitively. *These two basal conceptions of God could not, in this sense, be more different.* And only one is thoroughly rooted in the implications of the Christ event." (Italics original.)

It is the pellucid quality of Paul's vision, its irrevocable quality of under-standing, that makes him really the most important witness of the New Testament, apart from the figure of Jesus himself. We might protest that this vision of liberated human life is impossible to fulfill, too radical and extreme for ordinary mortals. Paul clearly did not think so. Rather, he saw the gospel as the inbreaking of an actual scheme of human possibil-ity even as the old might still persist. In a noteworthy passage, he tells the Corinthians to live as if their standard human undertakings—mar-riage, mourning, celebrating, commerce, etc.—were actually *not* the case: meaning that even as they fulfill normal human relationships, they live by an entirely new, superseding one, "for the present form of the world is passing away" (1 Cor 7:29–31). Paul's vision is the template of all possible revolutions, but beyond the generative violence of all revolutions.[42] It is rooted in the nonviolent cross and resurrection, the once-and-forever turn of meaning that reconditions all human meaning. Whether we be-lieve in its truth or not, the tenor of this revolution has entered our semi-otic universe, promising a world beyond violence and a God only known in that relation, a God beyond violence:

> What then are we to say about these things? If God is for us, who is against us? He who did not withhold his own Son, but gave him up for all of us, will he not with him give us everything else? ... Who will separate us from the love of Christ? Will hardship, or distress, or persecution, or famine, or nakedness, or peril, or sword? [Or gun or bomb?] As it is written, "For your sake we are being killed all day long ..." No, in all these things we are more than conquerors through him who loved us. For I am convinced that neither death, nor life, nor angels, nor rulers, nor things present, nor things to come, nor powers, nor height, nor depth, nor anything else in all creation, will be able to separate us from the love of God in Christ Jesus our Lord. (Rom 8:31–39)

42. Note the way contemporary secular philosophers like Giorgio Agamben (*The Time That Remains*, 62–68) and Slavoj Žižek (*The Puppet and the Dwarf*, 111–13) are attracted to this passage, as it dramatically reconstructs the possibility of human future in the face of social and political hegemony.

Brief Appendix on the Lamb

AFTER THE MESSAGES TO the seven churches in the first three chapters of the Book of Revelation, the scene shifts to an awe-filled moment of worship before the throne of God. A "scroll" is introduced and there is a "lamb standing as having been slain" (Rev 5:6, *arnion hestēkos hōs esphagmenon*). What is the scroll? It is a writing, a content of signified meaning. But "no one in heaven or on earth or under the earth [is] able to open the scroll" and read it (Rev 5:3). A meaning of extreme relevance to human existence is forcibly closed to all creation. But then one is found who "has conquered, so that he can open the scroll and its seven seals" (Rev 5:5). It is the lamb (a "little lamb," *arnion*), whose identity and value is that of "having been slain." This lamb now becomes the key protagonist and hero of the whole book, mentioned twenty-eight times throughout (twenty-eight equals 7 x 4, the number of named series of seven—letters, seals, trumpets, bowls, a complete set, as it were, of signified history). The lamb is one who has conquered through *having been slain*, and preserving that sign-value ("standing *as* . . .") continually throughout. Predictably in the commentaries and footnotes, the victory of the lamb is through its "sacrifice," although this is nowhere shown to be the case. Much more evident and powerful is the fact of the lamb "standing as having been slain," and "conquering" precisely in that role. To wit, the lamb communicates— semiotically, informatively, continuously, meaningfully—its identity as the nonviolent victim of violence, and thereby unlocks the meaning of history.

It's necessary at the end of this book to thus state succinctly the drama of the Lamb, given how the Book of Revelation has been hijacked as the standard proof text on ultimate divine violence. As the cliché has it, "Jesus first came as gentle, he will return as a warrior." There is no space, of course, to give a full commentary on this last book of the Bible. Therefore, the absolutely cardinal thing to understand is that all the metaphors and images of violence in this book are a mirror code of the world's own violence brought to light and crisis by the constant *standing-as-slain* of the Lamb. Standing in this way, the Lamb is the functional *mirror* of the world's violence. It is a trans-historical revelatory constant, reflecting the action of the world. It is seen, therefore, *as* violent by this world which continues incorrigibly in the generative principle of its own violent perception. The Book of Revelation is written partly as this mirror perception. It is a Wisdom concept, fulfilling the principle of "They have dug a ditch and fallen in it themselves." There is little doubt that this powerful mirroring concept helped sustain and motivate a community under severe social pressure and random persecution. It is a picture of triumph by a nonviolence which refers the enemy's violence back to itself. Brian Zahnd says that "the drama of Revelation is cast as an epic conflict between the Lamb (Jesus) and the Beast (Rome)."[1] He also quotes Michael J. Gorman:

> Revelation is therefore a *theopolitical* text. It makes claims about who is truly God and about right and wrong connections between God and the socio-political order; it challenges the political theology of empire and the religious ideology that underwrites it; and it reveals God and the Lamb alone as the true Sovereign One, source of all blessings, and proper object of worship. Moreover, Revelation tells us not only who is really sovereign but also what kind of sovereignty the true God exercises, namely what many have called nonviolent and non-coercive "Lamb power."[2]

If this is the case, it entails something other than the normal reciprocity of "victory." And the end of the book confirms this by its huge *coup de théâtre*. There is a final battle in which all humanity is "killed by the sword of the rider on the horse, the sword that came from his mouth . . ." (19:21). Unarguably this sword is the word of God (the figure is named as such just earlier, at verse 13) and the "killing" is itself the overcoming of the violence of the world. This is confirmed in the final chapters on the New Jerusalem, where "the nations [who have just been killed] will walk by its light" and the kings [who have just been killed] "will bring

1. Zahnd, *Sinners in the Hands of a Loving God*, loc. 155.

2. Gorman, *Reading Revelation Responsibly*, 43, quoted in Zahnd, *Sinners in the Hands of a Loving God*, loc. 157.

their glory into it" (21:24). Ultimately the Wisdom motif of "their own violence falling on their heads" (Ps 7:15) is undone by something much more profound. Because there is a battle of meaning and perception engaged, it is never simply "the measure you measure to others measured to you"—end of story! No, the Lamb-standing-as-having-been-slain is engaged in an epoch-long semiotic battle with the Beast, a battle for human meaning, and the end revealed in Revelation is of the conclusive victory of the sign of the Lamb. The nations "will walk by (the) light" of the city of the Lamb. This is not an image of the crushing of the enemies of the Lamb, but rather of their human and meaningful transformation. This cannot happen without a profound struggle at the level of generative anthropology. Revelation describes that struggle intensely and predicts its final outcome.

In several places in the book one can detect the trauma of the loss of the Jerusalem temple in the Jewish-Roman war (66–70 CE): many of the revelations come from a temple in heaven, and from the midst of a wondrous worship there (7:15, 11:19, 14:15, 15:5, 15:8). As if the brutal destruction of the temple is compensated by direct visions into a heavenly counterpart and its liturgies. But then, at the end, this compensatory revelation is brought down to earth, literally, with a bump. It is dissolved in an astonishing vision of "a new heaven and a new earth": "And I saw the holy city, the new Jerusalem, coming down out of heaven from God, prepared as a bride adorned for her husband. And I heard a loud voice from the throne saying, 'See, the home of God is among mortals. He will dwell with them'" (Rev 21:2–30). And a little later: "I saw no temple in the city, for its temple is the Lord God the Almighty and the Lamb. And the city has no need of sun or moon to shine on it, for the glory of God is its light, and its lamp is the Lamb" (Rev 21:22–23).

There is no longer need for exchange between holy and non-holy, for negotiation between violent sacred and day-to-day human life, between priesthood and lay. All violence is gone, and there is an entirely new principle of meaning and communication, a semiotic novum—the Lamb. And there is God-according-to-the-Lamb, a transcendence without violence.

The destiny of history is the overcoming of violence. The Book of Revelation, and its hero, the Lamb-standing-as-having-been-slain, reveal this to be the case: "The kingdom of the world has become the kingdom of our Lord and of his Messiah and he will reign forever and ever" (Rev 11:15).

Bibliography

Agamben, Giorgio. *The Time That Remains: A Commentary on the Letter to the Romans*. Translated by Patricia Dailey. Stanford: Stanford University Press, 2005.

Allison, Dale C., Jr. *The Historical Christ and the Theological Jesus*. Grand Rapids: Eerdmans, 2009.

Anderson, Bernhard W., Stephen Bishop, and Judith H. Newman. *Understanding the Old Testament*. Upper Saddle River: Pearson, 2007.

Aristotle. *Poetics*. Translated by S. H. Butcher. Mineola: Dover, 2012.

Augustine, *City of God*. Translated by Henry Bettenson. Introduction by John O'Meara. New York: Penguin, 1984.

———. *Confessions*. Translated by Henry Chadwick. Oxford: Oxford University Press, 2009.

———. *The Literal Meaning of Genesis*. In *On Genesis*, edited by John E. Rotelle, 168–506. The Works of St. Augustine I/13. Translated by Edmund Hill. Brooklyn: New City, 2002.

———. *A Refutation of the Manichees*. In *On Genesis*, edited by John E. Rotelle, 39–102. The Works of St. Augustine I/13. Translated by Edmund Hill. Brooklyn: New City, 2002.

Austin, Michael. *Re-reading Job: Understanding the Ancient World's Greatest Poem*. Sandu, UT: Greg Kofford, 2014.

Barker, Margaret. *Temple Theology: An Introduction*. London: SPCK, 2004.

———. *The Great Angel: A Study of Israel's Second God*. London: SPCK, 1992.

Barrett, C. K. *Jesus and the Gospel Tradition*. Minneapolis: Fortress, 1967.

Barthes, Roland, et al. *Analyse Structurale et Exégèse Biblique: Essais d'interprétation*. Paris: Delachaus et Nestlé, 1971.

Bartlett, Anthony W. *Pascale's Wager: The Homelands of Heaven*. Syracuse: Hopetime, 2014.

———. *Theology Beyond Metaphysics: Transformative Semiotics of René Girard*. Eugene, OR: Cascade, 2020.

Bellinger, William H., Jr., and William R. Farmer, eds. *Jesus and the Suffering Servant: Isaiah 53 and Christian Origins*. Harrisburg: Trinity International, 1998.

Blenkinsopp, Joseph. *Judaism, the First Phase: The Place of Ezra and Nehemiah in the Origins of Judaism*. Grand Rapids: Eerdmans, 2009.

Boadt, Lawrence. *Reading the Old Testament: An Introduction*. New York: Paulist, 1984.

Bouyer, Louis. *Eucharist.* Translated by Charles Underhill Quinn. Notre Dame: University of Notre Dame Press, 1968.

Brueggemann, Walter. *An Introduction to the Old Testament: Canon and Christian Imagination.* Louisville: Westminster John Knox, 2003.

———. *Isaiah 40–66.* Louisville: Westminster John Knox, 1998.

———. *The Prophetic Imagination.* 2nd ed. Minneapolis: Fortress, 2001.

———. *Theology of the Old Testament: Testimony, Dispute, Advocacy.* Minneapolis: Fortress, 2012.

Bultmann, Rudolf. *History of the Synoptic Tradition.* Translated by J. Marsh. Rev. ed. New York: Harper and Row, 1976.

Calloway, Joseph, and Hershel Shanks. "The Settlement in Canaan: The Period of the Judges." In *Ancient Israel: From Abraham to the Roman Destruction of the Temple,* edited by Hershel Shanks, 55–90. Washington, DC: Biblical Archaeological Society and Prentice Hall, 2011.

Campbell, Douglas A. *The Deliverance of God: An Apocalyptic Rereading of Justification in Paul.* Grand Rapids: Eerdmans, 2009.

———. *Framing Paul: An Epistolary Biography.* Grand Rapids: Eerdmans, 2014.

———. *Pauline Dogmatics: The Triumph of God's Love.* Grand Rapids: Eerdmans, 2020.

Caputo, John D., and Linda Martin Alcoff, eds. *St. Paul among the Philosophers.* Bloomington: Indiana University Press, 2009.

Chomsky, Noam. "Interview by Wallace Shawn." *Final Edition* 1.1 (Autumn 2004) 10–25.

Cohen, Shaye J. D. *From the Maccabees to the Mishnah.* 3rd ed. Louisville: Westminster John Knox, 2014.

Collins, John J. *The Apocalyptic Vision of the Book of* Daniel. Missoula: Scholars, 1977.

———. *Daniel: With an Introduction to Apocalyptic Literature.* Vol. XX, *The Forms of the Old Testament Literature.* Grand Rapids: Eerdmans, 1984.

Cone, James H. *God of the Oppressed.* Maryknoll: Orbis, 1997.

Cross, Frank Moore. *Canaanite Myth and Hebrew Epic: Essays in the History of the Religion of Israel.* Cambridge: Harvard University Press, 1973.

———. *From Epic to Canon: History and Literature in Ancient Israel.* Baltimore: Johns Hopkins University Press, 1998.

Crossan, John Dominic. *The Historical Jesus: The Life of a Mediterranean Jewish Peasant.* Reprint, New York: HarperOne, 1993.

———. *Who Killed Jesus?: Exposing the Roots of Anti-Semitism in the Gospel Story of the Death of Jesus.* San Francisco: HarperSanFrancisco, 1996.

Dell, Katharine J. "Reinventing the Wheel: The Shaping of the Book of Jonah." In *After the Exile: Essays on Biblical History and Interpretation in Honour of Rex Mason,* edited by John Barton and David J. Reimer, 85–101. Macon: Mercer University Press, 1996.

Dodd, C. H. *The Founder of Christianity.* London: Macmillan, 1970.

Douglas, Kelly Brown. *What's Faith Got to Do with It?: Black Bodies/Christian Souls.* Maryknoll: Orbis, 2005.

Ehrman, Bart. *Forgery and Counterforgery: The Use of Literary Deceit in Early Christian Polemics.* Oxford: Oxford University Press, 2013.

———. *The New Testament: A Historical Introduction to the Early Christian Writings.* Oxford: Oxford University Press, 1997.

Fohrer, Georg. *History of Israelite Religion*. Translated by David E. Green. London: SPCK, 1975.

Friedman, Richard Elliott. *The Exodus*. New York: HarperOne, 2018.

———. *Who Wrote the Bible?* New York: Simon & Schuster, 2019.

Friesen, Steven J. *Imperial Cults and the Apocalypse of John: Reading Revelation in the Ruins*. Oxford: Oxford University Press, 2001.

Funk, Robert Walter, et al. *The Five Gospels: What Did Jesus Really Say? The Search for the Authentic Words of Jesus*. New York: Harper Collins, 1993.

Galor, Katharina. "Plastered Pools: A New Perspective." In vol. 2, *Khirbet Qumran et Ain Feshkha*, edited by Jean-Baptiste Humbert and Jan Gunneweg, 257–86. Goettingen: Vandenhoeck and Ruprecht, 2003.

Girard, René. *Battling to the End: Conversations with Benoît Chantre*. Translated by Mary Baker. East Lansing: Michigan State University, 2010.

———. *Job, the Victim of His People*. Translated by Yvonne Freccero. Stanford: Stanford University Press, 1987.

Girard, René, et al. *Things Hidden Since the Foundation of the World*. Translated by Stephen Bann and Michael Metteer. Stanford: Stanford University Press, 1987.

Gorman, Michael J. *Reading Revelation Responsibly: Uncivil Worship and Witness: Following the Lamb into the New Creation*. Eugene, OR: Cascade, 2011.

Gottwald, Norman K. *The Hebrew Bible: A Brief Socio-literary Introduction*. Abridged ed. Minneapolis: Fortress, 2008.

———. *The Tribes of Yahweh: A Sociology of the Religion of Liberated Israel, 1250–1050 BCE*. Maryknoll: Orbis, 1979.

Gottwald, Norman K., Richard A. Horsley, eds. *The Bible and Liberation: Political and Social Hermeneutics*. Rev. ed. Maryknoll: Orbis, 1993.

Greenstein, Edward L. *Job: A New Translation*. New Haven: Yale University Press, 2019.

Gutiérrez, Gustavo. *On Job: God-Talk and the Suffering of the Innocent*. Maryknoll: Orbis, 1987.

———. *A Theology of Liberation: History, Politics, and Salvation*. Rev. ed. Maryknoll: Orbis, 1988.

Hays, Richard B. *The Faith of Jesus Christ: The Narrative Substructure of Galatians 3.1—4.11*. 2nd ed. Grand Rapids: Eerdmans, 2002.

Hengel, Martin. *Between Jesus and Paul: Studies in the Earliest History of Christianity*. Eugene, OR: Wipf & Stock, 1983.

———. *The Atonement: The Origins of the Doctrine in the New Testament*. 1981. Reprint, Eugene, OR: Wipf & Stock, 2007.

———. *Was Jesus a Revolutionist?* Minneapolis: Fortress, 1971.

Hooker, Morna. *Jesus and the Servant*. 1959. Reprint, Eugene, OR: Wipf & Stock, 2001.

Jeremias, Joachim. *The Eucharistic Words of Jesus*. London: SCM, 1966.

———. *New Testament Theology: The Proclamation of Jesus*. New York: Charles Scribner's Sons, 1977.

Josephus. *The Jewish War*. Translated by Martin Hammond. Oxford World Classics. Oxford: Oxford University Press, 2017.

Kidd, B. J., ed. *Documents Illustrative of the Continental Reformation*. Eugene, OR: Wipf & Stock, 2004.

Kugler, Robert, and Patrick Hartin. *An Introduction to the Bible*. Grand Rapids: Eerdmans, 2009.

Lacocque, André. *The Book of Daniel*. 2nd ed. Eugene, OR: Cascade, 2018.

Landes, George M. "The Kerygma of the Book of Jonah: The Contextual Interpretation of the Jonah Psalm." *Interpretation: Journal of Bible and Theology* 21.1 (1967) 1–31.

Lambert, W. G. *Babylonian Wisdom Literature*. Winona Lake: Eisenbrauns, 1996.

Leithart. Peter J. *Delivered from the Elements of the World: Atonement, Justification, Mission*. Downers Grove: InterVarsity, 2016.

Lessing, Gotthold. *Lessing's Theological Writings: Selections in Translation*. Translated by Henry Chadwick. Library of Modern Religious Thought. Stanford: Stanford University Press, 1956.

Limburgh, James. *Jonah: A Commentary*. Louisville: Westminster/John Knox, 1993.

Liu, Cixin. *The Three-Body Problem*. Translated by Ken Liu. New York: Tor, 2014.

Lundbom, Jack. *Deuteronomy: A Commentary*. Grand Rapids: Eerdmans, 2013.

MacCulloch, Diarmaid M. *Christianity: The First Three Thousand Years*. New York: Penguin, 2010.

Manson, William. *Jesus the Messiah*. London: Hodder & Stoughton, 1943.

Markus, R. A. *Saeculum: History and Society in the Theology of St. Augustine*. Cambridge: Cambridge University Press, 1970.

McKnight, Scot. *Jesus and His Death: Historiography, the Historical Jesus, and Atonement Theory*. Waco: Baylor University Press, 2005.

Meier, J. P. *A Marginal Jew: Rethinking the Historical Jesus*. Vol. II, *Mentor, Message, and Miracles*. The Anchor Yale Bible Reference Library. New Haven: Yale University Press, 1994.

Mendenhall, Georg E. *Ancient Israel's Faith and History*. Edited by Gary A. Heroin. Louisville: Westminster John Knox, 2001.

———. *The Tenth Generation: The Origins of the Biblical Tradition*. Baltimore: Johns Hopkins University Press, 1973.

Meyer, Ben F. *The Aims of Jesus*. London: SCM,1979.

Myers, Jacob M. *Ezra-Nehemiah*. New Haven: Doubleday, 1965.

Neusner, Jacob. *A History of the Jews in Babylonia, Part 1: The Parthian Period*. Illustrated ed. Eugene, OR: Wipf and Stock, 2008.

———. "Money Changers in the Temple: The Mishna's Explanation." *New Testament Studies* 35 (1989) 287–90.

Noth, Martin. *The Deuteronomistic History*. Sheffield: JSOT, 1981.

———. *A History of Pentateuchal Traditions*. Englewood Cliffs: Prentice-Hall, 1972.

O'Connell, Robert. "Augustinism: Locating the Center." In *Augustine: Presbyter Factus Sum*, edited by Joseph T. Lienhard, Earl C. Muller, and Roland J. Tesk, 209–33. New York: Peter Lang, 1993.

———. *St. Augustine's Early Theory of Man, A.D. 386–391*. Cambridge: Harvard University Press, 1968.

———. *The Origin of the Soul in St. Augustine's Later Works*. New York: Fordham University Press, 1987.

Philo. *On the Embassy to Gaius*. Translated by F. H. Colson. Loeb Classical Library 379. Cambridge: Harvard University Press, 1962.

Pliny. *Pliny the Elder, Natural History: A Selection*. Translated, introduction, and notes by John F. Healy. New York: Penguin, 1991.

Plotinus. *Enneads*. 7 vols. Edited and translated by A. H. Armstrong. Loeb Classical Library. Cambridge: Harvard University Press, 1966–1995.

Pope, Marvin H., ed. *Job*. The Anchor Bible 15. Translated with introduction and commentary by Marvin H. Pope. Garden City: Doubleday, 1965.

Redmount, Carol A. "Bitter Lives: Israel in and out of Egypt." In *The Oxford History of the Biblical World*, edited by Michael D. Coogan, 79–121. Oxford: Oxford University Press, 1999.

Rombs, Ronnie J. *Saint Augustine and the Fall of the Soul: Beyond O'Connell and His Critics*. Washington, DC: Catholic University of America Press, 2006.

Ruether, Rosemary Radford. "A Religion for Women." *Christianity and Crisis* 39.19 (1979) 307–11.

———. *Sexism and God-Talk: Toward a Feminist Theology*. Ann. ed. Boston: Beacon, 1993.

Sanders, E. P. *Jesus and Judaism*. Philadelphia: Fortress, 1985.

———. *Paul and Palestinian Judaism: A Comparison of Patterns of Religion*. Philadelphia: Fortress, 1977.

Schweizer, Albert. *The Quest of the Historical Jesus*. Edited by John Bowden. Translated by W. Montgomery, J. R. Coates, Susan Cupitt, and John Bowden. Minneapolis: Fortress, 2001.

Silva, David A. *Introducing the Apocrypha: Message, Context, and Significance*. Grand Rapids: Baker Academic, 2002.

Simonin, Antoine. "The Cyrus Cylander." *World History Encyclopedia*, January 18, 2012. https://www.worldhistory.org/article/166/the-cyrus-cylinder/.

Smith, Mark S. *The Early History of God: Yahweh and the Other Deities in Ancient Israel*. 2nd ed. Grand Rapids: Eerdmans, 2002.

Stalker, D. M. G. "Exodus." In *Peake's Commentary on the Bible*, edited by Matthew Black and H. H. Rowley, 208–40. London: Nelson, 1962.

Taylor, Glen A. "Review of Lundbom 'Deuteronomy.'" *SBL Central*, June 2, 2014. https://www.sblcentral.org/home/bookDetails/9357.

TeSelle, Eugene. *Augustine the Theologian*. Eugene, OR: Wipf & Stock, 2002.

Towner, W. Sibley. *Daniel*. Louisville: Westminster John Knox, 1984.

Trible, Phyllis. "Depatriarchalising in Biblical Interpretation." *Journal of the American Academy of Religion* 51.1 (1973) 30–48.

———. *Rhetorical Criticism: Context, Method and the Book of Jonah*. Minneapolis: Fortress, 1994.

———. *Texts of Terror: Literary-Feminist Readings of Biblical Narratives*. Philadelphia: Fortress, 1984.

VanderKam, James, and Peter Flint. *The Meaning of the Dead Sea Scrolls: Their Significance for Understanding the Bible, Judaism, Jesus, and Christianity*. 2002. Reprint, New York: HarperOne, 2004.

Van Seters, John. *The Pentateuch: A Social-Science Commentary*. New York: T&T Clark, 1999.

Vermes, Geza. *The Complete Dead Sea Scrolls in English*. New York: Penguin, 1998.

Westermann, Claus. *Continental Commentaries*. Vol. 1, *Genesis 1–11*. Translated by John J. Scullion. Minneapolis: Fortress, 1994.

———. *Continental Commentaries*. Vol. 2, *Genesis 12–36*. Translated by John J. Scullion. Minneapolis: Fortress, 1995.

———. *Continental Commentaries*. Vol. 3, *Genesis 37–50*. Translated by John J. Scullion. Minneapolis: Fortress, 2002.

Williams, James G. *The Bible: Violence and the Sacred*. New York: Harper Collins, 1991.

Wink, Walter. *The Powers*. Vol. 1, *Naming the Powers*. Philadelphia: Fortress, 1984.

————. *The Powers.* Vol. 2, *Unmasking the Powers: The Invisible Forces That Determine Human Existence.* Philadelphia: Fortress, 1986.

————. *The Powers.* Vol. 3, *Engaging the Powers.* Philadelphia: Fortress, 1992.

Witherington, Ben, III. *Jesus the Sage: The Pilgrimage of Wisdom.* Minneapolis: Fortress, 1994.

————. *The Christology of Jesus.* Minneapolis: Fortress, 1990.

Wright, N. T. *Jesus and the Victory of God.* Christian Origins and the Question of God 2. Minneapolis: Fortress, 1996.

————. *The New Testament and the People of God.* Christian Origins and the Question of God 1. Minneapolis: Fortress, 1996.

————. *Paul and the Faithfulness of God.* Christian Origins and the Question of God 4. Minneapolis: Fortress, 2013.

Zahnd, Brian. *Sinners in the Hands of a Loving God.* Colorado Springs: Waterbrook, 2017. Kindle.

Žižek, Slavoj. *The Puppet and the Dwarf: The Perverse Core of Christianity.* Cambridge: MIT, 2003.

Žižek, Slavoj, and Boris Gunjevic. *God in Pain: Inversions of Apocalypse.* Translated by Ellen Elias-Bursac. New York: Seven Stories, 2012.

Žižek, Slavoj, and John Milbank. *The Monstrosity of Christ: Paradox or Dialectic.* Cambridge: MIT, 2009.

Index

Milton Keynes UK
Ingram Content Group UK Ltd.
UKHW041512071024
2052UKWH00016B/40